WITHDRAWN
UTSA Libraries

SAINTS & REBELS

SAINTS & REBELS

BY

ELOISE LOWNSBERY

ILLUSTRATED BY

ELIZABETH TYLER WOLCOTT

Essay Index Reprint Series

BOOKS FOR LIBRARIES PRESS

FREEPORT, NEW YORK

Copyright 1937 by Eloise Lownsbery

Copyright © renewed 1965 by Eloise Lownsbery

Reprinted 1971 by arrangement with
David McKay Company, Inc.

INTERNATIONAL STANDARD BOOK NUMBER:
0-8369-2322-7

LIBRARY OF CONGRESS CATALOG CARD NUMBER:
72-156682

PRINTED IN THE UNITED STATES OF AMERICA

Salutation
to
The Immortals of all ages
Whose selfless labors
Sung or unsung
Evolve our common social state

FOREWORD

Blessed are those who cultivate in themselves
a love for their neighbors, and who respect before
everything the dignity of the human being.
Catherine Breshkovsky

If Thomas Paine were to return to earth today he would rejoice that modern youth is no longer content to be insular, bound on a little island by a little blue sea, as he found the England of his own day. He would applaud youth for reaching out to conquer time and space, for running in thought beyond the boundaries of four walls, beyond school, city, state, nation, out into the universe to help spin our planet Earth.

"The spiritual evolution of this universe," he would say to boys and girls, "is dependent upon you, upon your education, your culture, your way of solving human problems, your attitude toward social relationships. For a universal brotherhood of mankind rests upon your individual conceptions and working out of a kingdom of harmony in your own hearts."

And you would fling back your heads and answer that you are not afraid to accept his challenge, but that you are working as hard as you can to gain knowledge, since knowledge you know to be a key to that Golden Age of the future.

"Seize the sword of knowledge; with it and with love the universe is conquerable," cries the philosopher.

This seems to have been the secret of the twelve humanitarians described in this book. They all revered knowledge, and they loved much. For them, too, space was annihilated. Time did not exist. They had an eye to the needs of any man anywhere as their neighbor, was he next door or twelve thousand miles away. They were quite willing to struggle for a lifetime, not in the usual pursuits of acquiring possessions or fame or success, but for the emancipation of the forgotten man, for social justice whether in a political or a religious sphere. Humanity's redemption from exile was a life task for them. They cherished the gods by cherishing the unfortunate and the underprivileged.

Only twelve such Warriors could be chosen for this book, yet they are legion. We could go on adding chapters all the rest of our lives, stringing them like pearls on the thread of our remembrance.

They have taught us, these blessed saints and rebels, that in each reform, each step forward toward liberty and equality and justice, the word precedes the act. It was so with Herzen and Mme. Breshkovsky in Russia, with Thomas Paine and Sarah Hale in America, with Lady Christine in France and St. Antoninus in Italy, and with Wilberforce and Hannah More in England. Upon the word, spoken or written or living, depends the evolution of goodness and beauty; and back of the word is the thought, the idea.

These twelve, among all the happy warriors of their kind, are irresistibly thrilling to us. Nothing stays their progress: "All parts away for them . . . along the grand roads of the universe." They tower up like giants above rich and poor, Christian and Jew, uniting peoples and races into one family. Out of their struggle against evil or tyranny or ugliness, evolves our individual and corporate happiness.

From the ranks of the youth of today will come others like these twelve, to carry on the same struggle. For you are the power-wielders, the world-builders of tomorrow. On your ideals will depend the home, the village, the city and state and nation. Out of the utopia of your dream of today will flower the social well-being of the children of tomorrow.

When you have built the Golden Age, no more shall our world be bowed under calamity and poverty and fear. It will stand erect with its head in the stars, a place of enduring beauty for a rational, a loving and a god-like people.

I am deeply grateful to these twelve whom we celebrate. Grateful, too, for permission to include amplified studies of William Wilberforce, Lord Shaftesbury, Hannah More, St. Vincent de Paul, Sarah Hale, and Christine de Pisan, which appeared in condensed form in *The Portal*. Grateful, also, to the writers of all the books included in the Bibliography, without whom these studies could not have been made.

E. L.

New York,
May, 1937.

CONTENTS

HENRIETTA SZOLD

1860–

On December 21, 1935, a joint birthday celebration was held between America and Palestine. It consisted of an international radio broadcast, speeches, a huge cake glowing with seventy-five candles, services in many synagogues, with thousands of people all pouring out love and gratitude and gifts. To whom? To a slight wisp of a woman called Henrietta Szold, hiding away from all this fuss over her, too humble, too busy, too content with her sisters to pay much attention to it.

She had only a month to spend in America, she said, and so much to do.

"I have such a lot of work ahead of me." She spread out her small shapely hands in apology. "I really can't stop to think how old I've grown!"

Pathé News tried in vain to make a reel of her. As persistently she refused the dozens of birthday meetings, teas, dinners, to which she was invited. Did America think she could do nothing but eat and play? Then they explained that she ought to attend at least one birthday function for the sake of her children.

For Henrietta Szold is head of the Youth Movement in Palestine, the first youth immigration known in history. Backed by the American Women's Zionist groups, she has already adopted fifteen hundred boys and girls who, denied education and opportunity in Germany, may now start life over again in the land of their fathers, Palestine.

So she consented to address two thousand of her Zionist friends at a tea at the Hotel Astor in New York. But when she learned the price they were willing to pay for the tea with its elaborate menu, she was distressed. If they would be content with plain tea and a bit of plain cake, so that the money they so generously paid might be used for her children in Palestine, then she would consent to be present.

She was hard to please, that little, much-celebrated lady, of whom Mr. Morris Rothenberg, president of the Zionist Organization in America, said: "Henrietta Szold represents the highest type of personality which Jewish life has produced."

At one of the great birthday parties in New York, which she was too busy to attend, Rabbi Stephen A. Wise spoke of her as a "semi-mythical figure beyond criticism, beyond detraction, beyond envy, beyond blame, and because of her humility, beyond praise. She is world Jewry's Jane Addams, a transcendent spirit which touches the lowly only to lift them up."

"Yet I never heard of her," you say.

That is because you live in the land of the free, and are

perhaps a Protestant or a Catholic. But if you were a Jewish refugee, driven in terror from your home in Poland or Russia or Germany or Rumania, then you would know and love her; then you, too, young or old, would be one of her children. Then to you, too, this dynamic, witty, vivacious mite of a woman with soft gray hair and sparkling brown eyes and a great heart would be the grandest Jewish woman in the whole world, as she is to some sixteen millions.

Yet not only boys and girls are growing up in Palestine in her name. A whole future forest of ten thousand saplings has been planted on Mount Scopus. And named for her, also, is the broad white-paved boulevard which replaced the rough and stony road that leads from Jerusalem up to this same mountain top on which stands the proud new Hebrew University.

Among her many birthday gifts was one check for seventy-five thousand dollars for her Rothschild-Hadassah University Hospital, and another check for ten thousand dollars from the Junior Zionists to be used for her Youth Movement.

What a happy seventy-fifth birthday!

Henrietta Szold, who has lived for the past seventeen years in Jerusalem, was born in Baltimore, Maryland, on that day of the winter solstice which the Jews celebrate as *Chanukah*, the Feast of the Lights.

Although that year of 1860 was full of the unrest which preceded the Civil War, Henrietta's childhood and girlhood in her cultured, prosperous home was nurtured in happiness and freedom and security; three gifts which most girls and boys in America take for granted and so think little about.

Perhaps this would have been true of Henrietta too, had

it not been for the tide of immigration flowing from Russia in the early 1880s. It came rolling across the ocean into the harbor of New York, and thence down the coast and up the Chesapeake Bay to the docks of Baltimore, and from the dock right into her own home.

For, as the compassionate rabbi of the city, who should welcome the strangers but her own father, Dr. Benjamin Szold? It was natural for him to invite them, a houseful at a time, to gather around his ample table, welcomed by his beaming wife and their five lovable daughters.

While Mother Szold served generous helpings of steaming Hungarian goulash, Henrietta, the eldest daughter, seated always in the chair beside her adored father, listened to the stories of these weary immigrants who had never known happiness or freedom or security.

Through them she heard of the life in the dark ghetto, walled about, beyond whose gate the children dare not venture. They told of such hunger and privation as she had not known existed on earth; of studying the Torah in dark cellars by sputtering candlelight; of persecution and the denial of the human rights of free speech, or free worship in their own synagogue; stories of misery resulting from the recent May Laws of 1882.

These laws, she learned, proposed by Count Ignatiev and sanctioned by the Czar, Alexander III, drove the Jews from the land back into the crowded cities, where they must be herded into the narrow confines of the ghetto, the pale of settlement. Henceforth, no Jew could own any land, excepting those in already existing agricultural communities. Nor could he move from one village to another, but must remain in the one where he happened to be on the day of the census, no matter if he had come only on business to sell a calf, or on a visit to a friend, and though he had lived in an adjoining village for twenty years.

Moreover, if he were in the army serving for the Czar and consequently was left out of the census altogether, when he returned home he was accounted a nobody, without a village or any legal status. There was nothing to do then but leave the country.

Or again, if the ignorant official who conducted the census wrote down Jacob Gruzman as Ruzman, he too was expelled. Was it not plain? If Gruzman was not Ruzman, then he was not in the census; so, then, he was nobody. A man without a village was a man without a country. So he and his wife and children, if they wished to follow him, must become wanderers.

Now if a farmer could own no land, how was he to graze his cows and reap his grain? He could not very well take corn and cattle into the ghetto to live with him.

As millions of Russians could testify, when the head of the government was a despot, he soon communicated his despotism to every under-official all down through the long hierarchy; and the lower in scale of intelligence, the more cruel the tyranny.

Why didn't they rebel? Henrietta asked with her lips trembling. Because those who did were certain to be massacred, they and their entire village or ghetto. Small wonder, then, that hundreds and thousands of these Russian Jews were forced to leave their homes, their cows, their possessions and trek along the roads to the seaports, there to wait for crowded steerage passage to America, blessed free land of America. And here they were, actually arrived! So they lifted their heads and sang a song of rejoicing:

O give thanks unto the Lord, for he is good:
for his mercy endureth for ever.
Let the redeemed of the Lord say so,
whom he hath redeemed from the hand of the enemy;
And gathered them out of the lands, from the east,
and from the west, from the north, and from the south.
They wandered in the wilderness in a solitary way;
they found no city to dwell in.
Hungry and thirsty,
their soul fainted in them.
Then they cried unto the Lord in their trouble,
and he delivered them out of their distresses.
And he led them forth by the right way,
that they might go to a city of habitation.
Oh that men would praise the Lord for his goodness,
and for his wonderful works to the children of men! *

Fortunate indeed was this Baltimore group to find a rabbi and his family to serve them, at once so kindly and so practical.

Together, Henrietta and her father faced with the newcomers all their fresh problems: where to find lodgings for them in the crowded Jewish quarter; how to help them to earn their bread; how to teach them to master the new tongue; how to enable them to assimilate American ideals and still retain their own deep culture of Russian Judaism.

Economic problems, and those involved in the synagogue, Henrietta, of course, left to her father. She used all her efforts to establish a night school, the first in Baltimore, and one of the pioneer efforts at Americanization in the whole country.

* Psalm 107.

Something of the drama, the pathos, the romance of this immigration movement gripped her as she looked at her pupils. Bearded old men, stalwart men and women in their prime, sitting with their young towheads and their older boys and girls, bending over the same books, patiently repeating the strange-sounding letters of the English alphabet. How their eyes shone! Out of the alphabet came words, from words sentences, and from sentences a language. And the new language would unlock American treasures: wealth, dignity, social position, freedom, happiness.

The sense of hidden grandeur in her work compensated the young teacher for her patient perseverance and the discomfort of long nightly rides in a cold horse-car.

In a few short years, this first wave of immigrants had moved up into the avenues of the city and stocked their mansions with ornate gilt and plush, while their old homes were occupied by a fresh stream of exiles.

More and more the rabbi and his family withdrew from the ostentation of easy money into the fastnesses of their own citadel. Theirs was an aristocracy of mind and spirit. At ten, Henrietta read Shakespeare with her father, not only in English but in the German translation of Schiller, and compared the two. She sat at her father's feet as he taught her the Bible in Hebrew, or listened while he recited all of Homer in Greek. She read Faust with him in German and Voltaire in French.

She loved, also, to hear stories of his home in Vienna, or of her grandmother's Austrian estate, where he had met her mother.

"And then tell me of that year 1848," she would beg.

Ah, 1848! The year that the wind of revolution blew

across Europe. Her father was a student then, dreaming of devoting his life as a rabbi to the spiritual needs of his race. But he was fired by the promises of the great revolutionary leader, Kossuth. Banded together to support Kossuth were peasants demanding freedom from serfdom, middle-class merchants asking for a constitutional government, Jews begging for just taxation and for recognition of their own religion.

For a few glorious months, Kossuth's war of independence dethroned the government, and swept the country clean of despotism, liberating the Hungarian people.

Then came the overthrow, the flight of Kossuth into Turkey, the suppression of the revolutionists by the young emperor, Franz Joseph, and a rule of autocracy more tyrannical than before.

And Henrietta would look wonderingly upon the face of that very Franz Joseph which still reposed in the family album in the parlor.

Better than an emperor's face was that of Carl Schurz, her father's friend, of whose service for America the whole family was proud.

So Henrietta Szold was molded in this "Citadel of Ivory," this strong tower of her home, with its deep culture, its sunny hospitality to the congregation of rich and poor which surged in and out, unable to touch or to modernize its Old World sanctity, beauty and simplicity.

The perfectionism of her father, whom she idolized, drove his eldest daughter to a stern self-discipline in facing duty, while the practicality of her mother gave her a genius for homely detail. Added to these foundation stones for her life-work was the classical culture of her father, their discussions of world problems, her absorption of Jewish lore from all lands, her mastery of languages perfected by years of teaching in Baltimore.

Although rarely ill herself, she had a deep sympathy with those who were. When her beloved little sisters were taken ill in turn with scarlet fever and diphtheria, Henrietta offered herself as doctor's assistant, isolating herself in the sick room on the third floor, nursing her charges night and day, reading aloud, telling stories during the long quarantine.

As her father's secretary, attending to his correspondence, writing his notes of condolence or of rejoicing, she learned the art of responding to the need of each one with the very essence of herself.

POGROMS in Poland, massacres in Russia, persecution in Rumania, sent Jewish émigrés in such a tide that even America, "the great mother of exiles," was forced to restrict their number.

Henrietta Szold said to her father, "If only there were some place on the face of this earth that Jews could call their own, where they might found communities of social justice, and live on the soil in happiness and security."

"There is still the land of Canaan," Dr. Szold reminded her.

She opened her Hebrew Bible and read again the story of how the Lord told Moses he would give his people "a good land and a large, a land flowing with milk and honey." And the Prophet Ezekiel had added, "which is the glory of all lands."

Could it be possible that at last, this twentieth century would see the long-looked-for return?

Ha shanah ha ba be Yerusholaim
The year the coming in Jerusalem

During how many hundred Passovers had not this prayer been repeated to one another! "May this year bring us back to Jerusalem."

Yet the land had been held for centuries by Moslem Arabs, ruled by the Turkish Sultan. Henrietta knew that a few Jewish farm colonies had been started in Palestine, and a few groups of rabbinical scholars or deeply religious old people who wished to die on the land were there also. These groups she knew were supported either by sympathetic groups in Europe or America, or by such generous individuals as Baron de Rothschild of Paris, or Lord Shaftesbury of London. But there seemed little opportunity for large groups of immigrants to become self-supporting in Palestine, for the land was as poverty stricken as the Arab serfs who tried to till it for their absentee landlords.

Yet Henrietta grew to believe more and more in the Zionist movement which was inaugurated in 1897 at the International Congress of Jews in Basle by Dr. Theodor Herzl. His aim was to restore Palestine as a national shrine. Under the rule of Turkey, he dreamed of establishing a Jewish communal life that would combine agriculture with trade, industry, finance, scientific investigation, culture, religion, and art. In fact, he visioned a complete social organization of the growing Jewish population in the Holy Land. He would unite the prayer and study of the older settlements with the work and play of the new. He would build a Jewish utopia, with Hebrew as a common tongue.

To Henrietta Szold this became a glorious ideal which

she longed with all her heart might become a reality. It had been her father's ideal, also, to bring the classical language of the Talmud and the Torah into everyday use among all Jews. Now, after his death, she set herself to a deeper mastery of Hebrew, taking courses at the Jewish Theological Seminary in New York, where she had access to the finest Hebrew library in the world.

She had meant to translate her father's voluminous writings, the life-work of a scholar trained in the University of Breslau. But now, as so often in her life, the personal desire had to be given up for the larger impersonal need. She was asked to translate from Hebrew a Commentary on the Talmud. And next she brought out a translation from German of *The Ethics of Judaism* by M. Lazarus in four volumes. She steeped her mind in its lofty principles.

"The Torah, the Law, exists only for the sake of the Ways of Peace," she translated. "The blessed paths of peace are those which tend to demolish natural barriers and which permeate the universality of moral communion."

She thought of all her refugees, those of Baltimore, those of New York, a million and more wandering over the face of the earth. "Israel's mission is Peace." If only they might know peace for themselves and so help to bring it to the world.

She became secretary of the Jewish Publication Society of America, with headquarters in Philadelphia. It meant a wrench to leave home, to identify herself with national rather than with local Jewry. Yet she had inherited from her father the longing "to build into America's culture the spiritual heritage of Hebraic civilization."

In order to encourage writers, she set herself to translate a German manuscript, *The Legends of the Jews* by Louis

Ginzberg; and from the French, *The Renascence of Hebrew Literature* by Nahum Slouschz. She rejoiced that the Society arranged for the publication of works by Israel Zangwill and Sholom Asch.

But the call of Palestine in her heart became ever stronger until, in 1909, she went out with her mother to see it for herself, this ancient Promised Land. There she found that refugees of every type and description, rich and poor, wise and ignorant, came pouring in: from the Yemen in southwestern Arabia; and from Eastern Europe through the ports of Odessa for Russia, of Constanta for Rumania, and of Trieste for Galicia.

What tales they told, and what need there was for their welcome in the Holy Land. A need of shelters to house them, of soup kitchens in every city and port, of medical centers to fight typhus and smallpox and malaria and trachoma; a need for farmland, or tools for a trade.

Her heart ached most for the children; hungry-eyed, apathetic, nearly blind or trembling with fever; pitiful victims. Yet the whole future of the land depended on them. They must have fresh milk, and schools and playgrounds; a chance to grow up in the sun, round and laughing. They must be lifted out of bitter misery that they in turn might be ready to lift the coming ones.

She went out to visit the agricultural colonies of Judea peopled by refugees from the same May Laws which had sent her Baltimore immigrants. How valiantly they were striving, in spite of the small yield of the stony hillsides. She marveled at their patience.

"What is a generation, or a century even, in the life of our people?" they said to her.

She knew they were preparing the soil for brothers still

to come. Yet their own living was so meager. The citrus fruits were small and sour, like the land, crying out for water. Was this then the land flowing with milk and honey? No, but it could be, she told herself stoutly. With modern machinery and scientific research, there must be ways of reclaiming the soil. Surely the ancient prophecy could not fail.

In spite of the filth and squalor of the native Arabian homes, in spite of the disease lurking in the dark winding streets, of complete lack of sanitation, of back-breaking toil without water, of mosquitoes and flies—still, Henrietta Szold caught a vision of what it could become, this new Zion, with American money, American ideals of cleanliness, of medicine, of social service.

So she returned from the first trip with greater faith than ever in Zionism, the back-to-Jerusalem movement which she felt would redeem her people. But it needed money, vast sums of money. It needed an organization of American women banded together to bring her vision into reality. Where could she find such an organization? She must make one.

With characteristic energy and foresight, she started with a small group of her student friends who had been meeting with her in a study club on Jewish literature. To these, with a few others, she told of her longing to start a Women's Zionist Society to do the work for Palestine that only women could do.

She proposed to leave to the men the problem of grappling with that stony, worn-out soil, and the organization of coöperative colonies.

Nor could she and her friends grapple alone with the problems of malaria and trachoma, but they might do something to save the babies. They might perhaps send out a trained nurse.

Her friends were doubtful. The Zionist movement was not popular in America. Their families would think them very queer. None of this group had much either of money or worldly power. But they listened to Henrietta's stories of the misery and poverty of those Palestine mothers until none in the group could sleep at night.

"What matter," cried their leader, "if we here in New York feel safe and remote from misery? We are as near as our hearts. The great thing is to start."

And in order to dignify the undertaking, they agreed to meet Henrietta in the basement study of the old Temple Emanu-El on the Day of Purim, in February, 1912.

To their surprise, Henrietta Szold presented them with a Constitution providing for not only a local but a national organization. In each city or town there must be but one branch group formed. She wanted no distinctions of rich and poor, high and low, cultured or ignorant. All personality must be kept subservient to their cause. Nor could those thirty-six young women join this parent New York chapter without pledging themselves for life-service to Zionism.

Today, twenty-five years later, that small group has multiplied to three hundred chapters. The thirty-six members have become nearly sixty thousand, with hundreds of new members coming in every year, and thousands of outside supporters.

They agreed to call the new organization after the Hebrew name for Queen Esther, *Hadassah*. For it was Queen Esther who said on the first Day of Purim, that day of victory for the Jews:

How can I endure to see the evil
that shall come unto my people?
Or how can I endure to see
the destruction of mv kindred?

So this Women's Zionist Organization of Hadassah was to become to Palestine what St. Vincent de Paul's organization of the Ladies of Charity became to seventeenth-century Francc. For they too cared for the sick in hospitals, for orphan children, for the poor and the distressed of the nation.

So also the little band in New York were fired by Miss Szold to reach out their hands across the seas to that land far off. She could not stop hearing in her heart the words of the Prophet Jeremiah:

Behold the voice of the cry of the daughter of my people
From a land far off:
Is it not the Lord in Zion?
Is not the King in her?
For the hurt of the daughter of my people
I am hurt.

Is there no balm in Gilead?
Is there no physician there?
Why then is not the
Healing of the daughter of my people recovered? *

Thus the motto of Hadassah became "The healing of my people." Surely, if there were no balm left in Gilead, then America would send her balm.

* Jeremiah 8:19-22.

In a subsequent report for 1915, printed in the *Jewish Year Book,* Miss Szold plainly states the needs as she found them.

"Here was no paternal government giving homesteads to worthy men, but here were people paying back for Arab lands monies at high prices, land that had been abused by generations of bad farming, that had to be carefully nursed back into fertility. Here, too, was constant danger from bands of marauding Arabs, intensely hostile to these people trying to settle again in the land.

"Hardships were numerous. Physicians and nurses were too expensive to be even thought of. Swamps abounded and mosquitoes were numerous. Is it to be wondered at that malarial fever was a common occurrence? Water was scarce, and the ideal of biologic protection never had a hearing. As a result, typhoid fever claimed too many victims. The climate differed from that of Eastern Europe whence came most of the colonists; but who was to instruct these people in a necessary change of diet?

"There was no provision for caring for maternity cases, except a missionary hospital to which mothers might be admitted only if the child were to be baptized in the Christian Church. Naturally, Jewish mothers could not use it. Therefore the infant death rate was frightful."

So Hadassah set itself to heal, to turn death into life, to bring scientific health culture to the Holy Land.

Through Miss Szold, Mr. and Mrs. Nathan Straus offered to equip and send out two nurses for three months, provided that her new group would carry on their support for one year.

To some members of the band, this was a fearsome and a terrifying thing to guarantee. But nothing was impossible to Henrietta Szold. If the project were right, the support would come, and she persuaded the group to accept the gift and back it up. So two nurses were chosen, who sailed with Mr. and Mrs. Straus early in 1913.

With what high hopes did Henrietta wave them off! There was work to do now, money to raise, new groups to organize, incoming immigrants to welcome. And how eagerly did she await the first letters from the two nurses.

"It is like stepping back into the Middle Ages," they wrote. "Such poverty, such distress, as we could never have imagined. The mothers are hopeless of trying to save their new babies, without water or any sort of sanitation, without linen, sheets. A bed is a ragged quilt on a stone or earth floor. Please send us more layettes for the babies, and sheets and bandages and . . ." The list seemed endless.

So now Hadassah got to work in earnest.

At that time in Jerusalem there was no telephone, and no automobile for the two nurses. Calls for aid began coming in thick and fast, in Jerusalem and out. They had to walk, going from one filthy hovel to another, all the day long. If they carried clean sheets to a mother, with a can full of precious water to bathe the new baby, there was wonder, almost alarm. The instant their backs were turned, the mother rose from her spotless bed, removed the precious sheets and folded them carefully away, to lay them down again only when the children, posted at the end of the lane, brought word of the nurse's return visit.

Working under one of the doctors in the Straus Health Center, they were able to train four native Jewish women as midwives to assist them with the babies. Yet how hard it was to teach the commonest laws of hygiene: clean hands, a clean apron, boiled water.

And how hard they found it to break down the old ways of ancient midwives, with superstitious incantations, of tossings of the new baby over burning incense, and bundling it in filthy rags.

Their small home became a miniature Nurses' Settlement House, modeled on that of New York. Later that year, when Jane Addams visited them, she presented them with a guest book, after the gracious ways of Hull House.

Now with added help for their mothers, both Jewish and Arab, and Christian, too, if they wished to come, the two nurses could respond to the countless needs of other patients suffering with malaria, typhoid, and especially trachoma, the disease which caused blindness in more than sixty per cent of the population.

To combat this, they decided to begin with the children in the Jewish schools.

An eye specialist undertook to examine every single child in the schools. Now, each morning at seven, the nurses would start off on their school rounds. In each one they fitted up a small dispensary, and one by one as fast as they could handle them, they treated one hundred pairs of eyes, swabbing them with the good salve which would surely save their sight.

Today, one of the nurses looks back upon this as the happiest experience of twenty-five years and more of nursing, for she had the tangible result of saving eyesight for hundreds of children. During the first year they had treated five thousand.

How the children revered the American nurses! Though they were disappointed at first in the plain uniforms, they soon grew to love them, and would bring gifts of wild flowers to the clinics.

So through these nurses, Hadassah was gaining headway. Through them, Esther was healing her people. The nurses now opened their home as a training school for older girls, a Big Sisters' Club, so that they could assist in nursing and baby care. Progress would have gone forward steadily but for a terrible event, the World War. Unforeseen, it crashed like a thunderstorm, darkening the face of the world.

For Turkey broke with the Entente, joining the Central Powers, and immediately poured its soldiers into Jerusalem, making Palestine a base from which to strike at England by way of Egypt and the Suez Canal. This meant that, with the country overrun with troops and the ports blockaded by battleships, all supplies, all money and foods from America, all communication with the outside world were cut off.

Now the Arabs, who had been watching the Zionist activities on the land and in the cities with growing suspicion, openly revolted against further law and order by seizing tools or cattle or sheep, ravishing and looting. And who was to stop them? Surely not Ahmed Jemel Pasha, governor-general of Syria and commander of the Turkish forces. For what was it to him, this chaos of little Palestine? He had greater things to think of: the blockade of the Dardanelles, the defense of Constantinople, the stirring up of dissension in Egypt. Besides, his own Turkish troops were quite as devastating to the country as the Arabs.

And as if this were not trouble enough, there came sweeping upon the Holy Land one of the plagues right out of the Old Testament — a plague of locusts. Only this time it was not sent against Pharaoh "to let my people go" ; but against a people already bowed in trouble. The black swarm of locusts swept over Palestine, eating every living spear of green in those agricultural colonies, every leaf of the olive trees, every ribbon of corn, every blade of grain.

The brave Hadassah nursing unit was summarily driven from their post and shipped home, leaving their poor more wretched, more helpless than before, so that thousands died of starvation.

Miss Szold and her devoted band of Hadassah still heard the cry of their people, but were powerless to help. They could only work and pray with faith that England would save Palestine. Nor did they pray in vain.

For on two counts the year 1917 was one long to be remembered in Jewish history. Unable to take Constantinople, General Allenby determined to strike a blow at Turkey by the invasion of Palestine. Working up from Cairo, he captured the port of Jaffa, wheeled inland, climbed the hills, and on December 11th, marched into Jerusalem.

What a deliverer he became to those wretched people. He found their lands untilled, their stocks of horses and cattle dead or eaten by soldiers, their orange groves ruined for lack of irrigation, all commerce and trade at a standstill.

But the British soon changed that for Jerusalem, at least. Food was rushed in by lorries and by rail from Egypt. Schools and law courts were reopened. Ancient springs were discovered which had served the Roman armies in the days of Herod and of Pontius Pilate, and which once more supplied water to the city of Zion.

Best of all, communication was established with America by way of England.

The outlying country still suffered cruelly, for it was nearly a year later before General Allenby could rid the land of Turkish troops. But the calls for help to Henrietta Szold did not go unheeded.

The men's organization of Zionists, having decided to send over two nurses and two doctors with half a ton of medical supplies, asked Miss Szold and her women's organization to take charge of it.

The project grew and grew, encountering innumerable difficulties because of the long journey through war-torn countries and seas, until at last, in June, 1918, the Medical Unit of more than forty, including doctors, nurses, dentists, civil and sanitary engineers, got under way, with four and a half tons of medical equipment including X-rays, serums, and a complete hospital, which was set up on arrival in Jerusalem.

They had begged Henrietta Szold to go out with them. But there was work still to do in America, money to raise, new Hadassah groups to organize; work that only she could do, humdrum, hidden work. So she let the others have the joy of bringing healing to their people.

Within two months after their arrival, the Turks had been driven out of Palestine. At once the Medical Unit sent a truck with medicines and a staff up to Tiberias, where they found the city in an epidemic of cholera. Here was work to do indeed. Soon they had five centers in operation, and throngs of sufferers pressed in day and night for treatment. From this splendid war work has grown the large permanent medical work of Hadassah.

On yet another count was Jewish destiny linked with that of England in 1917. Five weeks before General Allenby's dramatic entry into Jerusalem, Lord Balfour, then Foreign Secretary, received from the Cabinet the confirmation of his recommendation that Palestine be declared a national home henceforth for Jewish peoples.

Now, having obtained the signatures of other European nations, and the ready endorsement of President Wilson for America, Lord Balfour so wrote to Baron de Rothschild and the Zionist leaders.

What if England's motives were not entirely dictated by humanity and philanthropy, what if she did want a friendly wedge between Turkey and Egypt, and an overland route to India? The glorious fact of the Declaration remained to stir Miss Szold's heart with glad thanksgiving.

And what rejoicing there was among Zionists all over the world! For this Declaration was followed by a Mandate over Palestine granted to England by the League of Nations. Now, even non-Zionists began to agree that this might mean a long step forward for this people who had been harried and hounded out of every country in Europe during twenty centuries.

With the 1917 recognition of Jews in Russia as a national unit, followed by the counter-revolution which plunged them into such suffering as had not been endured since the Middle Ages, refugees began pouring into Palestine now by thousands, soon swelling the 1914 population of sixty thousand to eighty-five thousand.

Bottled up during the World War, with Poland a battleground across which two armies shuttled back and forth, Polish refugees began swarming to Palestine, adding their quota. New problems confronted the country. To America came a cry from the Hadassah-Zionist medical group for Miss Szold herself. Only she would know how to assimilate all these people.

So it was that in 1920, Henrietta Szold answered their cry and went out to make her home in Palestine, to become the mother of refugees. She watched them come crowding in on every Egyptian train, on every boat. They brought lumpy bundles of treasures, the Torah, what clothing they could carry.

They spoke a polyglot of tongues: Arabic, Polish, Rumanian, Yiddish, Russian, Turkish, Greek, Italian, French, German, Spagniol or Castilian of the fifteenth century. Few had had opportunity to learn the Hebrew which was now the common language of the country.

In worship, some were orthodox, some liberal, some reformed, some believed in nothing. In politics, some were communists, some even anarchists, some believed in democracy, all believed in the law of human rights and in social justice.

Miss Szold had to become selfless, impersonal, universal, without prejudice. She had to help to find a shelter and food for all these thousands, and a place for each in the farm colonies or in trades, so that they could begin at once to work, and to earn their bread.

For to Henrietta Szold, these immigrants were not just a mass, shapeless, disheveled, weary, dispirited. No, each was an individual, to be treated with love and respect, with deep understanding of his own peculiar needs and problems and their solution.

She saw that her outstanding gift to them, backed always by Hadassah, must be not only the expansion of the whole medical work but also the inauguration of social service. Palestine must be turned into a huge Social Settlement

House. Instead of that first class in Americanization in Baltimore for a few hundred immigrants, she must now attempt "Palestinization" for many thousands of immigrants, until each man, woman and child could be melted, assimilated, fitted into his or her own niche, and so grow happy and content.

That Palestine became a haven of refuge alike to Zionists and non-Zionists is proved by figures alone, for by 1929, the Jewish population had increased to one hundred and fifty-seven thousand, and today to almost four hundred and fifty thousand. This, in a little country about the size of Wales, a bit larger in area than Vermont but smaller than Maryland, which must support in addition a large Moslem and Christian population.

So Miss Szold planned and worked among them, and Hadassah worked at home, standing behind her these twenty-five years, and growing great and wise in consequence.

Since "the healing of my people" was their chief aim, they have extended that first maternity work to twenty-three infant welfare stations, with eighteen pre-natal clinics. To these spotless blue-and-white havens come a stream of mothers: intelligent university graduates from Russia, blue-eyed and fair-haired; Oriental Yemenites, wholly untaught save in grace and dusky beauty; black-girdled Moslem women with snapping black eyes; all willing and eager to follow the instructions of nurses and doctors and so save their babies.

No wonder the rate of infant mortality has been decreased fifty per cent. These years of holding to standards of scrupulous cleanliness by the trim green-and-white uniformed nurses have convinced mothers that babies are better off without the aid of magic or of being branded with a red-hot iron. No wonder that, in a single generation, Hadassah has advanced medical standards from the Dark Ages to the twentieth century.

In addition to baby care, this organization has equipped and maintained four hospitals and five dispensaries. They have opened a sanitarium for sick minds, and clinics for sick teeth. Their nurses inspect twenty-five thousand school children for the dread trachoma, which, thanks to the work of the Rockefeller Foundation and other agencies has reduced trachoma to three per cent.

Single-handed, Miss Szold and Hadassah could not battle against malaria, but with engineers to drain swamps, and the Palestine Government to provide quinine prophylaxis and to destroy carriers, Hadassah nurses have carried on an educational campaign which is truly liberating the land.

Nor could malaria and typhoid and tuberculosis be stamped out without grappling with the fundamental problem of sanitation. But no problem daunts Miss Szold. Was it the work of men? But the women must be educated to coöperate, and this work of education no one in the world could do but Hadassah nurses.

When the Government took over their work for sanitation in the cities, the nurses moved out into country areas.

Although all incoming immigrants must pass a medical test before being allowed to disembark at the two ports, yet they brought with them seeds of disease from the crowded ghettos of Russia, Poland, and Rumania. So a new work was undertaken by the Queen Esther staff, in providing for six months' free medical care after arrival.

From the very early days infectious skin diseases had played havoc with children's heads. But thanks to their

X-ray institutes and specially trained nurses, Hadassah has been able to reduce these skin eruptions from sixty-eight per cent to zero. Now every child is cured before he is allowed to enter school.

Tuberculosis had to be fought from the ground up, by means of clinics for children, educational campaigns, prevention societies for grownups, and a hospital which, for many years, was the only one in Palestine.

All during these years of her work, Henrietta Szold has felt that no permanent healing was possible without sound education in common hygiene. In a land without ice, without much water, and that often defective, she had to teach the habit of boiling drinking water, and the use of dried milk. At last, through the generosity of Mr. Nathan Straus, she was able to set up a milk pasteurization plant in Jerusalem.

Now as the cities such as Tel-Aviv and Jerusalem, Tiberias and Damascus, have grown in wisdom and prosperity, they have been able to take over one after another of Hadassah's projects, leaving Miss Szold free to venture into new fields.

Social service called for trained workers to travel among the settlements and colonies which number nearly one hundred and twenty-five. For in the many experiments in communal, semi-communal or private ownership of land, as well as in forms of government, they have presented every sort of problem in human relationships. The social worker solves many of these problems through wise and impartial tolerance.

Under this department, too, come the playgrounds for children, the clubs for grown-ups, and the school lunches. All these were frowned upon at first, just as much of the medical work was. The people have had to be educated to accept proper food and supervised play for their children in Palestine, just as they have on the lower east side in New York. But today, the playgrounds of the Holy Land have become so necessary that the work has been extended to include traveling companies who go from colony to colony giving concerts, lectures, festivals, showing lantern slides.

So now those who labor for Queen Esther include, besides some twenty-seven physicians and fifty-five nurses, increasing numbers of social workers, headed of course by the founder.

Still another project was dear to Miss Szold's heart from the beginning of 1913. She dreamed of a nurses' training school for young girls. Today this school is run in her own name. Already it has graduated more than two hundred nurses for work in hospitals, clinics, rural settlements, growing cities.

And not only did she think of nurses, but also of the young doctors coming out to work in the Holy Land, ignorant of the unusual conditions to be met. For them, Hadassah opened a special training hospital where they might study the diseases peculiar to a sub-tropical climate.

But the crowning work of this busy, vital American women's organization is their growing gift of a medical institution of research in connection with the new Hebrew Hospital which crowns the hill called Scopus.

It was for this work that the birthday check of seventy-five thousand dollars was made by the three hundred chapters of Hadassah. The goal set of raising seven hundred thousand dollars for this work alone, is a long way from that first small beginning of maintaining two nurses for one year. For in addition to this gigantic project they must carry on the work of their seven hundred institutions in Palestine which they already support.

Most of Hadassah's nearly sixty thousand members have never seen the land of their fathers, so it is the more remarkable that they are able to sacrifice so much for its healing. Surely it will be one of the stars in the crown of America, that she sheltered these immigrants, whose children and children's children in turn, have ministered so ably to the restoration of other thousands in the home-land. Truly has Miss Szold been magnified a thousand-fold in her life-work, as her dreams have been made realities by this group.

Now the younger generation, organized in 1921 as Junior Hadassah, already numbering some ten thousand, are pledged to the work of education of the children.

Believing with all her heart that the future of Palestine lay in her children, Miss Szold had long been troubled by the orphan waifs thronging the narrow streets, sleeping in doorways, snatching food where they could steal it. So she proposed that Junior Hadassah take over this group and build for them a children's village. Not just a cold institution, but a village modeled on the best in America, so as to produce happy, healthy, loving, romping youngsters. Especial care must be taken in educational training in crafts, in order to fit them for life.

Now having provided for all these groups, having established the healing of her people, Miss Szold's family decided in 1933 that it was high time she came home to America to rest and enjoy life. At seventy-three, she was surely too old to continue further. So they urged her to resign from all her executive committees; to lay down her portfolios of education, public health, social service; to turn over her mass of correspondence, and her three secretaries, to younger hands. Consequently, one of her sisters went over to Palestine to bring her home.

Henrietta Szold thought her sister was probably right. Younger people could do her work better, she was sure. She thought wistfully of returning to Baltimore, of walking on green grass, of gathering spring wildflowers, and of watching the pageantry of color in the fall. She thought too of the books waiting to be written. Yes, perhaps it was best to leave: the younger ones could carry on now. The path was clear. The pioneer problems were faced. Palestine was set upon the Way of Peace, in spite of the trouble with the Arabs. Education and tact and patience would win them also, she felt. So she packed her trunks.

But she reckoned without Herr Hitler. There began now in 1933 a series of new edicts against Jews. Twenty thousand children were expelled from German schools, such good schools from kindergarten to university, among the best in the world. In addition to schools, all trades and professions began closing their doors to German Jewish youth.

In panic and terror, the Jews sent a deputation at once to Palestine to lay the whole matter before Henrietta Szold. She would know what to do. It was not for themselves that they pleaded, but for the children.

Her heart stirred strangely. What if in years she were seventy-three? She felt young with courage to face this big new problem.

She went straight to the Government, to talk with the High Commissioner, Sir Arthur Wauchope, and his advisory council of Arabs, Christians, Jews. Yes, a plan must be worked out for allowing new immigration quotas: so many capitalists, so many professors, skilled workers, laborers, elderly couples, each to present an entrance fee, each to be allowed families of children, each to come laden with bundles and bales, each with a health certificate of vaccination.

And for the children of parents who could not leave, or were not included in the quota? Well, she would have to work out her own plan, they told her.

"But I hope you will consider taking charge of the whole thing yourself," said the High Commissioner.

"We are putting the whole problem of the German youth immigration on your shoulders," said her two fellow members of the Palestine Executive.

She unpacked her trunks, a new light in her great brown eyes.

"You see, dear," she told her sister, "they seem to forget my age, so I may as well forget it too. In fact, I've decided never to have another birthday!"

She journeyed to Germany to see conditions for herself. Together with the leaders there, she worked out a plan for the saving of a generation of German youth. There, parents were to send their boys and girls between fifteen and seventeen to youth camps for three months of intensive training to see whether they were fitted for, or could stand, the hard agricultural work in Palestine. First they must pass a rigid physical examination. Then they must learn to milk cows, to plow, to plant seeds, to study how to care for citrus fruit and olive trees.

If at the end of this period they still had courage and enthusiasm, if they could bear the long separation from their families, they were to take ship for Palestine, each group of fifteen being shepherded by a teacher who, also, would join the agricultural group.

Youth Aliyah, she called the movement, youth immigration or "going up" to Palestine.

Miss Szold herself explains the terms. "The Hebrew word for immigration to Palestine is 'Aliyah,' which means 'going up.' Those of you who have visited Palestine know that to reach the center, the heart, the ancient city of Jerusalem, which to many means the whole of Zion, you must go up and up, because it lies high on the skyline. Therefore, immigration is 'going up,' and indeed, this whole movement is a progress upwards."

Meanwhile in the Holy Land, Miss Szold and her committees made preparation to receive the new recruits. Thirty-four agricultural colonies agreed to make room for them. The Government agreed to issue special Youth Certificates, provided that the Jewish Agency would be responsible for them up to the age of eighteen and would guarantee that they should not become a burden on the country.

When the cable came announcing the arrival of the first group of fifty-nine, Miss Szold went up to Haifa to meet them. How eagerly she scanned the row of fresh young faces crowding the ship's rail. And how lovingly they waved to her. For they knew her well, this mother of all youth.

She went up with them in the crowded busses to the colony of Ain Harod, in the shadow of towering Mt. Gilboa in the Plain of Jezreel. She stayed with them until she had learned to know them well. She learned of their parents, of their difficulties in being barred from their future at home, of their longings and their aspirations. She started them in Hebrew and watched them begin their work on the land. That was in February of 1934.

All Jewish Palestine watched to see how this first group would turn out. Could they stand it? Would they make good as pioneers?

In a message from Miss Szold to her American groups, dated January, 1936, she wrote: "The German Youth Immigration to Palestine is to my mind one of the most touching things that I have ever encountered in my long experience. I have never been connected with any work that has been so responsible, and yet so wonderful. We have brought to Palestine a thousand adolescents in less than two years; a thousand boys and girls . . . who lived in abysmal distress, in abject hopelessness . . . marred by bitterness, robbed of the birthright of youth which tells them they are the makers of the future. . .

"In Palestine these children are placed in our coöperative settlements for the first two years. . . These coöperative farmers came forward as soon as the news of the Hitler catastrophe reached us. They called a meeting and decided that they would accept a certain number of children at a low cost in order to pay for their maintenance and education.

"One of our groups will be graduated the middle of February when fifty-nine boys and girls will leave Ain Harod, in order to go out into the world on their own account. They will stand on their own feet. They will have received two years of instruction in practical work on the farm, in the stables, in the workshops; they have received two years of instruction in the Hebrew language and they will have made the difficult adjustment to the conditions of their new home through the study of Jewish history, Jewish literature and the geography of Palestine. They will have been given a fundamental understanding of their practical work because they will have had the auxiliary studies which make that work understandable, such as botany, physics and chemistry. They will have had the opportunity from time to time of wandering on excursions throughout the land with their leaders and teachers who are ready to give historical explanations, ready to point out the nature of the land, ready to tell them what the meanings of the social experiments are that are being carried on in this laboratory of Jewish life.

"We do not claim that they will emerge from the two-year period in the coöperative settlement perfect in any one vocation, but they will have been adjusted to this new life, into which fate has plunged them. Within a week after these fifty-nine leave their places at Ain Harod, sixty others will come who are at this moment in some training camp in Germany where they are being prepared for life in Palestine. A few weeks later another group of young people will be graduated from one of the settlements which has been their home during the first two years, and a second group will come from the Berlin training camp to fill their places . . . in a land of hope, work and achievement."

Naturally, she could not depend upon Hadassah alone to finance so large a project, so she organized twenty-two committees working in seventeen countries of the world to conduct campaigns for Youth Aliyah.

Now, as the time drew near for the first group to venture out alone, they held many conferences with the five hundred older members of the community as well as among themselves. They knew that Miss Szold and her committees both in Jerusalem and in Berlin eagerly awaited their decision. At last it was announced. They applied to the Jewish National Fund to purchase for them a piece of land in order to start a new settlement of their own; like the older pioneers, they would work up from nothing, from a rocky, back-breaking hillside, to a model farm.

Accordingly, forty-five of the original group of fifty-nine moved to a nearby plot of land which they called *Sheikj Aveik*. The others went into trades, or rejoined their families who had come over from Germany, or remained at Ain Harod for further training.

What a great moment it was for Miss Szold, when she could thus prove to the world that her faith had not been misplaced, that the plan really worked. How joyously she helped them design their own social hall for lectures, concerts, and games, their own synagogue, their common library. With what new courage she could greet the incoming groups.

A letter written by a member of a colony to Germany and translated for America describes graphically the arrival of one such group. As usual, Miss Szold had met them at Haifa to accompany them to their new home.

"The Youth Aliyah group from Germany arrived here today. [In Daganiah, Jordan Valley.] The water splashed high on both sides of the wheels when the heavily laden bus drove into the courtyard. It was a rainy day.

"The sixty youngsters were very tired, and some of them much shaken after the stormy voyage. They looked at the green fields and the blue Lake Tiberias, hardly believing that they had arrived in their own country, that they could inhale the free air of a land which they could call their own. The whole atmosphere seemed like a miracle to them, and they walked about as though in a trance.

"We had expected them. We had stopped our own work, because the new concrete house for the Youth Aliyah had to be built in great haste. The best and most suitable spot in Daganiah where the house could be erected had to be found.

"The completed house stands near the coast, with a fine uninterrupted view of the blue Lake Tiberias. Palms reach up to the sky, and olive trees spread their branches in front of the house.

"Beds, chairs and cupboards which the juveniles have to paint themselves were put into the rooms.

"The school children and those from the nursery looked forward to the arrival of the boys and girls with special joy. They prepared many presents for them. The older children decorated the dining room and others made banners of welcome.

"So splendidly were the tables laid that they reminded one of a wedding feast.

"And now they are all sitting at these tables, and I am looking on.

"Gradually the excitement on the faces of the boys seems to subside, and they fuse into one great mass, which one calls a 'people.' And I see the great tragedy of this people to whom all of us belong. . . Shall we find peace and rest in this country of our fathers?

"I catch the bright eye of a boy. Hopeful and consoled, I observe the looks of all the boys. . . The festival begins. I hear sounds of music from the piano as all rise from their seats and sing 'Techesakna,' a song of comfort and hope.

"Henrietta Szold begins to speak. She is a delicate little person, but full of vitality, power and personality. She said that she was grateful to Divine Providence for enabling her in her old age to coöperate with the work of the Youth Aliyah.

"She had helped many people during her life, she had helped to achieve much, but she knew that this work would be the most important of her whole life. She compared the festival with a wedding, with the fusion of the youth with the soil—their country. Just as a marriage should be an unbreakable tie, so should the fusion of the youth with the country also be unbreakable.

"She knew of the great responsibility lying upon all of us who have settled in the Jordan Valley. If she entrusted the greatest treasure of our people, its youth, to us, she knew that the young people would be in good hands.

"One of our comrades answers her. We know the great responsibility which we have undertaken. We are happy that we are able to receive the juveniles in our midst. We shall teach these boys and girls; but they must keep their eyes open, for we are men of few words. We shall talk to them through our plantations, our vineyards, and our stables, and by the nature of our work, they will understand our ways.

"Some more addresses were delivered which recalled the past to our minds. Many recall their own Aliyah (immigration), how difficult it was at that time, how hard the fight for existence, and how exhilarating the work.

"One of the juveniles rose from his seat, a tall fellow. He spoke in broken Hebrew of the necessity of their coming to this country. The pain of farewell could still be noticed in his faltering words. He referred to his parents in Germany . . . he hoped that the life in this country, working under freedom, would be the reward for painful separation.

"Music, pastoral songs, the compositions of a shepherd from Beth Alpha, and dancing concluded the evening.

"Was this a mere dance? No! It was more than that. It was as a man reels when he goes from the dark into the light. It was that intoxication which affects men who awake to a new existence after a long, long sleep; it was a storm of enthusiasm which carried everyone away. Even the seventy-five-year-old Henrietta Szold put her arms around the shoulders of a young man, and made the *horra* a solemn dance which none of the people present will ever forget." *

So groups have come until more than fifteen hundred boys and girls have been absorbed into thirty-four colonies. Miss Szold still makes the trips to Jaffa and Haifa to meet the incoming boats, and, whenever possible, she still stays with them for a week or two, telling stories, playing games, helping them over the first torturing wave of homesickness. She supervises the division of their day into part-time field work, part-time indoor study. On Sabbath they attend whatever form of worship they have been accustomed to at home, whether orthodox or liberal Judaism.

If the youngsters are musical, they must find time to carry on studies with violin or piano or flute. Above all, Miss Szold insists that they speak their own language, even though they must use Hebrew as a common tongue. She feels that there is something precious in their native culture which must be carefully fostered and preserved, that it may make its own contribution to the flowering of the new land.

They understand that if, at the end of two years, they find themselves unsuited to agriculture or dairying, they

* Published by the *Arbeitsgemeinschaft für Kinder und Jugend Alijah*, Berlin.

may turn to the crafts: wood or ivory carving, copper or brass work, jewelry, embroidery, lace-making, carpet-weaving; or to a trade; or they may even win a scholarship in the University, in training for one of the professions.

Best of all to them, at the end of this two-year period, they may send for their parents, their younger brothers and sisters. For to them the Government has granted the proud privilege of bringing in their families on an extra quota basis of kinship.

This separation from mother and father has been the hardest burden of all. The adjustment to work, climate, and conditions was not so difficult. Youth is strong and brave and loves adventure, and is not afraid to work. But homesickness has been the worst agony of the two years.

To Miss Szold, these letters from her children, pouring out their hearts to her, their foster mother—since they dared not write home and so make the burden there more bitter—these letters to her prove her most tragic burden. For she carries them all in her heart.

By means of card files in her office in Jerusalem, she keeps in intimate touch with each boy and girl. At a glance, she reads on his or her card qualities of character, dreams and hopes. She charts progress, sicknesses, development. Never does she think of them as a youth mass, but as fifteen hundred individuals, noisy, assertive, presenting a thousand new problems, but the hope and the glory of Israel.

"When I come into a coöperative settlement," she writes to her Hadassah groups, "and hear the presentation of problems—adolescent problems and therefore serious problems—when I hear them presented by our colleges of workers, as I like to call them, that is to say, by the young man or woman who has brought the group from Germany, having there been associated with it in the youth organizations; and by the teachers who are teaching the various disciplines, and by the house mother of the settlement who deals with intimate problems of these boys and girls, and by the master workmen who work in the workshops, fields and vineyards – when I observe with what intelligence and sympathy and understanding for youth they present these questions, then I am thrilled to be privileged to join in these discussions. I am more than thrilled, I am touched deeply to the very roots of my being.

"Sometimes representatives of these coöperatives will come to me at Jerusalem in order to present a serious problem. We may have to let this boy go from our settlement, they say, because he does not seem to adjust himself to collective living, he is not accustomed to it. However, don't take it as a final decision, I am cautioned, because we are going to look into the situation. After two weeks have passed, they come to me to say they think they discern progress; and then after a few weeks more have elapsed, they announce that the child will stay with them.

"When you have people like that, who undertake to work out the educational programs for these adolescents with their teachers and leaders and who hold conferences every three months in order to discuss such questions, after which they apply with intelligence and devotion what has been learned at these gatherings, then you know that you are in the midst of a stream of life that carries you along, away from old age and back to youth. That is the reason I feel as though I have been privileged in my old age to assist as a modest worker in what I consider a significant world movement.

"I say a world movement because we cannot stop at Germany; we must bring succor to the children of Poland, Austria, Rumania and to the children of refugees who have fled to France and other parts of Western Europe. We must take care of all the underprivileged, economically and socially. . . "

How her mind and heart do run ahead of her organizations and beckon them on. Yet she knows, too, that to admit ten thousand children a year would mean chaos. So she is forced to limit the waiting lists, taking only as many as can be given careful supervision and training, knowing that if the foundation laid is wise and safe, these boys and girls will mean the salvation of the country for the future.

Nor is it easy for her to refuse the hundreds of begging letters:

"Dear Youth Aliyah of Palestine," came a letter from Kassel, Germany. "We are forty-four children of the Jewish elementary school of Kassel, in our fifth-sixth year. Together with our teachers and near relatives we want to go to Palestine through the Youth Aliyah. Please reply soon. In the name of the whole class, Shalom."

It is but one of many. So few can be accepted, one out of thousands.

Hadassah tells the story of one boy who could not wait for permission to enter Palestine. So desperate was his need that, in spite of a club foot, he started out alone from a crowded industrial city of Poland. All the way he trudged across Poland, across Czechoslovakia, across Austria, down over the Carnic Alps and so into Italy, to the port of Trieste. What a great world it was. What a weary trek. And still the seas to cross.

One after another the boy begged passage on fifteen

ships bound for Palestine. He had no papers, no money. He was irregular, a waif. No wonder that no one would allow him passage.

The boy grew desperate. Finally, on the sixteenth boat he managed to slip aboard and stow himself among bales of merchandise. Crouched in the darkness, he sailed down the Adriatic, across the Ionian Sea to the Mediterranean. Driven at last by hunger, the boy crept up on deck.

He was discovered a few days before the ship landed at Haifa, and was taken to the captain. So hard did he plead to be allowed to land that the captain finally agreed to turn him over to the passport commission in the port. There, hearing the boy's amazing story, the Youth Commissioner sent him up to Miss Szold. So at last he came home. For she understood well that only an intense and bitter need could have driven him to endure those months of hunger, cold, and fatigue.

Her first act was to make use of the agencies of her own making. In the new Rothschild-Hadassah Hospital his club foot was successfully operated on. After weeks of care, of good food, of love, he was placed in one of the children's agricultural colonies. So eager was he to prove his gratitude that he threw himself into every department of the farm life. He learned the difficult Hebrew language easily. He developed unexpected marked musical gifts. To his supreme satisfaction he was at last given "the right to work."

Truly for him Youth Aliyah meant a "going up."

"I believe it is unprecedented in history," Henrietta Szold writes, "as, in my Zionist understanding . . . I look upon the whole of Zionism and what it has achieved in Palestine as an unprecedented movement in Jewish history.

We are really creating something out of nothing. We have achieved much—we know much remains to be achieved; and through this Youth Aliyah we are training and bringing into Palestine these youthful workers who will supplement the achievements still needed to make Palestine a true home for the Jew."

How difficulties melt before this army of agricultural colonists. In their hands modern science is transforming the barren rocky hills, denuded these centuries of all trees, into fertile productive land with a yield beyond their dreams.

Even the aridity is being overcome by piping water long distances for irrigation, so that the citrus fruits now rank with those of California.

A German scientist used his divining rod in one colony with effective results. That glad day when gushing springs far beneath the surface were uncovered, the young people went mad with joy. They danced and sang the whole day through, declaring it a holiday. They made new psalms of thanksgiving for the blessed gift of water.

It is but one more answer to Miss Szold's faith. Did not her Hebrew Prophets sing of a land flowing with milk and honey? Are not the new yields of bee hive and dairy, garden and orchard, proclaiming it daily? Surely these five hundred and eighteen square miles of the fatherland owned by Jews may one day become like the garden of Eden. Of agriculture she writes with enthusiasm:

"Farming has risen to the height of an intellectual calling, with the finest agricultural experimental stations, adding well-established theory to practice. It is the hope for the Youth to remain on the land, and still to enjoy theatrical performances, concerts and lectures, brought to them at regular intervals. Real farmers are thus created out of shepherds and students of the past."

Yet for all this reclamation work for land and human beings, Miss Szold does not ignore the varied problems presented by the uprisings of the Arabs, crushed for centuries, and scarcely emerging from economic and social slavery. Nor those problems presented by a society made up of Christians, Moslems, Jews of every nation, soldiers of Britain, all compressed within an area of some ten thousand square miles.

To her, however, no future development of the country is possible without a spiritual foundation for Jewish life. That four-volume work on Ethics which she translated in her youth is still the basis of her life. She would like to see this Jewish ethics shaping the general life of the country, eliminating "speculations, loud living, assertiveness, party strife and class war."

It is on a basis of brotherhood, of tolerance, of freedom from prejudice that she is able to recognize and call forth the worth of an individual—of any individual, whether Arab, Christian or Jew. The attainment of peace among them, she believes, will depend upon education and spiritual culture. For this she works ceaselessly.

No wonder, then, that she could ill spare the time for her seventy-fifth birthday celebrations. Although seemingly frail, her energy is still boundless. In a land where sickness prevails, even among doctors and nurses, she herself keeps buoyantly well, working from eighteen to twenty hours a day, tiring out her three secretaries. To one she dictates reports and letters in Hebrew, to another in German, and to the third in English.

She has an inexhaustible capacity for details, and brings to grave issues a clear and unbiased judgment.

Nor does she spare herself. Never in these sixteen years has she accepted a salary. When funds are sent explicitly for her own use, to make her constant journeys to and from colonies or seaports more endurable, she has spurned soft and easy ways, such as a car of her own, but takes the common bus and bumps along the rocky roads, or rejoices in the building of a new highway. She keeps only one room at the Hotel Eden. Nor does her light ever seem to go out. For she is upheld by a strength greater than human, and works on tirelessly, selflessly. Clearly "has she shown to what heights of self-dedication and responsibility one can rise in purely voluntary labor."

Loving greatly, she is also greatly beloved. Vera Weizmann, chairman of the Palestine work for London, writes of her:

"Henrietta Szold reminds me irresistibly of a woman who occupied a similar position in the Russian Revolution of my student days. Few know exactly who she was. She was called 'Baboushka'—Grandmother—not because of her age but because of her wisdom, experience, courage and self-annihilation. Very few were privileged to meet her, but her name was on everybody's lips. It is the same with Henrietta Szold, the 'Baboushka' of our movement, so deeply has the knowledge of her personality and achievements gone into the furthest corners of Zionist and Jewish life, so widespread has her influence become."

No wonder she considers that all her previous work for Palestine was but a training for this of Youth Aliyah. To it, she has brought fifty-five years of wisdom and experience. Through it, she is lifting youth en masse from the devastation of fear, hatred, persecution, denial of human rights, to the redemption of the individual.

No longer is the plight of fathers and mothers hopeless while they have the joy of hope for their sons and their daughters.

It is not to be wondered at, then, that Henrietta Szold is loved and adored above every other woman in all Jewry. The practical achievements of her inspired vision will live on for centuries still to come. And children yet unborn will rise up to call her blessed.

She is many sided: to one a mother; to another a wise executive; to still another a perfectionist, excelling in everything she undertakes; to Justice Louis D. Brandeis she is an able statesman; to a colleague she is a world-figure:

"Completely self-effacing, desiring anonymity in all her achievements, she is a woman of wisdom, strength, and statesmanship. She has lived a life of peaceful labor under the challenge of destructive forces, a life of human love and brotherhood in the face of cruel persecution. Her long career of service in the mitigation of the evils of persecution and bigotry should be crowned with world recognition, not only in justice and recompense for great tasks done, but in order that fellowship, good will and peace among nations should be advanced."

CATHERINE BRESHKOVSKY

"BABOUSHKA"

1844–1934

LIKE HENRIETTA SZOLD, Catherine Breshkovsky suffered from an enlarged heart. In it she carried the whole peasantry of Russia, numbering some forty million souls. For them she suffered every indignity; hunger and cold, prison and exile. They did not ask that of her. But she loved them, and believed in them. They had been tortured, abused, beaten, crushed down for centuries, until they were little better than human animals with hearts capable of human suffering. Catherine wanted to free them, to give them the education they had been so long denied, to liberate their minds and spirits.

She herself was of the nobility—of the landed aristocracy. Born in 1844 on an estate in Little Russia, she was christened Ekaterina Constantinovna. They called her Katya for short.

All the work of the estate was done, of course, by the peasants born on the soil. Like their fathers' fathers before them, they were born and chained to the land. It was against the law for serfs to escape. If they ran away, they were hunted with dogs and brought back in chains. For the slightest offense they could be flogged by the master or sent to the mines in far-off Siberia. But life here on the Verigo estate was like paradise. For Catherine's father did not flog his peasants. When a house burned down he helped them to build a new one. He was a wise judge when disputes arose. He called in the more intelligent older girls to work as maids in the great house. Thus they came to know and love his wife and children.

They liked to borrow the little Katya and take her home to visit in their huts, to show her off. To them she was like a princess in a fairy tale.

Katya herself loved these visits. She felt quite at home sitting at the scrubbed deal table on a log of wood and sipping tea from a wooden bowl. She liked to hear them talk—of how the men at the neighboring estate were flogged because they had not got in the hay before the rain fell; of how old Ivan dropped under the lashes.

"If only we could get word to the Little Father," they would say again and again.

"What would the Czar do for you?" Katya asked.

"He would free us," they explained. "See, we have been slaves long enough. It is getting harder and harder, this life."

They all felt restless with the wind in their faces—that wind blowing from Europe with a smell of liberty in it.

Katya saw that they had only coarse black bread to eat, and were allowed to cultivate only one small strip of land for themselves. All the rest of the crops, the wheat and oats and rye and barley, must be garnered for the master. The land all belonged to him.

One day, as she sat in one of the huts, the peasant father drew out a wooden chest he had made, and from it he unwrapped a treasure for Katya to see. The whole family gathered close with big eyes. The children were scarcely ever allowed to see this treasure. Katya herself wondered what it might be.

At last the linen cloth was unwound. It was a book—an old book with tattered leaves.

"Oh!" she said, looking at their ecstatic faces. "It's only a book!"

"Can you tell us what it hides within it, little Countess?" They whispered. One stepped to the doorway to keep watch. If they should be found out!

Katya turned the pages. "Of course I can." She smiled at them. "It's quite harmless—nothing to be afraid of. You won't be sent to Siberia for it. It's only a book of fairy tales—about how Prince Vladimir rescued the princess from the dragon. It goes like this."

As she read, they pressed closer. They stroked her pretty hair, her tiny hands.

Suddenly Katya, looking up, found her throat aching and her eyes filling with tears.

"You want then to learn to read so terribly?"

"Sh—it is forbidden." Hastily they wrapped up the precious book and laid it back in its chest, safely out of sight.

Yes, forbidden—like everything else in their lives but hard work. A rebellion grew in Katya's heart. Who was this Czar Nicholas I that he could allow his people to suffer like this?

"Some day they say we will be free," they whispered. "And then we will know all things."

What a dream. What faith they had. It wasn't the

fault of their Czar, they thought, but only of the hierarchy of cruel officialdom that stood between. If only they could break through and reach him — this Appointed-by-God-One.

Katya went home and talked with her father. He explained to her the operations of the governments of the world, the abuses that had grown up in great despotic monarchies such as their own. He told her of the ideal of democracy for which men in free America had fought and died. He told her the story of how England had freed her black slaves in the West Indies, and of the uprisings of the common people all over Europe in 1848. He agreed with her that their own Russian peasants must be educated and freed.

"Then I will begin right here with our own," Catherine said simply. And she did. She gathered in as many as would come and began teaching them the thirty-five letters of the Russian alphabet. She found the older ones often sunk in apathy and hopelessness. But the younger ones were eager to learn, a new hope stirring with thoughts of freedom.

At sixteen, she was devoting nearly all her time to her school. In the evenings, Catherine read with her father brilliant articles by Alexander Herzen, exiled in England, calling upon the nobles to demand of the Czar the freedom of his peasants. They read in French Diderot's brief that "it is the common people of a nation whose lot ought to be the main concern of a government." And Rousseau's theory that "the basis of all government should rest upon the consent of the governed." And Voltaire's fierce and fearless defense of all those unjustly burdened and oppressed by that same government which, jealous of its royal powers, had exiled him for so many years.

She began to realize that the peasants were deceived in the Czar—that his ears were stopped and his hands bound fast in his own terrible System, while all who opposed this System trudged along the road to Siberia, condemned as political exiles.

The year 1861 brought a crisis to Russia, even as to America: in the latter it marked the beginning of a four-year struggle for the abolition of slaves; in Russia it ended many long centuries of slave-serfdom. On February 19th by the old calendar, or March 3rd by the new, the Czar Alexander II signed at last a manifesto freeing forty million of his peasants, whether they belonged to the State or to nobles—freeing their souls but depriving them of most of the land to which they had been chained for generations. The wide fields of wheat and barley and rye, the vast dark forests, these still belonged to the landlords, as always. Only the peasants were free.

Quite true, each peasant was allowed a narrow strip of land—too often of the poorest soil on the estate—to till as long as he lived. But Catherine Breshkovsky heard the wailing cry that rose all over the country: "How can I nourish my little ones through a Russian winter? Such land means death."

With heavy heart, Catherine stood among them as they pressed into the church where the decree was read. Something was wrong—they well knew what it was. Some of the pages written by the Little Father had been torn out by the nobility before it was read. It couldn't be as it said, it couldn't! What use freedom without the land? Without the good black earth to give them bread? They wouldn't leave, that was all. So they stayed. They sat down on the land.

Then Catherine had to watch the floggings—the horrible brutal floggings with the knout. Her eyes said no but her heart said yes, and she went to the village where the peasants had been driven, lining either side of the road. Every tenth man was flogged.

When the officials returned in two weeks, to find the peasants still doggedly clinging to the land, every fifth man was flogged. Two weeks more and every man in the line bared his back. Some died under it. Some were crippled.

The Verigo garden was crowded with peasants pleading with the Count to tell them that this edict wasn't so; begging him to change things. Catherine saw her father grow haggard and worn. She could stand it no longer, and persuaded her mother to take her away to St. Petersburg. She felt she must study, must learn what was wrong and how to mend things.

In the great capital, she plunged at once into the group of aristocrats called the intelligentsia: young novelists, poets, scientists, doctors, lawyers, nobles, already considered "criminals" because, against the law, they had opened classes for women in natural and political sciences; because they met nightly to discuss the problems of the country, and to formulate plans for solving them.

Catherine was now nineteen. It was like going to a university, and she thrilled to it, all these discussions about freedom and democracy. She knew, also, that the group was ringed about by spies. The slightest criticism of existing conditions or of the System was punished by prison or exile.

Her parents grew terrified about her, and called her

home. Catherine's father understood the growing passion of her soul for social justice. But here at home she was safe. He built for her a boarding school to house the girls of neighboring well-to-do families, and a cottage for her peasants' school. Daring innovations these, to educate girls and peasants. Catherine rejoiced that her father was a liberal.

Here she taught until her marriage to a wealthy but liberal landowner, Count Breshkovsky, who was already helping his own people in their *zemstvo*, or local government. He established for Catherine a peasants' agricultural school. Naturally their home became a center for all the liberal nobility in the district. After long search, they discovered among old laws and edicts, long-neglected but actual rights of peasants to local suffrage. They taught the people how to vote. Naturally, the peasants elected this group of liberal landowners to offices in the *zemstvo*. Thus were ousted the landowners who still believed in graft and in beating the peasants into submission to the old régime. Naturally, in return, these landowners lodged a complaint with officials higher up, charging the young liberals with conspiracy against the government.

As a result, several were sent to Siberia. Catherine and her husband were put under police surveillance. Her father lost his government post.

Together the Breshkovskys faced the future. The last vestige of respect for the System of the Czar fell from them. They knew now that behind it there was no will to peace or security or well-being for the people. Someone had to champion them. The people were helpless by themselves. Yet to champion them meant to be spied upon and watched like a criminal, to become a revolutionist, to face prison or exile.*

Should they give up their home and move to the city, to cast in their lot with the newly formed People's Party? They looked down at their tiny son, not two years old. Catherine's husband decided to stay on at his estate, to help where he could, and to let events move of their own momentum.

Catherine had to think of him, of their son, of her beloved parents and her sister. They formed the dearest and nearest group in her heart. But then she had to think of those millions of peasants who, when at last they succeeded in reaching "the very Czar," were only repulsed by him and thrown into deeper misery by his System of "iron and blood." Else she would have no peace. Which duty was greatest?

Long afterward, she wrote: "This consciousness of duty toward the people is so mighty a force that no personal affection . . . can displace it. When once it has sunk into the depths of one's soul, it drives out all other aspirations and leads mightily toward the chosen goal. It gripped my soul and became my master."

So she made her choice: of such choices the drama of human life is written.

At twenty-six, Countess Breshko-Breshkovskaya, aristocratic landowner, turned her back on her family, her home, her social position, her wealth, to become a revolutionist. She was willing to make any and every sacrifice for her passionate belief that only by educating the peasants, and by overthrowing the System of absolutism, could freedom

* Several years previously, exile in Siberia was substituted for capital punishment.

and happiness result to all the millions of souls in the Russias.

At Kiev she offered herself, heart and soul, for life, to the young revolutionary party. She put on peasant dress: "enormous bark shoes, coarse shirt and drawers, a heavy cloak." She stained her fair skin brown with acid. She ate and slept among the peasants. She traveled on foot from village to village, using forged passports and a new name. She lived "illegally" in defiance of the Government.

Nor was she easily discouraged because she found many of the people apathetic, listless, dull of soul. She had expected it to be uphill work, this, of firing them with her own spark. During the day she unpacked the big sack on her back and set to work at the dyeing of heavy cloth. By this she earned her food. At night she invited the peasants to gather in her mud hut. Out of curiosity they came, until it was packed with men, women and children. Above the low wooden rafters over their heads rose the thatched roof. She watched the firelight play on their stolid faces as she recalled their sufferings. Gradually, she made them see that they themselves were to blame for their submission to floggings that crippled some and left great welts on their backs.

But they were used to this: what good would it do to complain? Then she would reach into her sack for a story book of fables. How the dull eyes would begin to gleam! How they reverenced a book—a holy thing "full of laughter and tears and ideas." How it stirred their age-old longing for freedom.

These books were printed in great secrecy in cellars or attics in the slums. Gifts of jewels, of libraries of rare classics, of gowns and furs went into the Fund and came out as precious books, with propaganda hidden and woven into the fables. If, while reading, Catherine were warned of an approaching spy, she would gather up her sack and rush from the hut, out across the back fields, leaving behind the treasure book which was carefully hidden away until the people could find someone to read it. In a few weeks, along would come another wanderer to repeat the same fables. Thus the seed she had planted was kept watered and green.

By 1874 there were two thousand of these educated revolutionists traveling among the peasants of thirty-six provinces, spreading the gospel of ownership of land, of freedom of the mind and spirit. They were supported and directed by an underground system of communication, with a code for letters.

Mingling freely with the people, Catherine was often able to deceive the police, and often the peasants themselves.

But in her *Memoirs*, she tells of climbing over a fence one day to talk to one of the leading peasants in a village while he threshed. She led him on to tell of his own tortures, of beatings and being thrown into the "black hole" for trying to follow the teachings of Jesus literally.

"Stephan's tale helped me to picture conditions of people elsewhere. I told him of those who ate bread mixed with grass, of the famine on the Volga, and in North Russia, of the miserable wanderings of the landless peasants, their hunger and beatings as they are driven from one village to the next, of the heavy taxes, and the indifference of the Czar to the sufferings of the people."

It was in Stephan's hut that she talked to a group of peasants that night. Next day he said to her:

"'I do not know, sister, who you are and whence you have come, but when you came to me, as I threshed my corn, I thought you were the Empress or the Emperor's daughter.'

"I was surprised.

"'Why?' I asked. 'I spoke against the Czar's power.'

"'It is said in the Bible that their own kind will condemn them,' he answered."

In spite of her brown face and hands, her coarse garments, Stephan knew her for a noblewoman.

YET for all that, Catherine Breshkovsky found that her mere words were often of little weight in convincing the peasants of her burning message. They always said:

"If you would write down these words you speak and spread them everywhere they would be of real use, because the people would know then that they were not invented."

That was because their whole lives were governed by written orders and decrees posted in the villages. And though no one in the village could read, the official who posted it there had read it in a loud voice, so it must be so.

For this reason, whenever our revolutionist ran out of her "illegal" leaflets, she had first to write out her appeal on paper to read to her nightly audience.

Not infrequently, however, she spent many days in assembling even a first audience. It was so in the village which was the scene of her first arrest. Not even the peasant from whom she rented half his hut suspected her, and was bewildered when the Commissary of Police came to his house to search her papers. Holding up her copied message, he began to read it aloud, his voice rising triumphantly with every sentence.

A score of peasants began crowding in, listening wide-eyed. For Catherine had not as yet been able to talk revolution to any except those miserable wanderers — those half skeletons, driven from the land — whom she had found at the marketplace of the nearby town. Now as she sat beside the wooden table, unconcernedly eating her dinner of apples, she watched their astonished faces as the peasants stood bare-headed at the reading of this new "edict." They thought it was from the Little Father at last, with its promises of education and a new life for them.

When the officer had finished reading it he shouted for his clerk to fetch the village priest. His excitement rose as he thought of the glory of bringing in a political prisoner. He, with his own hand, had found her.

"Listen, Reverend Father!" He drew in the priest, commanding his clerk to read the thing.

Now the clerk, unmindful of the peasants, read it again distinctly and solemnly in a loud voice.

"He is doing my work for me," Catherine thought gleefully as she went on munching apples. But in her heart she knew too that she was caught. She should have been more cautious — but somehow, anyhow, she must escape. She went on munching and planning.

The crowd gaped at the priest and the officer. Was it true then? Justice and learning for all! They kept their eyes fixed on that paper.

Now came the Magistrate of the town, sent for by the officer. He was older and sterner. Again the clerk read through her plea for revolution, a third time. Again the audience made the sign of the cross. It was like a word from God. Catherine was delighted. Her arrest was not in vain then. The yard was filled with people, all listening. They crowded every window. They pressed close against the little group by the table.

They waited as hours passed. Finally the chief Commissar of Police for the district pushed in. He had driven thirty versts in answer to a summons. The fourth reading began, but he interrupted it at the end of the first page.

"What is this?" he demanded of the accused woman who sat meekly by the table with hands folded in her lap.

"Propaganda," she answered him mischievously, "with which the officer, the gendarme and the priest are viciously inciting the people."

"Sizt! Take her to prison under a strong guard. First search her well!"

Next morning, after sleeping on a bench in the local prison, Catherine found a group of sentinels and soldiers peering in at her window. She asked them what they had heard of the "edict," and one soldier stepped forward and repeated it word for word. They agreed with her that she was right. But it was impossible to make demands for just taxation, ownership of land, representation in government, education, singly.

"If you would distribute such leaflets all over the country it would be another thing," they told her. "If we tried to enforce these demands, we would only be flogged and sent to prison like you."

Little did they know that such leaflets were being distributed far and wide over the great lands of Russia; that this was her life-work. And yet here she was in prison!

But surely not for long. Surely there was some means of escape.

That night she was taken by cart to the district prison and thrust into a "black hole," the first of many. She dare not step forward for her feet felt slimy filth and ooze. With her hands she tried to feel for a bench, but there was none. The walls were too damp and cold to lean against. So she faced about and stood as close to the door as possible, standing still as long as she could. Then she sat down where she was. In a few moments she sprang up again, covered with insects. Now her body itched from head to toe so that it was impossible to doze or even to stand still.

"I tried to shake off the lice, which gave me no peace," she tells in her *Memoirs*. "In my heart I laughed at the annoyances and thought, 'You won't scare us with this. We knew what was awaiting us, what we should have to bear. But our duty is to go ahead; yours, to torment us. . .'"

Mercifully, she could not look into the twenty-three years ahead. So she lived just one day at a time, knowing that she could get through that, and always planning escape, always dreaming her dreams of liberty for Russia. She saw every form of cruelty, of misery possible to human beings. She had to suffer every form of indignity and insult. She saw and heard her fellow-prisoners become depraved to the status of wild beasts, or go insane.

Yet she lived through ill health, partial paralysis from cold, rheumatism, half starvation, without medical aid of any kind. She learned to dance to keep her muscles fit, even in a tiny cell too small for pacing up and down.

Once, when goaded beyond endurance by a bestial

warder, she prayed intensely for many hours that he might be taken from the prison. He was the terror of hundreds of women and children. By a strange coincidence he suddenly died.

Never did she stop trying to make converts to her strong belief in the ultimate power of the peasants to redeem themselves through education. Often she found keepers and officials who agreed with her secretly, but were powerless to remedy matters, caught as they were in the meshes of the System.

"It is a horrible thing to develop in one's self the instincts of a hound," she told one of them. He had had to help round up some two thousand of her accomplices during the three years that she waited for her trial.

She was to know every type of prison cell in many cities and towns, but as she lay for the first time on her iron cot in St. Petersburg prison, to her delight, she heard a curious tick-ticking sound close to her ear. She listened. It came with regular beats. Tap-dash-tap, tap, along the pipe through her cot. It must be a code, but what code? If only she knew it. Could it be that the letters of the alphabet had each its own number? During a pause she tried it, tapping out the whole thirty-five. Someone responded, tapped it back. She asked a question, laboriously. To her joy it was answered by a comrade—one whom she knew. Patiently, by means of spelling words according to the place of letters in the alphabet, her comrades taught her a much less complicated code.

So now she was joyously enrolled in the prison Social Club of more than a hundred members. Now, every night between the passings of the guard, she could carry on a lively conversation, tapped on the common iron rods that ran from cell to cell through the cots. There was news of the Party, of the organization of a Youth Movement all over Russia, the cheering of comrades who were ill and depressed, bits of gossip, fairy tales, plenty of love-making and even a chess game. What matter if the days were lonely and long, when the nights were jovial and short?

So Catherine waited for trial with her comrades. When it came, in 1878, one hundred of them had died or gone insane. The remaining one hundred and ninety, brought suddenly into the court room, looked into one another's white faces and spoke with burning eyes. The five months of trial were but a mockery, a farce. At its close, Catherine rose to protest against its palpable injustice, and heard her sentence: five years of hard labor in Siberian mines — the same sentence as for a murderer. So, for the first time in her life, she became an exile.

Yet what a tower of strength was Catherine Breshkovsky to those frail ones, less able to endure than herself. For now began the long five-thousand-mile trek along the Great Siberian Road * — partly on foot, mostly by cart, in a *telega*, a springless wagon, without even straw. Hard going it was over the deep ruts, bumping furiously for two weeks at a time, stopping no more than ten minutes night or day to change the three post horses or to put out the flames when the axles caught fire; never out of sight of her three guards for one moment.

Existing on tea and potatoes, and seldom sleeping, she was forced to watch the ragged, unkempt, bitter army of cursing or sobbing human beings marching along that Great Siberian Road. A million had already passed. A million would follow. Yet she endured the journey far

* The Trans-Siberian Railroad was not begun until 1891.

better than many of her younger companions whom she cheered and cared for, regaling even the stolid guards with jokes and stories. She was determined not to make a tragedy of exile, nor to let it make a tragic end of her. She had work to do and Russia to save.

"Hard labor in the mines of Kara," read her sentence. And Kara was followed by a journey into the bleak Arctic Circle, to a group of forlorn huts. At once she gathered the dreary little children into her hut to teach them. But the guards drove the children home. Teaching was not allowed. She heard that one of the mothers was desperately ill, and went to her hut with medicines and ointments. The guards forced her to leave. No doctors or nurses were allowed. She learned that an old man was dying. As fast as she could walk through the snow she went to give comfort and relief. She knew the prayers for the dying. She would dare even administer the last sacraments. Once more the guards interposed.

Desperately, then, she watched for a chance to escape. Never a day had passed in captivity but she had plotted and planned her freedom. After two years in Siberia it came—the chance to set out with three young men revolutionists. Secretly they had gathered supplies as they waited to start the long thousand-mile trek to Vladivostok, and thence by boat to America.

After walking six hundred miles and enduring many months of hardships, and just when they considered themselves safe, they were caught, brought back, and resentenced. Now the seven hardest years of Catherine's life were endured in a hut in the Buriat country, on the borders of China. Because her nature demanded people about her, hundreds looking to her for succor, comfort, strength, inspiration, it was punishment indeed to live alone.

Besides, upon her forced return she learned two sorry facts. The first concerned herself. Her mother had secured her pardon, made impotent and useless now by her escape. And while she was attempting to escape, the Russian Chief of Police had authorized the *Kishinev*, the dread 1881 pogrom or massacre of thousands of Jews. Hundreds of exiled ones had already arrived in Siberia. She longed with all her heart to go about caring for them. Now her own party would be swelled by four hundred thousand Jews waiting the moment of revolution. Ah, yes, they knew well, these officials, how to punish her with solitude.

Moreover, in that same year, 1881, the Czar Alexander was assassinated. Would Alexander III continue the blood and iron tradition of his father? Already there were uprisings as the revolutionary ideas gained momentum. There was famine on the Volga, too, and vast work for her to do. How long, O God, how long?

During these seven years, she used to run out into the deep snow shouting grand opera rôles, or make long oratorical speeches to the wide white wastes at forty-five degrees below zero. She had her sanity to keep, her gaiety, her sense of humor, her faith in human nature.

She saw only three men with whom she could talk for a short time during these long Siberian years. Strangely enough, one of these was an American. Mr. George Kennan went out to write a book about the thousands of political exiles, and was told to go to visit Mme. Breshkovsky. He was deeply impressed by her, and wrote thus:

"Her face bore traces of much suffering, and her thick,

dark wavy hair, cut short in prison at the mines, was streaked here and there with gray. But not hardship nor exile nor penal servitude had been able to break her brave, finely tempered spirit, or to shake her convictions of honor or duty. . . There was no other educated woman within hundreds of miles. What had she to look forward to? Yet she had unshaken courage and faith in the ultimate triumph of liberty."

These were her last words to him:

"We may die in exile, and our children may die in exile, and our children's children may die in exile, but something will surely come of it at last."

Nothing, no one had power to destroy her faith. Mr. Kennan added:

"I have never seen or heard of Mme. Breshkovskaya since that day, but I cannot recall her last words to me without feeling conscious that all my standards of courage, fortitude and heroic self-sacrifice have been raised for all time, and raised by the hand of a woman."

Many years later, he was to hear of her again, and indeed to see her in America!

A blessing it was for Catherine Breshkovsky that she was never embittered by anything that the System did to her. Years later she wrote: "I was never disillusioned; even as a child I learned from the biographies of great men that aspirations toward high ideals always lead to cruel penalties."

However much she might suffer outwardly, nothing could touch her inwardly. She was safe. She seems all the more remarkable when one realizes that out of the hundreds of women exiled during those years with her, only two besides herself survived.

But at last, in 1896, after eighteen years in Siberia, "thoroughly reformed," she was allowed to return to Russia.

She found a new Czar on the tottering throne, the tragic Nicholas II, in whom the people could have no hope either of reform or of a voice in government. For when they had appealed to him, he had denied them any voice whatever, denouncing their plea as a senseless dream. "Let all know," he concluded, "that I intend to defend the principles of autocracy as unswervingly as did my father."

So what could the people do but rebel?

Now Baboushka, Little Grandmother, as she was called, found that her People's Party had become the Social Revolutionary Party. They were still teaching thousands of peasants that the land must be owned by themselves, and that the System of the Czar must be swept away. This, in spite of the many arrests, and the increased vigilance of police and spies. The organization was formed on the lines of a hierarchy, with scores of presses in Switzerland sending propaganda through underground mails to the central committee in Russia, and thence to its district, town, and local committees, until it was distributed to thousands of peasants and laborers in huts and tenements.

For six years, Mme. Breshkovsky traveled through twenty-six provinces, stopping from two weeks to a month in each, holding meetings and telling stories on boats, in cellars, huts, attics. Again and again she was nearly caught, as the police were always trailing her. She became a clever actress, able to assume a new disguise in an instant; now a French Countess, now a cook, always calm, merry, equal to any emergency.

After all these years of struggle, she found that Czar Nicholas II had refused money to equip village schools, and was still afraid to allow newspapers to be circulated among peasants. But she found, too, that these same peasants had grown to have a passion for books, for learning. She felt that the constant breaking out of open rebellion could be handled without violence or bloodshed if only the peasants could be educated.

There was so much to do — to teach moderation and restraint. It was like unloosing a torrent and then trying to control its course.

The year 1902 found her in Switzerland organizing the scattered groups of exiles and strengthening the work of the presses.

And 1904 found her in America, that longed-for land of liberty, which in the years of her exile had made great strides forward. She found a host of friends waiting for her — at Hull House, Denison House and Henry Street Settlement. For who but Jane Addams, Helena Dudley, and Lillian Wald could better sympathize with her ideals and her life-task? Had not they, gentlewomen all three, also chosen voluntarily to spend their lives among immigrants and refugees?

Hidden away for a brief rest in an American home, Mme. Breshkovsky's hostess describes the charm of her guest; * of how she bewitched the children with her stories, her swift cutting and folding of paper into shapes of ships or cocks or bears or dolls; of her joy in music and art; her keen sense of humor; her noble faith in the future, without even a taint of bitterness.

"How is it, dear Madame," asked her hostess, "that after all these cruel years you are without bitterness?"

* From *The Little Grandmother of the Russian Revolution*, ed. by Alice Stone Blackwell, by courtesy of Little Brown & Co.

"Oh, it is just because I believe in evolution," she answered smilingly. "Bitterness gets crowded out by faith."

Her hostess thus describes her:

"Sitting in the twilight by the fire, with her shining eyes, her noble face, her melodious voice, she seems a splendid sibyl bringing to our modern materialism the simplicity, the poetry, the devotion of the mighty past, with its primitive virtues and its prophetic inspiration."

Newspaper reporters were welcomed as her dear boys. Kellogg Durland wrote of her in the *Boston Transcript*:

"To look upon the face of this silver-haired Apostle is like receiving a benediction. Her outward and inward calm are superb. Her hands are beautiful in their delicacy and refinement, despite the years in Siberia. Her voice is low and sweet, her smile winning and childlike. Only her eyes betray the suffering of the years. In repose her face is strong like iron. The shadows of her eyes speak of deepest pathos."

In behalf of her people, she addressed crowded mass meetings in Boston, Philadelphia, New York, Chicago. Strong men carried her on their shoulders as they acclaimed her Baboushka, Little Grandmother. They listened spellbound to her stories of "man's inhumanity to man."

She spoke of sitting in her prison cell one day as a white envelope fell through the slit in the barred iron door. A friendly guard must have smuggled it in. The letter was from a group of sympathizers in Switzerland sending her cheer.

"All Russia is an immense prison to every Russian of progressive ideas," she said to her audience. "It is worth everything to the men and women working for freedom to know that free and civilized nations sympathize with them and wish them success."

It was Julia Ward Howe, the "Grand Old Lady" of America, who helped Baboushka, the "Grand Old Lady" of Russia, to organize, at Faneuil Hall in Boston, "The Friends of Russian Freedom."

In the beauty of the lilies, Christ was born across the sea,
With a glory in His bosom that transfigures you and me;
As He died to make men holy, let us die to make men free,
While God is marching on.

How the great hymn rang out—out over free America to that land across the sea still enslaved by tyranny.

How comforted she was by the men and women who rushed to support her. She returned home with ten thousand dollars in her pocket and with life-long friends in her heart to help carry on her work for freedom. She, who had loved so much, had found herself in turn beloved by thousands.

In 1905, after the uprisings following in the wake of the Russo-Japanese war, the Czar was forced to promise the long-waited-for constitutional government. Instantly, his people lifted their heads, found their voices. Had it come at last, the breaking of his iron will of despotism? The people were jubilant. The officials were fearful. So in terror of consequences, the Czar retracted, tightening the System, hiding behind the cruelty of his officials. Now forty-five thousand souls were exiled to Siberia. Again despotism triumphed.

For three years longer Baboushka worked, trying to bring

reason and peace to troubled hearts, trying to restrain the peasants from deeds of violence. But ever closer about her spread the net of spies until once more she was caught and shut up, this time in the dread Fortress of St. Peter and St. Paul.

Here she lived two of the hardest years of her life, deprived of all companionship, not allowed to speak or write on any political subject. But even this did not break her spirit.

"Everything here is stone, asphalt and iron," she wrote; "it is very dark in the cells of the first floor, for the wall which surrounds the buildings is high enough to keep out the light of the sun, and you never see the sky and stars. An old creature like me can support all the privations of air, light, motion, but the young suffer seriously. Its silence . . . is like a tomb. No human sounds . . . Many young souls have perished in this awful place, the best souls and best characters."

Here there was no gay tapping, no contact with other prisoners. Yet she was allowed non-political books, and she could write letters, read by the censor.

Thus she began now a correspondence with her only son who, brought up as an aristocrat all these years, had no sympathy with his mother's strange way of life. Indeed, he was finally prevailed upon to visit her only through the efforts of an American woman, Mrs. Isabel Barrows, who had twice crossed to Russia to try to save his mother from prison. Intervention failing, Baboushka was grateful for this crumb of comfort in her forced solitude.

She wrote to beg him for a book of travels with pictures —"nothing about cruelties in it," she cautioned him. She told him she had been reading Dickens but had to skip whole pages. She had seen and endured too much. Her heart was too quick to suffering. She now found deep solace in Scott and specially adored his *Ivanhoe*, even if she did have to omit four chapters about battles.

It was to her son that she wrote the Beatitude which is the keynote to this book. She tried very lovingly to break the hard shell encasing his heart, this novelist son of the aristocracy.

"Life is a great teacher for all who wish to learn," she told him, "and he is fortunate who gets on to the proper road to learning, otherwise one may go through life without learning anything or thinking anything."

Once when he had inquired if she followed the news, she replied: "I follow the news! My dear, I am entirely in the position of those fabulous creatures that have been stolen away and are kept living in such places that even the ravens and the wolves cannot peep in. . .

"Yesterday I saw one blade of grass climbing from under a stone, on the sunny side. It represented a very sad contrast with the rest of the surroundings, the bare trees and granite walls. A small patch of sky also looked upon me."

Yet in her mind and her heart, she was able to escape these dreadful prison walls and fly back to the dear land of that happy America where all her dreams of freedom had come true.

Among the institutions that had held out wide arms to her was Wellesley College. She had loved to sit among the fresh eager faces—"the lovely blond heads"—talking to them in her delightfully piquant broken English. And how they had loved her! The whole college was indignant to learn of this new imprisonment. A fiery protest was sent to the Czar. A fund was gathered for books and a warm shawl. In reply, there came out of that grim Fortress one of her radiant, loving letters to a new generation of girls who loved her even as the old. How she marveled at it.

Many of the faculty members treasured her friendship all their lives. One of them, Sophie M. Jewett, wrote to her while she was in the Fortress of St. Peter and St. Paul a sonnet which begins:

The liberal summer wind and sky and sea,
For thy sake, narrow like a prison cell
About the wistful hearts that love thee well
And have no power to comfort nor set free. *

Nor was Baboushka forgotten by her own people, though shut away from the sun these two years. For at the end of a two days' trial, the news of her new sentence "to Siberia for life" spread like wildfire. Crowds came to the court room for a glimpse of her.

"Do not let this trouble you," she said, as she kissed a young English newspaper correspondent on both cheeks. "I have been through it all before."

So off she started again, at sixty-eight, in that year 1909, with a company of one hundred and fifty political criminals and one hundred ordinary criminals, for the long five-thousand-mile trek, by cart, by boat, on foot. At stations along the way hundreds ran to offer her a bit of chocolate, a cup of tea. Yet they found "Granny's" face unwrinkled, even rosy, her eyes sparkling. She was ever the gayest of the party, always joking and laughing, for the sake of the younger ones.

* From *The Poems* of Sophie M. Jewett, by courtesy of T. Y. Crowell Company.

The news ran ahead of her, and the whole of Siberia waited to see her, their "miracle woman."

From Siberia she wrote gallant letters to her friends in America. "See how happy I am—persecuted, banished, and yet beloved!" For in every letter she thanked her friends for their lavish gifts to her, among them copies of *The Outlook*, which had published the story of her own life.

This time a series of George Kennan's articles on Japan interests her:

"How well it is that science is making a successful advance toward giving different countries a knowledge of each other! It is so dull to have only strangers around us in every place on earth, when we are really brothers, all coming from one source. The soul is the same, the habits alone are different."

All the American gifts of money and boxes of food and clothing sent to her she shared with her boys who, she said, "came naked out of prison in midwinter."

"You understand my situation," she wrote in 1911. "I am an old mother who wants to aid every one of them. I help, I scold, I hear confessions like a priest, I give advice and money, but still it is only a drop in the ocean of misery. With all this, I feel myself strong and ready, always ready—perhaps because of this."

Truly she had found the secret of the victory of "mind over matter." It was quite true that she kept fit and strong in spite of everything, just because she had a great work to do, so great that she never stopped doing it. She had been astonished on her return to Russia in 1905 to find her sister frail and miserable. Baboushka marveled that her sister, who all these years had lived in luxury, worried about little things—her coffee, her garden, the servants; while she herself, "without baggage for thirty years," owning nothing of her own, had no worry and was strong and eager for work.

So now in Siberia she found an immense work to do, for another seven years. Her great regret was that she was so hampered by police restrictions that she could scarcely do this work.

She wrote to a friend that she felt "like a salted herring in a big but immovable hogshead, conserved, nobody knows why, and waiting, waiting without end. My straining and activity are limited now so narrowly that I see myself like a sea urchin in its shell, only thinking and endeavoring to understand the meaning of what mankind as a whole is doing."

Then, suddenly, a telegram: a moment in history changing the course of the sun! The System overthrown; the Romanoff dynasty ended; her own Socialist party in the seat of government. That was on March 2, 1917. Russia was free. She, Baboushka, was free now to do her great work. Delirious moment! A sleigh, a *troika* with jingling bells, flashed her over the snow to the nearest railway station. For the first time she boarded the great Trans-Siberian Railroad and traveled without officials and guards.

At every station, every train stop, she was lifted from her coach by strong arms and held above the throngs who had come to greet her, so that all might see this Baboushka whom they so revered. Children, peasants, soldiers, workers, all kissed her; all brought her food and flowers.

She found everywhere only reverence, deep joy; no anger, no sense of revenge, but only a great hope ready to flower.

The thousands of beggars—descendants of those peasants driven from the land in 1861—plead with her now to restore their fields and to give them books. The thousands of workers in the towns plead with her for better wages, saner living conditions, more schools. The bourgeoisie plead for political freedom. They all looked to her, to this little old woman of seventy-five. Little Grandmother could do anything, could work miracles.

What a glad moment of triumph for her, to be driven through Moscow in the gilded carriage of the Czar; to arrive at St. Petersburg in a railroad coach filled with flowers—this little laughing, humble Bride of Russia. No wonder the whole city came to meet her, singing the *Marseillaise.*

In the royal apartment of the station, reserved for visiting kings and queens, Baboushka held her court. A comrade introduced her:

"Comrades, the Grandmother of the Russian Revolution has returned at last to a free country. She has been in dungeons, in the penal settlements of the Lena, has been tortured endlessly. Yet here we have her with us, brave and happy. Let us shout 'Hurrah' for our dear Baboushka."

In the midst of the wild acclaim, she could only look down at those faces and repeat in her heart: "*Moia lubov' knarodu moe velichaishee socrovische*—My greatest treasure is my infinite love for my people." She would give the rest of her life to their service.

They knew this as well as she. They lifted her chair high on willing shoulders and bore her through the streets of the capital of all Russia, streets lined by cheering, laughing, sobbing people, past the grim Fortress of St. Peter and St. Paul to the Czar's Winter Palace, where she was to establish her headquarters. She had seen all Russia on this last long journey, all her children and her grandchildren. Now she had come home.

Not to fêtes and ceremonies, but to work. What a world of work to be done. She had no time to eat or to sleep. For, as she had explained to the members of the Douma at Moscow, "at every station and crossroad there is only one demand, one groan of the people — for literature, for books, for teachers."

She proposed a conscription of every man and woman in the nation who could read and write to teach groups at once, in schools, homes, churches, and so wipe out as quickly as possible this stain of illiteracy from the land.

Education had been the dream of her life. Now that Russia was free of the System, she could fulfill that dream. Blessed moment, lasting eight short glorious months!

She cabled the glad news to her friends in America. They must share her joy even as they had shared her misery. She wrote to them to beg for a rotary press, since in Russia she found only small hand presses, slow and laborious. She must turn out books now for one hundred and seventy millions. In spite of eighteenth-century equipment, by September of 1917, she had one hundred and forty presses in operation. Surely it would not take long, now, to illumine that darkness of ignorance.

In October she was chosen temporary chairman of the first provisional Parliament, to honor her as the eldest member. "We must unite to work together, free and happy, without discord, as one man," she told them. "Let us substitute constitutional liberty for tyranny in the hands of any man, worker, peasant or noble."

After fifty-two years of prison life, and eleven years of the underground, she was free at last to work and to live in the open. Baboushka, more than most, could appreciate liberty. Out of her infinite love and wisdom she would create a new social order.

What plans she made for the education of her Russia! Also in her heart she carried four million children: orphans, waifs, vagabonds. For them she must organize settlements near the Ural mountains. Then there was all Siberia to re-create; the poor persecuted ones, Jews and Christians alike, needing doctors, nurses, schools, tools, seeds.

But her mind outran even her vast Russia. Her dream now was to make one family of all the nations on earth. No more wars, or hatred, or ignorance of one another. Tyranny was ended for Russia. With it must end the World War for Europe, for the Near East.

So she worked and she dreamed.

THEN the crash. For the hidden forces of evil, the long repression of hate, the slow starvation of mind and spirit had bred a flood of fury and rage. Now the black tide, unleashed, was forced into new channels. The Socialist party was overthrown. Driven by the Bolshevists—the Majority—pricked by the bayonets of the Red Army, the leaders were forced from the Winter Palace, from Russia itself.

So again, in 1918, Baboushka was exiled, this time for life.

If you can watch the things you gave your life to, broken
And stoop to build 'em up with worn-out tools. . .

And she did stoop. In her place of refuge in Czechoslovakia, she still found work to do. For she knew well that freedom, liberty, was a precious gift that must *follow* education, not precede it. Even now she did not lose faith. She knew that her "dear dark people," usually so patient, so long-suffering, so deeply religious, would grow calm again, would cease their mad violence and come home to themselves.

An American newspaper friend, Mr. William T. Ellis, who was in Russia at the time of her last banishment, ten years later sent her a box of candy to cheer her in exile. Her letter of thanks was first published in *The Outlook* for June 15, 1927. She wrote in her quaint English:

"I have never doubted the brotherly lights that exist between the two great nations—your splendid United States of America and our Russia-all-in-the-future.

"It is worth while to spend one's life in work and suffering having in prospect the day when your people will be able to take an honorable place among those who were so happy to succeed before, and to develop its capacity for the welfare of humanity. . .

"As I worked till my seventies for the delivoretion of Russian people from the despotism of Czar's régime, I continue to fight against tyranny . . . to aid our young generation to encounter consciously the resurrection of our freedom. The lot of Russian refugees is a hard one. Great many were buried before grown up, and more are doomed to it. Europe is tired to give refugees and to sustain Russian students, and to give work to our workers.

"Nevertheless we believe the hour will be when all of us will return at home to do our best for the rehabilitation of moral and mental progress that were trampled by the enemies of all what is noble and can serve to the brotherhood of peoples. An immense work awaits us. I am sure that the terrible lesson given by the history will not fail to render all nations more cautious, and less selfish in their mutual intercourses. The lessons must be learned by heart."

And so, in a village near the city of Prague, Catherine Breshkovsky, growing deaf and nearly blind, lived on until her ninetieth year. There, on September 12, 1934, after her last seventeen years of exile, her great spirit was liberated.

Among the dear American friends she had met at Wellesley College was Katherine Lee Bates, whom you know as the author of *America the Beautiful.* She voiced for us all our own love for

Baboushka *

Thou whose sunny heart outglows
Arctic snows;
Russia's hearth-fire, cherishing
Courage almost perishing;
Torch that beacons oversea
Till a world is at thy knee;
Baboushka the Belovéd,
What Czar can exile thee?

Sweet, serene, unswerving soul
To thy goal
Pressing on such mighty pinions,
Tyrants quake for their dominions,

And devise yet heavier key,
Deeper cell to prison thee,
Baboushka the Belovéd,
Thyself at liberty.

Thou thy martyr body, old,
Chains may hold,
Clearer still thy voice goes ringing
Over steppe and mountain, bringing,
Holy Mother of the free,
Millions more thy sons to be.
Baboushka the Belovéd,
What death can silence thee?

* From *The Retinue and Other Poems*, by Katherine L. Bates, by courtesy of E. P. Dutton & Co., Inc.

Quotations from *Memoirs* are from *Hidden Springs of the Russian Revolution: Personal memoirs of Katerina Breshkovskia*, by courtesy of Stanford University Press.

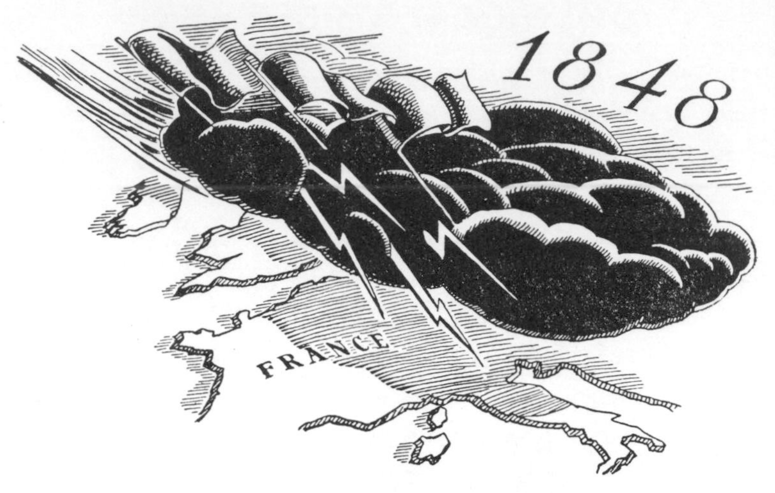

MALWIDA VON MEYSENBUG

1816–1903

A LOVELY child of the lesser German nobility, Malwida von Meysenbug grew up close to the palace of the reigning prince of the province of Hesse. Her father was prime minister, so Malwida's parents formed an important part of the court life. At thirteen, she was still a little girl, sheltered and happy. Her mornings were spent with her sister and their tutor, her afternoons in the garden, at her piano, or driving about the country.

When rumors reached her through the servants of strange uprisings of the people and demands for a constitutional government, she staunchly defended her prince and her father, whom she adored. She was a little aristocrat, with great blue eyes, like periwinkles, calm and pure.

At fourteen, she experienced the terror of seeing a mob of revolutionists, who had stormed the palace to demand a constitution, now threaten her own home. She clung to her mother and sisters as stones came hurtling through the windows. She heard the angry roar of the crowd and saw their brandished clubs. Would they storm the house? Whatever did they want with her father, who was defending his prince at the palace? Would they kill her mother?

Just then two officers dashed up to their door. One of them, the fearless young prince, talked to the crowd until the State troops had time to march up and disperse them, still muttering threats against Prince William and his prime minister, Baron von Meysenbug.

Yet in spite of her mother's indignation, such demands were not to be denied. Paris, too, was inflamed with revolutionists, she learned. The year was 1830. The very air in Europe was electric with coming storm. Malwida's father began the drafting of a constitution, his great concern being to appease the people and yet keep the throne intact for his Elector Prince.

But the new constitution was no sooner proclaimed than the feeble William fled, leaving his son as constitutional monarch. And he insisted upon taking Baron von Meysenbug with him. Henceforth, Malwida, her mother and sisters were exiles from Hesse, following the faithful nobleman and his broken prince from one watering place to another, up and down the land. Malwida, longing for a real education, could do little more than eagerly read books and work at her music and her painting.

Her passionate young soul groped for an ideal, something great to follow, something to give her whole life to, something that would satisfy her craving for perfection. Instead, she was offered travel in Switzerland and Germany, dances and balls, music and gay conversation, always among the aristocracy of her family's choosing.

Then love came, a love that changed her whole life, that

wrenched her from her family, turned her into a revolutionist and made her an exile for life.

Her lover was Theodore Althaus, a young minister of a reformed or independent Lutheran church, a fiery spirit, who was a radical and a democrat.

Naturally, her family looked upon him with horror. But Malwida looked with the clear eyes of love and began to comprehend through him the whole tremendous struggle of Europe against the despotism of rulers. Now she saw her own Hesse in a new light. She understood the desperate need of that mob for a voice in government, for lower taxes and for education.

How her cheeks burned with excitement at the letters from Theodore—for they could scarcely exchange a word in private though they lived in the same town.

"The wind of freedom is blowing in Switzerland," he wrote. "The old religious controversy between Catholic and Protestant is settled. The Swiss, like the Americans, are free to worship as they please."

Brave land of white peaks! Malwida thought of all the souls sheltered on its free soil, the exiled ones. What a terrible thing it must be to be unwanted by one's own dear land. And how blessed must be liberty, worth fighting and dying for. Happy, fortunate America! She sat down to pour out all her thoughts to Theodore.

Another day he wrote: "Now the wind has blown over the peaks down into Italy. Sicily and Naples are in revolt. How I long to go there and take you with me. Even in Turin, Charles Albert's throne is toppling."

So! All that day Malwida kept his letter close, her cheeks flaming to hear how her family indignantly supported Charles Albert, King of Sardinia, who had just declared himself King of all Italy. She knew more than they, she knew how one called Giuseppe Mazzini, even though exiled, in spirit led the Piedmontese to the gates of the palace to demand a constitution, a share in government. And Charles Albert yielded!

Little did she dream that she was later to know intimately that great exiled Mazzini who spent his life working for the freedom of Italy.

Through Theodore, too, she read later a description by the Russian exile, Alexander Herzen, of that night in Naples; of how, when the people shouted for justice, King Ferdinand appeared on the balcony to make them promises—promises, alas, which he did not keep. But the city went mad with joy, turning the night into a Walpurgis, a Halloween orgy.

"One felt everywhere the rumblings of a volcano," wrote Herzen. "Each dreamed his own dream of a world remade in justice and in brotherhood."

Little did Malwida think then that she was to know intimately this Count Herzen, to become one of his family.

And still the strong wind blew. Malwida writes in her *Memoirs* *: "One day, returning from a lonely walk, I found everyone at home in great excitement. News of the Paris revolution of February 24 (1848) had arrived. My heart beat with joy. The monarchy had fallen; the republic had been declared . . . and the great watchwords Liberty, Equality, Fraternity were again inscribed on the banner of the movement."

Eagerly she read all she could lay her hands on of the ideas of French leaders: Lamartine, a simple workman,

* Several quotations from *Rebel in Bombazine: Memoirs of Malwida von Meysenbug*, tr. by Elsa von Meysenbug, ed. by Mildred Adams, are included, by courtesy of W. W. Norton & Co.

Thiers, Louis Blanc, Ledru-Rollin, who had helped to formulate the new creed.

"All men are brothers," they declared. "Liberty is only a dream where there is no equality. We cannot attain to equality without a democracy. A democracy recognizes the right of the people as its first principle, universal suffrage as its origin, and for a goal, the realization of liberty, equality, fraternity."

It was a good creed, she thought. But in reality there was still an angry dethroned Louis-Philippe, with ministers and nobles still believing in the divine right of kings, in the despotic power of royalty. How violently was the pendulum of government to swing in poor France, now toward monarchy, now toward democracy, before it could come to rest!

In despair, Thiers was to cry out later: "I have no faith in France. We are not yet ripe for a Republic and we cannot live longer under despotism."

How agonizingly true this was for all of Europe!

In Brussels, Friedrich Engels and Karl Marx had already formed an international democracy built upon Marxian principles. Government must be dominated by the mass —the proletariat must rule, with unlimited power vested in its leaders as the State. It promised material well-being for the mass, at the expense of the individual.

Which principle would dominate the future of Europe? Malwida questioned. If the State were to be all powerful, then would it not but exchange one despot for another, with no true liberty of speech or of life?

She learned that Bakounine was working to form an intellectual alliance of all Europe against tyranny. He had leaders in all countries to draw upon: Mickiewitz of

Poland, Garibaldi and Mazzini of Italy, Herzen of Russia, Kinkel and Schurz of Germany, Kossuth of Austria.

Each leader had a burning passion to liberate his people by his own method; one by violence, another by peace. Yet all were agreed that royal tyranny was the cancer eating into the life of the common man.

"Citizens," cried Ledru-Rollin to his colleagues in the first national assembly of 1848, "when the fruit is ripe, there needs but a little wind to detach it from the tree."

Was the fruit ripe? Malwida wondered.

Now Theodore rejoiced with her that the wind of freedom was blowing a gale in Austria. For the news of the Paris revolution had inflamed Lajos Kossuth. Following his release from imprisonment for high treason during the 1830 revolution, he had been publishing a liberal newspaper and ceaselessly suggesting reforms. Now he boldly demanded a parliamentary government for Hungary and a constitution for the rest of Austria. By fiery speeches he roused the Hungarian people to rebel against the high-handed autocracy of Count Metternich, the power behind the Austrian throne.

These speeches, printed and read aloud in the streets of Vienna, denounced the mad weak Emperor Ferdinand I and his *alter ego*, the powerful Metternich, who was bent on maintaining Austria as the mailed fist of Europe and repressing her people.

This time the people would not be denied but shouted for reform and a constitution. In haste Metternich resigned as prime minister. Both he and the Emperor fled. At once Kossuth was elected president of the Committee for National Defense, and virtual dictator. The Government retaliated by proclaiming him traitor.

On April 19, 1848, Kossuth issued his great Declaration of Independence, demanding freedom of worship and of speech, the liberation of all serfs, universal taxation for nobles and commons alike, and religious tolerance for Jews. Rushing on horseback through the villages, calling his people to arms, he stirred them to fight for their liberty.

Four months later his army was overthrown. Kossuth fled into Turkey. The revolution collapsed. Metternich returned to Vienna in triumph. His eighteenth-century principles still prevailed. All talk of a democracy, a republic, was mere nonsense. All the same, in December of that year, 1848, Ferdinand abdicated in favor of his young nephew, Franz Joseph, who actually promised a constitution. In two years, however, Franz Joseph had revoked his promises, and as Emperor of Austria and King of Hungary, declared himself an absolute monarch holding in his young hands the whole weight of government.

Evidently Hungary was not yet ripe for democracy. All the liberals had to flee or be silenced again while they watched their neighbor Switzerland stand up strong and brave to throw off the old yoke of Prussia and proclaim herself a republic.

The wind blew now over Germany, stirring her from her old dream of individual state monarchy, to that of a united nation. For long years the people had been forced down by their nobles and petty tyrants. They remembered the revolution of 1525, repulsed by knights at the point of sharp lances. Surely it was time, after three hundred years and more of submission, to overthrow tyranny and reign themselves!

In the duchies of Baden and Württemberg, as well as

Hesse, the people united to demand liberty of press and of speech, jury trial, universal suffrage, just taxation.

> *O wind a-blowing all day long,*
> *O wind that sings so loud a song!*

It was in the then free city of Frankfurt, seat of the insurrection of 1833, that the wind blew hardest. And to her joy, it was just here in Frankfurt that Malwida found herself. She writes in her *Memoirs:* "The news that a German preliminary parliament would meet in Frankfurt filled me with intense joy. The city was in boundless excitement. At the meeting of the Free Congregation, which I had attended all winter, the speaker did not ascend the pulpit to deliver a regular sermon but from the altar spoke fiery words of inspiration, exhorting the people to be ready to fight a joyous battle for the most sacred rights of humanity. Outside we could hear the clang of weapons, as the burghers hurried into the arsenal close by to arm themselves. I was wildly happy. I wished that the enemy were standing outside the door of the little church and that we might all march out singing Luther's *Chorale* to fight or die for freedom.

"The people came forth from their caves (of thought) with the curious gaze and naïve astonishment of men who have long been kept in darkness and who see daylight again."

Here, in this windiest city in Germany, Malwida thrilled to see the flag of Father Johann's young gymnasts hoisted above the new Parliament. Here she saw long-silenced dramas of Schiller produced, awakening men to his dream of freedom. Here she mingled with groups of working men staring into shop windows at the faces of liberal leaders, German and French. Malwida forgot her rank, her family, her upbringing, herself.

"I tried to explain everything to them," she tells us, "to point out the men whom they could trust, to make clear the significance of the days ahead."

For so much would depend upon these leaders, and upon the ripeness of the people for a new life of human rights. It would take so much more than cannon shots and ringing of bells and glad huzzahs. Would the leaders hold together in their demands that the citizens be armed, and that a parliament be elected by universal suffrage? The old order of despotic power was fighting a desperate battle to regain control by secretly undermining the counsels of the liberal leaders. Which would win?

Malwida felt certain of democracy now. "Never had I loved Germany so intensely," she writes. "Only a few weeks before I had wished to be in rebellious Italy. Now I would not have wanted to leave Germany at any price; I felt myself bound to it by mighty bonds of love, and was convinced that nowhere would development be so thorough and so beautiful."

She was deeply grateful that a friend could smuggle her into St. Paul's Church where the first provisional parliament of April, 1848, was sitting. There, hidden behind the flag-draped pulpit, she could look down upon the five hundred members and distinguish the party leaders. Some wanted to enforce drastic measures to secure the upper hand. Others counseled moderation. Hecker, who had come over from Baden, insisted that Frankfurt unite all Germany under her banner. "Unity is the mother of liberty," he affirmed. Carl Schurz and Herr Kinkel agreed.

After the decision that a parliament be assembled at once by popular vote, the shouts within were echoed by the shouts of the hundreds without. Malwida says: "I was seized with a delirium of joy; I saw my dreams coming true, a rich, free, life-giving future opening for Germany."

So our young Baroness von Meysenbug, obeying the law of her inner being, must now renounce her family and attach herself to this cause of the people, to help form a new humanity.

She pored over Fichte's *Discourse to the German Nation,* written forty years before. "All human progress in the nation must come from the people," he declared. "Only when the cultured group can meet with the toilers as men of good will, will we have unity."

And Fichte it was who gave Malwida the idea of taking her place in the world of education, even though she was a gentlewoman. For he believed in putting boys and girls together in the same schools and giving them exactly the same courses. Scandalous radicalism! But how Malwida delighted in it. How she had longed to do something to emancipate girls from the position of mental underlings, of mere ignorant housekeepers and baby-tenders. Now Fichte called women to take their own place in social progress.

She rejoiced to be part of this revolutionary movement and wept with happiness when the new parliament at once made education obligatory. Now she saw the old and fragile Empire of the Hapsburgs cracked in every part. Fortunately, her Prince of Hesse and her dear father had not lived to mourn its crash. But she was of the new order. And she set herself vigorously to the task of teaching in one of the schools of this new world, a college for women in free Hamburg. Here then was her life-task, the education of the girlhood of Germany.

Alas, with November of that year, 1848, came a counter-fever of reaction. Frederick William IV, King of Prussia, refused haughtily any such united empire as Frankfurt's dream. Blum was executed in Vienna. Kinkel was thrown into prison. Many of the others fled to England or to America. Her beloved Theodore was arrested for high treason. He had published in his magazine his fears that a deluge of cruel materialism would cover the whole earth unless the spirit of man could rise and conquer.

"I am like a good patriot," he wrote to Malwida. "In the same situation as the whole country, in a temporary prison."

It was unthinkable that the King of Prussia, entrenched at Berlin, should have been more powerful than all those eager souls at Frankfurt. But as they admitted, sorrowfully, Germany was not yet a united nation. And without unity liberty was powerless.

It was a crushing blow to Malwida. Not only the failure of the whole grand republican plan for the nation, but the exiling of the leaders, and especially the harm done to that one nearest and dearest to her own heart.

For within two years, the brilliant young socialist minister had contracted a fatal illness in prison, and was released to die. Close upon this tragedy came the spying of officials on the Hamburg college and its enforced closing. Malwida fled to a friend in Berlin, but was followed by the police who seized all her letters, even those dear ones that were all she had left of Theodore. Commanded to yield herself the following day at police headquarters, she appealed to her friends in panic.

What would it mean to her family, already incensed and hurt by her strange conduct? For her brother had a high official government post here in Berlin. And her mother's whole life was still bound up in the old régime of aristocracy. Prison, a trial, a sentence! What a horror for them.

She decided to flee alone, and at once, to England, still fighting against "the fear which despotic, unclean, suspicious governments instill, and against which innocence is no protection. I thought with horror of all the noble souls who had fallen into their hands and been sacrificed as veritable martyrs in the prisons of my fatherland, in the murderous climate of Cayenne and other sad places, in which brute force held imprisoned intelligence, virtue and patriotism."

In her heart she felt that she could never return home until her fatherland was free. Would it come soon or late?

Well for Malwida that she could not look into the future, that she had no sibyl to prophesy for her that sixty-nine years must pass before Germany should become a republic. Then, in 1917, "in outward response to President Wilson's demands, and in inward response to the uprising of the people against the leaders who had led them into a world disaster," the ancient eagles would droop. It was well that she could not know what further suffering would result to her people. How, nearly a century later, Jew and Gentile alike would be steeped in the woe of oppressed and oppressor, and still freedom was not.

During that journey from Berlin to London she felt in her heart "that it is bitter to be forced to flee from home into exile," a leaf blown by the wind of revolution.

Blessed England! Strong safe harbor for government-wrecked souls. In spite of her prejudices, her dislike of foreigners, her reluctance to depart from the established law and order; in spite even of a Young Ireland rebellion in Tipperary and, in Birmingham, a Chartist demonstration of working men demanding manhood suffrage and further parliamentary reform, yet England sheltered revolutionists from every nation of Europe. For all the fears of her conservatives, she was liberal of mind and large of heart to these poor feverish exiles. Free speech and free assembly were theirs by right of England's constitution. In spite of a conservative ministry, Victoria and Albert reigned.

Arriving alone, unheralded, uninvited, with little money and her own way to make, Malwida timidly knocked at the door of the only German revolutionists she knew in all London, the kindly, hospitable Kinkels.

Rescued from his German prison by the daring strategy of Carl Schurz, who had eluded the police, Gottfried Kinkel was now the head of the Frankfurt exiles. At home Malwida had corresponded with him, as she had with Richard Wagner and many other courageous rebels. Now the Kinkels helped her to start life in a strange land, to find pupils to tutor, and to plunge at once into the large body of European émigrés.

Through the Kinkels she met Kossuth and the whole Hungarian group. She writes amusingly of Kossuth, of the pomp and circumstance of his entry into a room, of the adoration of his group for this man who was the acknowledged leader of all Europe in that fatal 1848. His grandiose manner, "with the language of a Shakespeare and the delivery of a Gladstone," did not make Malwida long to know him intimately, much as she admired his brilliant mind and "his distinguished face, framed by a full graying beard, serious and dignified."

His was a stormy life of ups and downs of power, with times of intense political activity followed by enforced impotence, and then by adulation during his visits to America and to England. After working with Mazzini for eight years in London on the Central European committee, he rushed to Italy when she threw off the yoke of Austria. Late in life he is said to have reversed his policy of fierce nationalism, and advocated a federation of Danubian peoples. Although elected to the Diet he never took his seat, and indeed was deprived of citizenship and exiled for life.

Ironically, after his death his body was taken from Turin to Pest amid the mourning of the whole nation.

No, it was not Kossuth whom Malwida loved, but his fellow revolutionist Mazzini.

"For a long time," she tells us in her *Memoirs*, "I had wanted to meet the great Italian, the Roman Triumvir, the fiery spirit through whose ardor a whole nation had kept its patriotic enthusiasm for twenty years, notwithstanding the despotic opposition of the priests."

He did not mingle with the other refugees as his circle was entirely English—so she had waited long to meet him. Now she was invited by Herzen to spend an evening with him.

"Just as I had been unpleasantly affected by the almost courtly ceremonies with which Kossuth had been surrounded and the supercilious attitude he took, so now I was surprised by the absolute simplicity and modesty in attitude and appearance of the man whom Herzen introduced to me as Giuseppe Mazzini, the man whose thought inspired and led a whole nation, and before whose political importance powerful princes trembled.

"Mazzini was of medium height, well and slenderly built, rather thin than stout, not an imposing figure. His head alone resembled the picture one had of him, and when one saw the noble features, the brow on which thought was enthroned, the dark eyes which bespoke both the fire of the fanatic and the mildness of the man of feeling, one felt the charm of this man's presence and realized at once that he was one of those rare personalities to whom one could not be indifferent, but must either follow or oppose."

She describes the argument in the group, some affirming that the lack of powerful organization in the democratic party was responsible for its defeats, and advocating a mere verbal protest against conditions of evil in the world. But Mazzini insisted upon "sacred action" . . . and "that the only true task of revolutionaries was to instill into the people the consciousness of having to fulfill a duty. He assured us several times that he cared nothing for Italy if it desired only material greatness and material well-being; the only thing that seemed to him worth struggling for was that Italy should fulfill a great mission in the progress of mankind by becoming more noble, more moral and more faithful to duty itself, by achieving a union of states.

"He then touched upon his almost mystic belief in the importance of Rome. The name alone suggests its superb destiny: Roma, backwards, spells Amor—an omen that Rome will rule the world a third time, but this time by the power of love, of true brotherhood, which will go forth from there and with the strength of a shining example draw the other nations after it."

Malwida was reminded of the sad prophecy of Rome's ruin by Nostradamus in 1543:

Oh, great Rome, thy ruin approaches,
Not of thy walls, but of thy blood and substance,
The printed word will work terrible havoc,
The pointed steel driven home to the hilt.

With all her heart she hoped that not Nostradamus but Mazzini was right. One can imagine her sitting enthralled before this man, drinking in his words with her great blue eyes fixed upon his, storing away his ideals in her heart. For her the rest of the group vanished. She saw only this man and understood his dreams for a free Italy—that it might fulfill its destiny of transmuting power into love.

Later on, Malwida was invited to dinner one night by Mazzini's English friends who made a second home for him, and who honored and loved him as a saint.

They begged him to tell their guest of his view of life. "The fundamental basis of all existence for him," she writes, "was a spiritual principle which he called God and from which the ideas of the good, the beautiful and the true were given us at birth. The perfection of the world was his dogma and to work toward that end he believed to be the duty of mankind.

"He compared life to a spiritual winding around a high mountain; from each higher point a greater part of the trodden path could be seen, but only upon reaching the peak could one see the whole, and only then would the real purpose and aim of existence be made clear. . . But belief was nothing to him without action, and had he translated the Bible he would surely have said: 'In the beginning was the deed.'"

Malwida accepted an invitation for open house to this home every Friday evening. "Mazzini dominated the gathering as a remarkable personality always will among people who gladly recognize it. However, there was a great contrast between the natural domination of a superior personality and Kossuth's pretentious appearance. No one, not knowing Mazzini, would dream, when the door opened noiselessly and a slender figure in a simple black coat, usually buttoned to the top, glided almost timidly into the room, that it was the celebrated agitator. It was only when he took his usual place by the mantelpiece and, with dark eyes flashing, began to talk, that one felt the presence of an unusual man."

His great longing was that all socialists give up their personal aims of material well-being alone, and unite in *action.*

Malwida also joined his reading circle—works in French and English followed by lively discussions. In between these weekly meetings, she and Mazzini carried on a vivid correspondence. He was much concerned lest she lean too far toward communism and become a "firebrand."

He came to depend upon her for articles and reports for his Italian paper, *Dio e il Popolo—God and the People.* She wrote in French and Mazzini translated. She found him always kindly, tender-hearted. She quotes one of his notes:

"'I wish that from time to time we could have a survey of the political trend of events in Germany from the heights of a philosophic viewpoint. Could you not also give one hour to a survey of present political German press and its tendencies toward France, England and Russia?

"'Forgive me for all these demands, but you are good and equal to your task. . . Your friend and brother. . . Joseph.'"

One of the deeds dearest to his heart was to organize the

working men in every country into a brotherhood of ideas—of progress, liberty and reason. He felt that only through imbuing each individual with these ideas, could there be any coöperation of action. And this was the exact antithesis, he felt, of communism with its mass leveling, its promise of merely material gains.

So at his request, Malwida got together twenty German working men in London—refugees like herself—and invited them to her home to meet Mazzini. How noble he was to them. He did not descend to their class, he lifted them up to his, to teach and advise them. He tried to make them see that living for the great underlying ideas for the future was better than blindly following individual systems of organization. He urged them each day to ask themselves: "What have I done today for my cause?"

But alas, Malwida saw that even among this twenty, there were soon at work the same forces that had split the larger party of democrats into many fragments; the same personal ambitions, ego, greed, envy, jealousy, love of power. How, then, was Mazzini's great dream of unity of action to be achieved?

As she worked with him during these years, she came to know the depths of this man with the soul of a Dante, the life of a saint, the faith of a hero, drinking the bitter cup of exile and of poverty. She sensed the tragedy of his life in that "he committed the error of all fanatics, of wanting to enforce a form for his ideal which was opposed to the tendency of historical development."

Through their mutual friends, Malwida was able to look back to the brilliant promise of his youth. With such a gift for writing that he might have become one of the great literateurs, he gave it up for what St. Vincent de Paul would have called his *vocation*, his mission, the struggle for the liberty of Italy against tyranny at home and the despotism of foreign powers.

He had organized a youth movement in those early days —*La Giovane Italia*—that young men might early catch the spark and so help to unify Italy into a republic. The means he chose were education and revolt—the self-same means used by so many revolutionaries the world over. This was in the 1830s after his imprisonment and decree of exile.

When Charles Albert assumed the throne of Sardinia, Mazzini wrote to him from France begging him to unite all Italy under one banner of freedom. The King replied by demanding that France refuse longer to harbor the traitor Mazzini at Marseilles.

From the safe crags of Switzerland, Mazzini directed his campaign, and gathered together all young exiles from European radical groups. When even Switzerland grew hostile to him, he fled to England. Here he struggled with language and poverty until his English friends found him and gave him a home.

Not an idle moment did he know. Not an outbreak in Italy that he did not foster. In 1848 he had rushed to the aid of Garibaldi in Milan. Then it was that Rome had declared itself a republic and elected him a member of the Assembly. Later he was given supreme executive power as a Triumvir.

But like most of the other revolutions of that decade, his party was forced to surrender and Mazzini was again exiled with a price on his head if he should set foot on Italian soil.

And now in 1859 he was going off to join Garibaldi again. For France had united with Sardinia this time to shake off the Austrian yoke, and Mazzini hoped passionately, and Malwida with him, that at last it meant freedom for his beloved Italy. As she bade him good-by, she felt in him the grandeur of a Giordano Bruno or a Savonarola.

She was never to see him again. But her feeling of intense sadness at parting was later borne out. For the burning dreams that must result in action in his life were given no outlet. His principles of individual freedom were rejected later even by his workmen, in favor of a mass consciousness. Mazzini could not work with communism, and died brokenhearted at Pisa in 1872, two years after the new constitutional monarchy had united all Italy. Then, ironically, as with Kossuth, the government expressed national sorrow, and gave him a public funeral.

Mercifully, neither Malwida nor Mazzini, on that farewell night in London, could look into the future.

Yet if Mazzini passed out of her life outwardly, Herzen remained. No one of the great exiled leaders played so large a part in Malwida's life as Alexander Herzen. For his two small motherless daughters were given to her to educate, and Olga, the younger, became her adopted daughter for life.

It is interesting to look back with Malwida upon Herzen's early life. Born in Moscow of Russian nobility, his father a cousin of the Romanoffs, the boy Alexander early developed an astonishing sympathy for the peasants. At the age of ten or twelve he formed a life friendship with Nicholas Ogareff, a boy of a different social strata. Both were intensely sensitive, with a growing rebellion in their young hearts against the system of despotism of the Romanoffs.

Together they read *William Tell*, thrilling to the struggle of the Swiss for freedom from tyranny. Schiller was forbidden in Russia, as in Germany, and the boys had a delicious joy in smuggling the book and then expressing to each other in writing their thoughts about it. Often they used to walk together outside the city, to the Mount of the Monks.

One night, sitting there just after sunset, with the first stars glowing above the church towers, on this hill where Alexander had wanted to build a temple to liberty, they joined hands and made a solemn vow—that they would both fight all their lives long against absolutism, for the good of Russia.

The following day the two boys were horrified to learn that on this very hill the Decembrists had been executed—those who revolted against the coming-to-power of Nicholas as Czar. The blood of these, whom they considered martyrs, made of their vow a sacred thing, never to be broken.

Later on, in the University, young Herzen joined a group of liberals among the nobility. They read Lafayette and of his glowing admiration for the new American Republic he had helped to free. They tried like Tolstoi to follow Saint-Simon's law of a society of brothers built on Jesus' rule: "*Aimez-vous les uns les autres*—Love one another."

At nineteen, Herzen was seized by a spy and exiled to a distant province. Six years later he was discovered there by his cousin, Prince Alexander, who was touring the provinces. Under royal wing he was taken back to St. Petersburg and given a post with one of the Cabinet Ministers. Surely he was safe there. But in three months another letter of his had been spied upon, and he was again exiled —to Novgorod. Here he plunged into study: science, philosophy, all the revolutionary literature of Europe. Upon his father's death, leaving to him a large fortune, he escaped to Italy, then finally settled in London.

Here he established the first Russian printing press, and translated from one language to another, all the greatest revolutionary literature. Although not one word of his prolific writings could he smuggle into Russia, yet for three years he kept on printing, writing ceaselessly.

Of course he had rushed over to Paris to take part in the uprising of 1848, and on its fall had returned again to London to continue his writing. Of course he helped the young revolutionists of Poland. He accepted the universe as the field of his labors. The written word must win at last. It was education that the peasants of Russia needed —how else prepare them for liberty?

Upon the accession of his cousin Alexander II to the throne of Russia in March, 1855, Herzen wrote him a long letter. That boyish vow to Ogareff was ever in his heart. He must now make a supreme effort to free Russia from the top. Later his printing press would be useful in helping to free her from the bottom, from the peasant grade.

After reminding the Czar of their last meeting in Novgorod, Herzen continued:

"Exiled, obliged to live in a city far from the Volga, I am reminded of the simple love with which the poor people of that district flocked to see you. I said then, 'Whence comes that love?'

"Now the time of payment for it has arrived: and that is easy for you. Give them liberty with all your heart.

Surely you love Russia and you may do so much for your people.

"I, too, love the Russian people. I left them for my love. I cannot rest, with my hands crossed in silence, and be a spectator of the horrors that they have endured in the past through their landlords and the system of officials.

"Distance has not changed my views; in the midst of strangers, I have not lowered my banner. . . Not many days ago the English people saluted in me the whole Russian people. It goes without saying, my flag is not yours; you are an absolute Emperor; I an incorrigible socialist. But between your banner and mine, we may yet find a common ground—our love for the Russian people. In the name of that love, I am ready to carry on an immense sacrifice—greater than prison and exile and wanderings from one foreign land to another.

"I am ready to efface myself, if I may have the living hope that you will keep your promise to Russia. Sire, give liberty of speech to Russia. Our very thoughts are oppressed, our lungs lack space to breathe. We kneel in chains of censure. Give us liberty of expression. We have something to say to the world as well as to our own.

"Give the land to the peasants. It has always belonged to them, spiritually. Efface from Russia the stain of slavery. Heal the welts on the backs of our brothers, those terrible traces of men's cruelty to humanity.

"Your father said on his death bed that he had not the time to do all that he would have liked for his subjects. Slavery came like remorse to trouble his last moments. [Nicholas I died March 2, 1855.]

"He had not the time—in thirty years—to free the peasants. Hasten then. Save the peasants from their ill-deeds to come, save your blood which will have to flow. . .

"You, surrounded by flatterers, will be astonished at my impertinence. Perhaps you will laugh.

"But it would be better not to laugh. I cannot but speak—that is why I have placed on foreign soil the first Russian printing press—like an electrometer, it shows the activity of the tension of a force long compressed. There suffices but a little pool of water with no outflow to break a granite rock.

"Sire, if these lines reach you, read them without hate, all alone, and reflect. You will not often have occasion to hear the voice of a free Russian." *

Did the young Czar read this passionate appeal? Malwida tells us: "It was just now that Herzen's propaganda was at its height and his paper had an ever increasing influence. It was said, on good authority, that Emperor Alexander read it and took it to heart."

At last Herzen was able to smuggle into Russia all that he had printed in three years. Like wildfire his pamphlets, articles, papers and books spread over the country. One magazine called *Kolokol (Bell)*, and another, the *Polyarnaya Zvyezda (Pole Star)* became immensely popular, and he himself a living word. Though it was many years before his *Memoirs*, novels, and essays, could be collected and published openly in Russia, yet at least he could flood the whole country then with his brilliantly written pleas for the abolition of serfdom.

Malwida tells us that her friend Professor Kinkel started a German paper in London at this time, and asked her for

* In Russian : cf. *Complete Works of Alexander Herzen*, Moscow, 1929. In French : cf. *Malwida de Meysenbug par Gaby Vinant.*

contributions from her conversations with Herzen, especially everything said or written about the emancipation of the serfs. She writes:

"This question was now being discussed so eagerly on all sides that a decision on the part of the government seemed an imminent necessity. Even if the Czar were not in favor of this, as was said, he would have to acquiesce in the end. . . Not only had Herzen unceasingly demanded it in his paper, the *Bell*, which has become a real power, but from other sources too, pamphlets and articles appeared on this subject. This gave me an opportunity of studying the question thoroughly and of reading several pamphlets on the subject.

"I was especially interested in the question, 'Will communism in Russia hold if freedom is granted? Or will individualism gain the upper hand as in other countries in Europe? Will Russia then have to go through the same process that the rest of Europe went through in centuries of struggle between the tremendous claim of the individual and the claim of all? Will this struggle, which can be ended only by a perfect government where every individual is protected and satisfied, be in harmony with the common interest?'"

Burning questions, searching her pure soul; with clear eyes she tried to look into the future. Yet she realized, too, that this problem of freedom for the peasants must come first before the future could unroll.

Thus, due to Herzen's *Bell* and the radicals in Russia, it is certain that as early as 1857 Alexander II authorized a committee to study this whole desperate problem. Two years later they brought to him their findings.

Many young liberals threw themselves into the drafting

of the edict which was to liberate forty million peasants. But at the last moment, due to the pressure of nobles and landowners who saw ruin for themselves, it was but a modified edict which passed into law in March, 1861.

Yet what a victory for the abolitionists. Herzen was beside himself with joy, with love for his Czar, for all Russia. With Ogareff at his side he organized a gigantic banquet and reception in his London home. Its façade was festooned with lights, and hung with banners proclaiming to all London the glory of that victory. Abolition of serfdom! Russia a free land at last!

A crowd gathered to watch the guests arrive, the liberal élite of England, the émigrés who had worked so long to help bring this to pass. In the midst of the happy toasts to Alexander II, with whom Herzen felt he could now resume friendly relations, someone rushed in with dreadful news. An insurrection in Poland followed by a massacre, a wholesale execution of young liberals by order of the Czar!

Poor Herzen! He would be accused at once of stirring up this Polish rebellion. There was then no possibility of harmony between him and his Czar.

Moreover, as he was to learn to his sorrow, by the terms of the edict of abolition the poor peasants were freed without their land, and must now be driven from it by the same dread whips that had already bowed their backs for so many generations. Ultimately, this freedom might be a glory to Russia. Just now, thousands were actually worse off than before.

If you can bear to hear the truth you've spoken
Twisted by knaves to make a trap for fools. . .

All the nobility and strength of Herzen's nature rose up now to sustain him. For the remaining nine years of his life, he lived much in Paris, writing his six volumes of *Memoirs*, a valuable record of the thoughts and strivings of this group of internationals.

Malwida described him as she first knew him, "a square-built, powerful man, with black hair and beard. He had rather broad, Slavic features and wonderfully brilliant eyes, which, more than any others I had ever seen, reflected his soul in the animated changes of thought."

She owed him so much, this man whose book she had read in the old Hamburg days at home. One of her workmen friends had brought it to her with the recommendation, "This man is one of us." In London, Herzen's home became her own for three idyllic years. Days spent with the children, evenings when Herzen translated for her his own Russian literature. Several evenings each week the house was filled with émigrés. For his home was a center of the leaders of all nations. Here she met Mazzini and Garibaldi. Here she lived with the best thought of her age.

It was Herzen who gave to her his own little Olga, and allowed Malwida to carry on her education, now in Paris, or in Florence or in Rome, thus giving Malwida an outlet for all her pent-up idealism. It was his largeness and generosity that liberated her from the harrowing struggle to earn a living in a strange land; that supplied a family in place of the one she had forfeited; that gave her exile dignity and her life graciousness and peace.

She was proud, too, that London liberals recognized his greatness. Indeed, England's very readiness to harbor these revolutionaries proved how vast a change she had undergone since 1775.

Malwida and her friends rejoiced that even the ban on the writings of Thomas Paine had now been removed. How they gloated over his *Common Sense*, republished by Mr. J. Watson of London with this significant foreword:

"The principles maintained in *Common Sense* are applicable to all times, and to all mankind. They should be carefully studied by every one who is at all desirous to possess that information without which he must ever remain a stone at heart."

Having quoted a series of appreciations for Paine's writings, he adds:

"Testimonies of this sort from friends and enemies alike could easily be multiplied, and proofs almost without end could be added to show how much the cause of mankind was promoted by Thomas Paine in thus assisting to lay the foundation of the American Republic—the example of which will in time be followed by every people on the earth." *

A grand prophecy, truly, and one for which Malwida and her friends were willing to give their lives to bring to pass.

They were able to keep in close touch with the progress of American democracy through the colorful adventures of their comrade, Carl Schurz. Exiled in 1848, he had no sooner braved German police to rescue Professor Kinkel from prison than he took ship to America, feeling rightly that if Europe spurned his fiery zeal, the new republic might find use for his gifts. And what spectacular gifts they were.

* *Life and Writings of Thomas Paine*, Vol. 2.

Now he threw himself into the frontiers of the new country, advocating for Wisconsin a liberalism which was to set its character for the future. Now he worked for the Lincoln campaign, or advocated abolition for slaves, or served as minister to Spain, or plunged into the Civil War, with conspicuous distinction. His bill of rights for the South spurned, he became a liberal editor, then United States Senator, and finally part owner of the *New York Evening Post*, and thus in large measure, molder of national opinion.

His letters to Malwida show his clear insight into the dangers which beset a democracy; the possibility of power being seized by a minority of the rich, to the exploitation of the poor or vice versa; the danger that the ideals of social justice be swallowed up by personal ambition and greed of power.

Malwida was astonished that the theoretic ideal of democracy should in actual practice be open to a reversion to the old rule of autocracy. Evidently, then, democratic freedom as well as all governing power was useless without wisdom, without a willingness to serve the common good, without education of mind and spirit.

Indeed, during the years of intimate contact with these world leaders of revolutionary thought, she had time to ponder much. Why was it that revolutions failed?

Was it because, as Mazzini and Hecker and Thiers had said, that victory was only possible in a nation where there was a will to unity?

"United we stand: divided we fall." She knew this to be the slogan of the American forefathers.

Was it because each leader had his own ideas of how to work out democracy, and the people ran unthinkingly after one or another, plunging headlong into good ways or bad?

Surely no revolution alone would bring justice and right living for each human being. She saw that clearly now.

"These thoughts," she writes, "led me to one conclusion—that we, who were supposed to have smashed all idols and false gods, had voluntarily made for ourselves a new god, a new idol, namely The People."

At home in the Germany of 1848, she had longed to have "the people take their destiny into their own hands, and that sovereigns may submit to them."

Now she saw that power in the hands of the people might be no better or wiser than in the hands of the king. For the people no sooner overthrew a tyrant than they mounted his throne and drew on his boots and pulled out his sword.

So in France Ledru-Rollin had said: "This revolution will not destroy the throne, but will simply reverse the normal process: the people will sit on it."

Malwida saw that full freedom with lust for power, with a spirit of revenge toward one's enemies, was as evil in one hand as in another. No, in order to use freedom, the people must have education, so that cruelty, moral cowardice, selfishness might fall away and each man stand free to develop his latent powers and so contribute to the good of the whole humanity.

This was why, in her later life, Malwida von Meysenbug turned to music as the avenue of greatest release for the life of the spirit. This was why so many great souls found inspiration and understanding in her—men like Richard Wagner and Franz Liszt, and young ardent spirits like Romain Rolland to whom she became a spiritual mother.

All her life, whether in London or Paris or Rome, she remained the pure idealist, living her idealism, and lifting the world through her efforts to share love and peace and education and beauty.

Her books were read widely in England and in France. And, curiously enough, her *Memoirs* in three volumes had a great vogue in Germany during the last ten years of her life. Surely the seeds she planted then, lying still and fallow now, will come forth one day and blossom in her own fatherland into the flowers of the liberty she so craved for it. Not a material liberty alone, but rather a spiritual emancipation which she had formulated after reading the three books written by Richard Wagner. She saw for Germany a new path to glory by means of a "great redeeming art."

May your dreams come true, dear Malwida.

DON BOSCO
1815–1888

THE YEAR 1815, which you associate with Waterloo and the downfall of the most brilliant and daring egoist of modern times, Napoleon Bonaparte, brought to birth one whom thousands of boys and girls hail as their hero, but of whom you may never have heard at all—Don Bosco, the modern "Boys' Saint of Turin."

Whether men admire or condemn him, all the world knows of Napoleon, of his bold attempt to dominate nations, boundaries, maps, kingdoms, men; to become a glorified trilogy of Alexander the Great, Cæsar and Charlemagne rolled into one. In the end, when his castle of nations had collapsed like toy blocks, he left the common people neatly flattened beneath his steam roller of conquest.

In that year of 1815, his idea of despotism which he had failed to focus longer in himself was seized, instead, by the monarchs of Europe.

Now at the Congress of Vienna they met to sign the Holy Alliance of Russia, Austria and Prussia. So there were three lords of creation now, instead of one Bonaparte languishing on St. Helena. They could now rearrange the map for themselves, uniting to resist all demands of liberals and revolutionaries alike.

Alexander returned to brood over his vast Russias plus most of Poland; Frederick William III gloated over his four new German states which would insure the future power of Prussia; Emperor Franz I with the cunning Metternich lorded it over Austria, Hungary and Italy, much to the discomfort of the latter.

It is with Italy that we are concerned, not the Italy of today but of yesterday, a country as yet disunited, made up of small independent principalities and dukedoms, united only by sunshine and beauty.

So on a morning in August of 1815 we climb the French Alps, flounder through the snow of the Modane-Monte Cenis pass, and drop down among the blue hills of Piedmont to a white-washed farmhouse near the village of Castelnuovo d'Asti and the hamlet of Becchi. Under the cerulean blue sky, the long red-tiled roof looks very decorative, sheltering as it does the small house in the middle, with a cow stable under one wing and a shed for goats and pigs under the other.

We tiptoe noiselessly up the narrow outer stairway and peep into the low-ceilinged white room. The brown-eyed, brown-haired bronze baby looks lost in the big white bed beside his mother. He does not feel the tick of corn husks nor the hard high pillows nor the coarse clean sheets. His grandmother has just bathed him in aromatic olive oil and bound him up in his swaddling bands.

"Eh, *bambino mio.*" She pats him. "What big hands you've got." The tiny strong square fingers curl about hers.

"He'll want them to work with," says his mother, smiling with happiness.

"What will you call him?"

Mother Margherita Bosco answers quickly, "And why not Giovanni?"

So Giovanni—John—Bosco he was: a peasant boy destined to lead not armies but boys; destined, in the midst of the struggle of his country for political unity and for a constitutional government, to become one of her great humanitarians, an "apostle of youth."

First, he must be carried next day the three miles and more to Castelnuovo to be baptized in the church of St. Andrew.

Then, he had to grow up. And for a small boy life on a small farm is much the same the world over, especially if that boy has an elder half-brother to boss him. Not being blessed with a sweet temper, Antonio was glad enough for a minion to order about. So Giovanni as herd boy minded the two cows in the pasture, or he gathered sticks for the fire; he fed the chickens and tethered the goats.

When Antonio shouted at him, ordering him this way and that, and Giovanni, stung with injustice, answered back, their mother would call out,

"Remember, God sees you."

Giovanni would hang his head, his face flushed crimson, while Antonio's grew blacker than ever.

"A house divided is a house in ruin," their mother would remind them as she served the bowl of minestrone. "If your father had lived he would know how to make peace in his house."

That night Giovanni would pray for forgiveness and resolve never to rebel again, but next day, Antonio was just the same, overbearing and tyrannical toward him. Often his mother would call him in to untangle her flax or to sweep out the kitchen.

Whenever he could he would run to his secret hiding place in the deep niche of the massive walls to unwrap his treasure and laboriously trace out the words:

"Q. What is faith?

"A. Faith is the substance of things hoped for, the evidence of things not seen."

Giovanni sighed. His mother echoed his sigh.

"Don't you want to become a good farmer and help your brother? You seem to care for nothing but that Catechism."

"I would care for another book, too, if I had one, my mother. Is it so wicked, then, to want to learn?"

"But as Antonio says, a book will do you no good on a farm. You should be out with him this moment, helping with the spring plowing. No wonder he gets cross with you when you care more for your Catechism than his work. I declare, you act more like a little priest than a peasant."

"That's just what I mean to become, a priest," Giovanni confessed shyly. "I've wanted to for ever so long."

His mother caught him to her, this sturdy, brown-eyed boy of ten. Her lips trembled. Could it be possible? Her boy, a peasant, to become a priest of the church?

"It must be because you were born on the day after Her festival," said his mother. "I gave you to Our Lady then."

"I've known Her for ever so long," the boy said.

"Then I will help you to study. I will shield you from your brother. Here, run to the village to borrow of your grandmother a bowlful of lentils. And stop a bit to play with the boys." Her heart was tender toward him. "But see that you don't get into a fight today."

Yet Giovanni came home with a black eye and a cauliflower ear. His mother shook her head, as Antonio taunted him. He liked so well to play with the boys, even if he usually came home smarting. How could he tell his mother that it was because he would not abide their cursing and swearing? Seeing how hot it made him, the boys would swear all the more. Out would fly Giovanni's fists. He was not going to let God and Our Lady go undefended. In the Middle Ages he would have been a Crusader. In the nineteenth century he was only a battered small boy.

Soon he found an odd way to win them over, these country louts of Piedmont. The idea came to him on a sunny day in September when his mother took her boys to the fair. Here Giovanni saw conjurers pulling white rabbits out of a hat, and jugglers who kept balls spinning in the air, and a man balancing a stick on his chin, and a slim lad walking a tight rope. Giovanni stared with all his eyes. His face was sober with the effort of concentration, but his heart was laughing.

Next day when he went to the meadow to mind his cows, Giovanni stretched a thick rope between two pear trees and began his perilous stunt practice. He tumbled often enough, but when he had mastered the delicate art of balance, he tied the rope higher. Next he tried ball juggling, and stick balancing and sleight of hand tricks. When he was ready, he invited the boys of the hamlet to come up on Sunday afternoon to see his show. No admittance—free!

Well, nearly free. All they had to do was to recite together a prayer before the show began. The boys grumbled and joked at this odd entrance fee.

"All right then, perhaps you don't want to see my tricks, after all."

But they did very much want to see them, and so all the boys knelt down on the grass and said the prayer.

"And now we might as well sing a hymn to Our Lady. She would like to hear us, and then I shan't be breaking my neck when I walk the tight rope," coaxed Giovanni.

Ave, maris stella,
Dei Mater alma,
Atque semper Virgo. . .

If the boys punctuated the hymn with giggles, Giovanni took no notice, but mounted a stump to preach them a sermon. At least he went over the main points in the one he had heard that morning at Murialdo. But Giovanni somehow made it human and brought it close to their own world.

And before they could grow restless, the small preacher turned into a showman. To the astonishment of his audience, he mimicked the clowns and the mountebanks. He made butterflies appear and disappear. He walked the tight rope as well as a professional. The field rang with laughter and applause when, after perilous-looking contortions, he managed to regain his balance and jumped lightly to earth.

The show over, the showman turned preacher once more and closed with a short talk on honesty.

As the Sundays passed, not only children but grown-ups came from miles around, until Giovanni had an audience of a hundred and more. Who wouldn't walk miles in Italy to see a boy trickster? He was every bit as good as a fair. Besides, these came but once a year, and Giovanni's show was every week. The voices rang out with the sweet hymns to Our Lady. The sermons on obedience and control of temper struck home.

"*Come parla bene,*" said the neighbors to his mother. "How well he speaks. You have raised up a boy for the circus."

But Mother Margherita shook her head, laughing. Well she knew that instead of the circus she was raising her boy for Our Lady. Indeed, already he had begun his life-mission.

His tricks were all very well for now, but what about the boy's future? How was he to gain his coveted knowledge? How could he study and go to school? Boy and mother faced the problem together. For on this Antonio had put his foot down. And Antonio was head of the house, wielder of the stick, *la verga.*

"Giovanni was born a peasant on the land, wasn't he?" he would demand. "Then a peasant he remains. Let him set his face to the soil instead of into a book."

So, though his mother tried her best to help him, for the next six years Giovanni had a hard uphill struggle. Whenever his spirit rose like a lark, he felt forces pulling him back to the earth.

One day, coming home from church, Giovanni caught up with a kindly priest from Murialdo.

"You are young for so long a sermon, my son, but tell me, what have you remembered of it?" For they had both heard the sermon of a visiting priest come from Rome to announce the Pope's jubilee.

"Do you wish the beginning, the middle, or the end, Father?"

"Bless me, boy, begin where you like. Tell me anything you can remember."

So Giovanni began, and repeated the sermon word for word, exactly as if he had engraved it on the wax disk of his mind, and was now putting on the record for Don Calosso.

The good Don was astonished at this feat. First he learned the boy's name and his village.

"Where do you attend school, Giovanni?" he asked.

"I can't go to school, Father."

So the story came out. But when he confessed his longing to study because he must become a priest, then his companion insisted upon talking with his mother.

It was agreed between them that her son must be meant to till wider fields than those of her little farm, and that she must send Giovanni to the Don for a foundation of Latin.

At first the boy gladly walked the six miles a day. Then, as Antonio still objected, his mother sent him to live with the good Don, herself bringing bread each week to pay for his keep.

Now Giovanni was in heaven, assisting as altar boy at church services, in between his eager studying of Donatus. And he was all the better pleased with this first Latin grammar, when Don Calosso explained how the very same book had been studied by all the boys of Europe for the last fifteen hundred years, ever since Ælius Donatus, the tutor of St. Jerome, had compiled it in the fourth century. It was the very same book that Gutenberg printed on his press soon after 1450, before he began his great Bible.

So here Giovanni was, no longer a cowherd, but cramming in his Latin as if he could not get it fast enough. It was the foundation, his master told him, on which would rest the working out of his destiny, the fulfillment of those longings he had felt stirring in his heart since he was nine, longings to be a leader of boys.

For the time being, the boy was a lark, and Don Calosso an angel from heaven. For the Don had promised to see him through college.

But Giovanni Bosco was to have no easy road in life. For his master and friend was no sooner stricken from him by paralysis than distant relatives turned up to claim his life-savings which he had given for Giovanni's education.

There was nothing for the lad to do but to return home, and take his books with him into the fields. He would have to teach himself. Yet he reckoned without Antonio who hated the very sight of a book. Nothing so infuriated his brother as to see him plowing with one hand, and studying with the other. At last Antonio made his life so unbearable that their mother decided that Giovanni had best go away for a time to find a place where he might work for his keep.

"Try the Moglio farm," she suggested, wiping her eyes. "I will come soon to see you."

In a snowstorm he trudged off down the road till he

came to the Moglio farm. No, they did not need him, nor want him, they said. So, laughing with good nature but with desperate resolve, he sat down in the shed where they were cutting withes to tie up the vines in the spring. So what could they do but let him stay? And stay he did for two years, helping with the herds, or with plowing and reaping, vine-culture, or threshing.

He had little time for his books. Yet for all that, he had his memory. Antonio had not been able to take that gift from him. Never a day but he would rehearse in his mind the Donatus. Over and over at night he repeated the conjugations, forcing himself to stay awake.

On Sundays he would gather the younger children of the parish under the great square church tower. First came his tricks. Then he taught them the Catechism. No need to look at the book; he knew it by heart.

Yet as more of the farm work fell to his strong shoulders, ever more desperate grew his longing for an education. Had Antonio won? Must he give up his idea of becoming a priest? For on that depended his future mission, and priesthood rested on Donatus. Who would help him?

Then, just as if he had stepped into the pages of a Horatio Alger story, at that moment an uncle turned up, an uncle who transformed him from a clod to a lark once more. For the uncle insisted that Giovanni drive back his herd to the Moglio barns, take up his bundle and return home to continue his studies with some neighboring priest.

Gladly the boy obeyed, but they both reckoned without his ancient enemy, brother Antonio, who raised such a storm of protest that his mother repeated her adage: "A house divided is a house in ruin." She bade Antonio divide the property, and go to live on his share.

Then the uncle decided that Giovanni had best go away to the school in Castelnuovo. Alas, his purse was less large than his heart.

"Providence will find a way," said Mother Margherita, and went off to the village to spread the glad news. Her son was to go away to school. He would start off as soon as she could manage a new pair of shoes.

So! And how the neighbors wagged their tongues. That Giovanni Bosco was to become a great man after all. He was to go away to school. But how would Widow Bosco manage his keep? No one had much to spare; still, they would do what they could.

Soon up the hill to the Bosco farm trudged a stream of visitors bearing gifts: one a sack of lentils, of millet or wheat, another a coat, a jar of olive oil, a sack of corn, and still another a pair of shoes, or rather those stout boots called *scaddini,* made for traveling these hill roads, of thick soles they were and studded with nails.

All the laughing and weeping and embracing drove Antonio out of the house. Yet no one minded him now in the excitement of sending this stalwart Giovanni off to school. What if he had no money? Their provisions could be sold in the market for his books. He could earn his way. So they waved him off down the hill, trudging along the muddy road to Castelnuovo in the new shoes and coat, his big sack of gifts slung on a stout stick over his shoulder.

Though he was a tall lad of sixteen, he had never gone to a real school. He squared his shoulders and set himself to overcome the heavy odds against him. For he must start down among the little boys, submitting to their taunts and jeers, and worse still to the scorn of his schoolmaster, a heartless priest who thought him only a stupid peasant yokel, and so made gibes at his expense. Yet in spite of the master's cruel indifference, Giovanni set himself to make up a year's work every two months.

Now in order to earn his keep, Giovanni worked early and late at many jobs. First with a tailor who set him at sewing on buttons and making buttonholes, and later to cutting out breeches and waistcoats. Next with a cobbler who taught him to cut lasts and to hammer soles to thick leather boots. Even in a pastry shop and a pool room he worked, where he heard rough talk among the soldiers and hangers-on.

He could have made plenty of new friends among them. They lived a gay and exciting life. One tried to take him to cheap theaters, another to risk his small capital on a gaming table, a third invited him to make a raid on a nearby vineyard and on the fruits of gardens, while a fourth suggested his stealing a watch and selling it to buy sweets. He had to set his will against each of them, and hide away in his small cupboard with a stub of a candle to commit to memory long portions of Dante.

"One rotten apple will spoil a whole barrel," his mother had often reminded him.

His life seemed lonely and hard at the time. It was only later that he was glad of these experiences, for through them he understood what boys had to strive against, what temptations they faced, how easy it was to follow bad companions instead of struggling for an education which no one seemed to want to give him.

But due to his efforts early and late, Giovanni was at

last enrolled in the Seminary of Chieri. His Donatus had led him to Cicero and Ovid, Tacitus and Virgil. Now he delved into church history, into arithmetic, and tasted the joy of the poets, of Dante, Tasso and Petrarch. Here, also, he had lessons in music and in drawing.

He still earned his living as apprentice to a joiner, learning the Italian art of carpentry and getting a feeling for wood. But if he still worked hard he now had companions among whom he could make life-long friends, boys like himself pledged to become priests of Mother Church.

With his fellows, Giovanni formed a *Società dell'Allegria*, a society of gay comrades. Perhaps, as Johannes Jorgensen suggests, the idea came to him from St. Francis of Assisi, who called melancholy "the Babylonian disease," and insisted that his brothers wear shining, joyous faces. Perhaps Giovanni knew the French proverb: "*Un saint triste n'est qu'un triste saint.*" That is, a saint who is sad makes but a sorry saint.

At any rate, his Companions of Joy were the best students in the college. For, thanks to his brilliant memory, Giovanni could keep up with the ablest. And thanks to his merry heart, he was popular with rich and poor.

On Sundays the Companions would strike out for the hills, in their pockets a lunch of bread and roasted chestnuts. Picking wild berries or mushrooms by the way, they would explore the neighboring age-old shrines and churches where they would stop to confess and hear mass.

If some boys held back from these excursions, Giovanni would resort to his tricks — more intricate ones now — such as climbing to the top of a tall tree and standing on his hands, or leaping across a wide brook. Or he sang and played his violin or made endless nonsense rhymes, or he gave readings of Dante and Petrarch from memory. So the shy and the weak-willed were drawn into his band. They set themselves never to shirk, never to grumble, but to enter wholeheartedly into the services and rules which many boys tried to evade.

At last, in 1841, after ten long years of work and of study, Giovanni was ordained a priest. The peasant boy of Becchi had won the first goal of his obstacle race. And who should walk all the way to hear his first mass but his little Mother Margherita! There she knelt, bowing her head under her black shawl, with her great brown eyes riveted on the back of that tall young priest in his new vestments. How strong and low his voice! How strong and good his face as he turned to administer the sacrament. A peasant face, but good; with his brown hair falling over his broad forehead; the deep-set brown eyes courageous, steadfast; the wide mouth kindly and generous, ready to break into a smile; the chin determined, forward thrusting. It was worth while, all her years of sacrifice and toil on the farm. And though she wept into her black shawl, yet it was the happiest moment of her life.

"And where will you begin your labors, my son?" she asked him later, as he shared his minestrone with her. She hoped that he might be sent to a village near home.

"I'll go to Torino, *madre mia*—to Turin, my mother. I hear the city is crowded with peasant boys looking for work."

"Ah, Torino!" She compressed her lips. "When you grow rich in the great city, then I can never come to see you."

Her son laughed. "Never fear, Mother. There are many poor still left in Turin."

Neither mother nor son had ever been to the city, the capital of Piedmont, the kingly city where Charles Albert lived in his palace. Ah well, all young men yearned for a city. So Mother Margherita looked deep into her young priest's eyes, kissed him on both cheeks, and plodded back along the dusty road to Becchi, while Giovanni set forth to Turin.

To TURIN, the Paris of Italy, one of her important industrial centers. Turin on the Po, for seven hundred years ruled by the House of Savoy, the *Casa Savoia*. Time and again it had been overrun with French troops, as Piedmont belonged now to Burgundy, now to Savoy. In 1818, twenty-three years before, when Giovanni was three years old, the city had been made capital also of the Kingdom of Sardinia which was then united to that of Savoy.

Just as during the sixteenth century, and again for most of the seventeenth, so in the eighteenth this French domination oppressed again. Giovanni's mother was ten years old when the soldiers had come marching down from the peaks, bearing the banners of fleurs-de-lys, to drive the Piedmont king, Charles Emmanuel II, out of Turin and force him to retire to the Island of Sardinia.

But two years before Giovanni's birth, Napoleon had commandeered Piedmontese troops "for fodder," and Piedmontese mellow church bells to melt into cannon. For in 1805 Bonaparte had had himself crowned Emperor of Italy in Milan—a crown which rolled off at the feet of Wellington. That was why, in that important year of 1815, King Victor Emmanuel I had returned from Sardinia to reascend the throne in Turin. After the last sixteen years of French occupation, the foreign soldiers had marched off, across the bridge over the Po, to climb again over Cenis back into France.

Once more the standard of Piedmont was raised over the city, the *bianca croce di Savoia*, the white cross of Savoy. You will find it still stamped on Italian coins with the letters F.E.R.T., which means: *Fortitudo Ejus Rhodum Tenuit* — to mark the heroic defense of Rhodes in 1522 against the Sultan Suliman.

Now, in 1841, the young priest Don Bosco found Turin full of those contrasts which seem inevitable in a royal city. Palaces of the King and his nobles, the palace of the archbishop beside his cathedral, stately buildings of the University, all crowned the new city; while in the old town, built on the ruins of the ancient Roman city, swarmed the poor. Artisans of building and leather trades, workers in wood and in iron, peasants driven in from the country by famine, all elbowed for a chance to earn their bread.

Here too were bandits and thieves, ready to entice green country boys into their gangs. Don Bosco, walking the arcaded streets, spoke to one boy and another, inviting them to his church, but they only spat out at him. So he helped his countryman, Don Collengo, who had established a soup kitchen, a home for the aged, and, at Valdocco, a hospital of four thousand beds for strangers and incurables.

But Don Bosco was restless. Don Collengo's work was not his. Somewhere in the dark doorways of this big city, he felt there must be boys who needed him. But how to find them?

A month after his arrival, a boy found him. Don Bosco was robing before mass in the sacristy when he heard the sacristan driving out a boy who had come to look in. Don Bosco rebuked the man and called back the lad.

Sixteen he was, but small for his age, this Bartolomeo, an orphan who had come to the city to find work. But no one needed a bricklayer, so he had slept for a week in doorways and snatched food where he could find it.

"Have you never been to school?" asked Don Bosco.

Bartolomeo shook his head.

"Would you like to learn to read?"

The boy nodded, a new light in his eyes.

"Then we'll start today. Come back here to me after the mass."

So they sat down together while Don Bosco gave him his first lesson in reading and writing. Then they had dinner. The priest found a place for him to work during the week and invited him to return the following Sunday and bring anyone he liked with him.

Bartolomeo turned up with six street boys. They played games, had a lesson, a dinner of bread and nuts, and heard mass.

Soon there were twenty boys; lusty-voiced, dirty of hands, ragged of clothes, apprenticed to cobblers or masons or tailors, or just looking for work. Soon they had increased to a hundred.

Don Bosco was delighted, but nobody else was. For who wanted a lot of noisy street hoodlums? At first they had been allowed the yard adjoining the orphanage where Don Bosco was chaplain. But they soon outstayed their welcome. To one church after another in Turin, Giovanni led his flock, but once mass was over, their young shouts could be heard for blocks. For no one could play games like Don Bosco, they discovered; no one knew so many tricks, nor such funny faces. No wonder they shouted.

The neighbors complained. Don Bosco's colleagues refused them shelter. Even from a cemetery they were driven. For five years they were shunted about, with never a *portiuncula*, a little place of their own.

In summer they took to the fields. They would meet at dawn like a modern scout troop: those who could brought lunch along. For those who had none, Don Bosco provided a basket of bread and sometimes chestnuts for a treat. Off they would go through the city gate out on the open road. Don Bosco would lead them to a village church or a chapel where he would say mass. Then a hymn was sung with their fresh clear voices. For they had quickly developed a fine choir.

Then breakfast, and games in an open field. Don Bosco could leap farther, climb higher, do more tricks than any of them. How they admired him! Then to a stream or a fountain to quench their thirst, or a dip on hot days. And then they would press about their leader for stories—stories of heroes of Greece or Rome, stories of courage, of poor boys who became great.

After lunch, Don Bosco would turn priest again and hear confessions, talking privately with one after another, hearing their troubles, giving counsel and advice.

Then as Vesper bells began ringing across the fields, they would recite the prayers as they walked. And so at dusk they would come back to the city, tired out but thoroughly content and satisfied. No wonder that by the end of summer Don Bosco had four hundred boys chattering and laughing and fighting for places to walk beside him.

But he needed a permanent chapel now for winter, with a big yard beside it for games. Where was he to find pasture for his flock? His fellow priests began to think him mad, and tried to have him committed to an asylum. His boys were only budding criminals, they scoffed. In refusing regular parish appointments, Bosco would find himself penniless, his career sunk for life.

Their arguments having no effect upon their colleague, they appealed to the police. So now Don Bosco was haled before the Chief of Police, the Marchese Cavour, father of a young man who was to become the great liberal statesman of Piedmont, and one of the Fathers of Italy. Perhaps the priest was in league with the exiled Mazzini, the Marchese suggested. Perhaps his street urchins belonged to Mazzini's *Giovane Italia*, young revolutionists who were demanding a constitutional government and union of all the independent states of Italy.

The courts still imposed sentences of death or imprisonment on all liberal suspects, so the Chief ordered the priest's room searched for dangerous papers. However, since the officers found nothing more incriminating than baker's bills, the case was dropped.

Don Bosco only laughed at his tormentors, and for answer he rented three rooms in a house and began teaching his boys in the evenings; this was the first night school in Italy, just as Henrietta Szold's was the first in Baltimore. He taught them arithmetic and principles of craft work, in order to improve at their trades. But each Sunday he was at a loss to tell them where to meet. Not a church in the city wanted them now. The boys knew it.

"They think we're not good enough," they grumbled. "Nobody'll give us a chance."

"Never mind." Don Bosco hid his worries from them. "Don't you know that cabbages grow better if they are planted out? Yes, sir, they like being pulled up and stuck into fresh earth again. The only trouble with us is that we haven't prayed hard enough."

One of the boys spoke up: "If God sees us, like you say, then why can't He see for Himself that we need a place of our own?"

"Yes," chimed in another. "And if Our Lady loves us like you say, then why can't She find a house for us?"

"Perhaps She thinks we are not yet ready for it," Don Bosco suggested, smiling.

"Yes, we are ready too. I'll tell Her so," said Carline.

"All right, you tell Her. And we'll meet out in the south field next Sunday. I'll set up an altar and we'll have mass with the birds."

Sunday came, with its games and shouting, its whispered confessions and open-air service. In the midst of it a man entered the field to speak with Don Bosco. Did he want to buy a large yard with a shed in it for his boys? Don Bosco's heart leaped. Leaving a friend to carry on in his place, he followed the man at once.

The property was in the district called Valdocco, on the outskirts of the city. It had been named "Valley of the Slain" for two Roman soldiers who, in the year 300, were martyred there for their faith. Now the place was half wasteland, half refuse dumps, with shacks of the poor clustered around small wine taverns. On Sundays it was noisy with drunken riotings. Its one redeeming feature for Don Bosco, other than its size, was its vicinity to the great hospital of his friend, Don Collengo.

Yet it seemed a strange place to begin his work. He had dreamed of classrooms for study, shops to learn trades, a dormitory and a chapel. He found only a low tumbledown shed with leaky roof and sagging beams. The large fenced-in yard with its one mulberry tree faced a tavern where men and boys drank cheap wine and plotted cheap crime.

Was this where he was meant to build? How was he to guess that within his own lifetime he was to transform the whole district into a place of order and beauty, and was to create an institution which would serve as model to thousands of others all over the world?

And the price? Could he meet it? Strangely enough, Don Bosco had recently received a gift from a sick man in gratitude for his sudden healing. The amount was the exact sum required.

When he returned to tell his boys that at last they had a place of their very own, where they could shout and pray as much as they pleased, they threw up their caps and yelled for joy. In a crowd the whole four hundred rushed to see it for themselves.

"Do you think you can perform a magic trick and transform this old shed into a chapel?" their leader asked them.

"Sure we can. Just watch us. The place couldn't be better!" They kissed his hands and his robe in their exuberance. And they set to work with a will, all who knew anything of carpentry or masonry trades. The magic worked. Soon the small chapel was crowded with boys outside and in singing *Angioletti del mio Deo*—Angels of God. Even if they were only Turin *ragazzi*, they had angelic voices. At night the chapel became a classroom, and again it was crammed with boys eager to learn.

At last, Don Bosco felt he must do something to shelter the boys who had no homes. He must have someone to mother them. So he walked the twenty miles along the road by the Po, past the blossoming acacia trees, out toward the blue hills and above them the shining peaks of Monte Rosa, out past the hamlet of Becchi to the whitewashed farmhouse on the hill, to persuade his mother to walk back with him, back to be the mother of his boys.

He rented three rooms in the house close to the yard and filled the loft with orphans. It was true that the first group ran away with the blankets, and the next homeless boy got locked in the kitchen for safe-keeping, but they soon learned.

Mother Margherita had never before been to the city, and no wonder she thought the place sordid and ugly. She had been afraid of riches for her son, so she had to make the best of his poverty.

Opening the bundle he had brought on his back, she took out her wedding gown which she kissed and cut up into altar vestments. Next she kissed her gold wedding chain and sold it to buy corn for her growing family. And Don Bosco himself made the corn into *polenta*, which the boys said tasted like nectar.

One by one the neighbors fled: too many hymns, too much noise, too many scrapings of violins, too much goodness. Even the taverns lost business and sought other quarters. Meanwhile Don Bosco's house was a hive of industry. For by means of gifts for more healings, he was able to buy the whole house and to fill it with boys. He found jobs for them; he taught evening classes every night in the week except Sunday. He still played games with them. He heard their confessions. He taught them to love Our Lady and to try to imitate Her Son. He trained young priests to help him.

All Turin knew him now, this sturdy black-robed priest striding along with his noisy gang hanging onto him. Even his former persecutors were content to forget his attack of insanity. The rich and the poor flocked to Valdocco to see his boys. For no less a personage than King Charles Albert himself favored the work. On New Year's Day of 1847 he sent a liveried servant with a gift of three hundred lire, marked "For Don Bosco's little rascals."

ALTHOUGH Don Bosco had been proved innocent of revolutionist propaganda, yet he was forced to study the whole problem of the country in order to answer the eager questions of his boys.

During the year 1848, the independent states of Italy were shaken by the same wind of rebellion as blew so hard over Europe on the other side of the white peaks. First the Sicilians, long fretting under the rule of petty despots, revolted; Sicily was followed by Naples, Naples by Tuscany, Tuscany by Milan, Milan by Venice, Venice by Rome, and Rome by Florence and Piedmont.

Everywhere the common man rose up to demand a constitution. If America could have one, why not they? Some rulers felt strong enough to rebuke their people, while others were forced to give in. Thus Ferdinand of Naples granted a constitution, and the Grand Duke of Tuscany a charter and a few liberties. After five days of hatred and terror in Milan, a provisional government was set up. Venice followed. Rome, led by Pope Pius IX, called down God's blessings upon Italy and set up its own constitution. It was no new idea that the head of the Church should assume the temporal power of his kingdom.

In Turin, the people stormed the palace led by the editor, Count Camillo Cavour, and the noisy Mazzini liberals until Charles Albert was forced to grant the constitution they demanded. While the people danced about the city with delight, the king mourned at the downfall of his house. For how was he to know that this self-same charter was destined to form the constitution of the future Italian Kingdom, and his son its first monarch?

No wonder that Don Bosco's boys were excited by all this stirring up of high and low, rich and poor. Aside from the airing of grievances, heavy taxation and plunder by armies quartered on the land, the people became aware of the need for union of Italian states. Mazzini and Cavour led the party which advocated this union under the present King of Savoy-Piedmont-Sardinia, their own Charles Albert. Others were pushing the idea of the same union of states with the Pope as president. Still others wanted a union only of the northern states as a barrier to France and Austria. While the fourth group were concerned only with a union of Rome and Naples under the Pope.

On one point only everyone agreed, that the time had come to free the country of foreign domination. France had marched off, except for the legions of the Pope. Now Austria must follow. For had not Austria lorded it over large sections of the country ever since Charles V was crowned Emperor in the sixteenth century? And the sting of Bonaparte's gift of free Venice to Austria still rankled.

So Charles Albert proclaimed a war in 1848 against Franz Joseph, and called to arms under the white cross of Piedmont men of Venice and Florence and Rome and Naples and Modena, to swell his hundred thousand soldiers of Turin.

The city was filled with young troops. All of Don Bosco's older boys rushed off to the barracks to drill. Alas, Charles Albert learned well that without unity there cannot be strength. His army of eager volunteers was no match for the disciplined Austrian troops, accounted the best in Europe. Defeated, beaten back, he had to watch Austria gain new cities in the north, while Venice surrendered through famine.

The times were perilous to royalty: the problems of constitutional monarchy were manifold. Within a year the King abdicated his throne in favor of his son, and retired to a Portuguese monastery to die. Truly it was no little thing that the people demanded of nineteenth-century princes. Few men find it easy to lay aside power.

Meanwhile a counter-revolution had crushed Naples and Sicily, Florence and Tuscany, beneath the ancient rule of despotism. Only Rome remained a republic, with Mazzini as chief Triumvir. The Pope fled to Gaeta, and the fiery Garibaldi and his red-shirted legionnaires escaped to America.

It was a time of violence and storm, of the economic confusion following war. Turin was crowded with refugees, with brigands, with orphans. Don Bosco had to deal with them all.

When his boys outgrew Valdocco, he opened a second center in the city, and soon afterward, a third.

"If the hive overflows, the bees must swarm," he said, smilingly. These were the first of many such swarms during these troublous years. Soon other cities heard of his success and wanted a branch. He sent his older boys and his trained young priests to open them. He called them Oratories, houses for work and for prayer. They were the first trade schools in Italy, the first boys' clubs, the first scout troops. They kept thousands of boys out of prisons and reformatories.

Soon France wanted an Oratory of Don Bosco, then Spain. Again he sent his sons and followed them with visits himself, and wrote hundreds of letters to individual boys. He called them the Order of Salesians, after St. Francis of Sales who had gathered the children of France about him and won them with gentleness.

"One catches more flies with a drop of honey than with a spoonful of vinegar," St. Francis de Sales used to say. And Don Bosco adopted that same principle in all his dealings with boys.

Five years after the revolution he had completed his new church on the Valdocco site, and had erected a large evening school. Now he added shops where his boys might learn a trade or brush up on their own. The tailor, bootmaker and joiner crafts he taught at first himself. It was not for nothing that he had put himself through school, those ten years. Now he added cabinet work and inlay, the fine *intarsio* work of setting one wood within another in design. Also a smithy, a hatter's shop, and best of all, his printing establishment.

For he wrote practical books for practical people and wanted his boys to learn the printing trade by publishing these books. One, on the metrical system which was just being introduced into Italy, furnished good copy. Another small book was on the culture of vines, those good vineyards spreading over the hills from which came the red Baròla and Asti wines. For his Oratories he wrote histories, one of the Bible, another of the Church, a third of Italy. His prayer book, *Il Giovane Proveduto,* has gone into many editions.

Thirty years later, at the Turin Industrial Exposition of 1884, Don Bosco and his boys filled one whole pavilion with a demonstration of how a book comes to life, from the wood-pulp to paper, to the founding of type, to composition, to a bound volume. It was justly acclaimed one of the marvels of the Exposition.

One of Don Bosco's chief contributions to his age was a little book called *A Preventive System in the Training of Youth.* To the thought of the times it was quite as revolutionary as Mazzini's dream of a united Italy.

For he taught the danger of repression and coercion. "Let the boys scream and shout as much as they like," he said. Something was certain to be wrong if they didn't. But a boy must not be regimented into outward goodness. He must not be made to attend mass or even the customary evening prayers of the Oratories. He must come of his own free will. He must not be forced to tell the truth: he must be led to want to be truthful.

One is reminded of the ancient advice of Krishna to Arjuna:

> *Since all men conform to their natures,*
> *Of what shall coercion avail?*

Nor did he believe in punishment of boys by master, teacher or parent, but rather in constant vigilance, in their ability to foresee difficulties and so give warning in time.

Many of his boys found under their pillows at night a little note from Don Bosco, who had anticipated a deed they would always regret, and so warned them in time.

He found that in all his boys the most serious lack was an untrained, undisciplined will. Here, in the will, lay the secret to a boy's nature.

"It is a fallacy," he maintains, "to cultivate only a boy's feeling and intelligence, no matter how highly developed these be. For his brilliant qualities often conceal the most incomprehensible weakness. The child, and later the young man, will intoxicate himself in his own enjoyment of the senses, but will be incapable of correct thinking or action. He will be entirely lacking in sound judgment, tact, or restraint. He will recognize judgments and opinions ready made from the outside because they please his feelings or his imagination.

"Do not look for order and method in such a boy, for he knows no law but his whim and his moods. Thus, susceptibility and inconstancy are the fundamental traits of his character. There has been no attempt by teacher or parents to form a human being, with the sad result that he is an intelligent, emotionally refined but weak and unreasonable creature—a highly developed animal."

Therefore, Don Bosco threw the whole weight of his dealings with boys, with thousands of boys during forty years, upon certain fixed principles.

First and foremost was the friendly, happy relationship and companionship of his trained young Salesians with groups of boys in play and work. His rascals, his *ragazzi*, were far better off in the company of an elder brother than alone, either in work or in play.

But underlying this were deeper factors in molding character. The first was confession. Not confession publicly or to one another, but a shy, whispered confession to that one which stood to the boy as his spiritual father.

Heretofore, the Church had taught that confession must be used only within the church. Don Bosco took it outside from very necessity, since during the five years of his struggle to find a foothold in Turin, he was literally pushed outside. So he formed the habit of confessing his boys in the open field, on the streets, in fact wherever he found them. And not only his boys but grown-ups profited by his willingness to allow them to unburden a tortured mind and heart: sitting beside a liveried coachman as he drove to the sick-bed of a nobleman, on railway trains, during the plague, in hospitals, on the streets, anywhere at all. Even the thieves who tried to murder him, found in him that large impersonal compassion, that deep understanding, that healing which their souls had long craved.

But confession was not the only necessity for his boys. He believed that for them the sacrament of the mass had a powerful efficacy. Never did he force them, never did he urge them to the altar by rows, or by a section. One and another came as they wished. Or a boy might live in one of his Oratories for months without once coming, though sooner or later the magic usually worked. But he came of his own accord.

His third principle was that of prayer. If the baker came to wake him at two in the morning to say he would positively not deliver another loaf of *grissini*—those long thin rods of Piedmont bread—unless his bill were paid, Don Bosco would ask a dozen boys to pray in the church while he went forth along the streets of Turin to "meet Providence," as he called these errands. How else were the bills to be paid, the schools built, the churches raised? The boys learned by vivid and countless experiences that prayer did work.

Don Bosco would return with the exact sum needed. He had met a man on the street; he had called on a nobleman whom he knew must be grateful for a recent healing.

By these means, and by the love of his boys for him and for his carefully trained assistants, Don Bosco was able to capture the will of the boy and return it to the youth strong and able to cope with the life about him.

For those were chaotic years. Counter forces of tyranny and democracy were struggling for power, now hidden below the surface, now bubbling up to demand a voice. Europe was like a gigantic cauldron over a hot fire. Yet the forces up-thrusting were in harmony with the progress of the nineteenth century, and would not be denied. This very principle of unity among states, already so strong in America and in England, so slow to develop in Germany and in Italy, must no longer be held back. Progress demanded it, and progress ruthlessly swept aside tyranny, selfish power, greed of men or of states or of nations. Surely unity of states would lead on one day to unity of nations.

Meanwhile all the dregs at the bottom of the cauldron rose to the surface. Turin was a hotbed of brigands, as everywhere else in Italy; Don Bosco had reason to know. For time and again as he searched for his boys through the night, drew them from pool rooms or dens back to the Oratory of Valdocco, he was beset by murderers and thieves. But for him, his boys would have been swallowed up in the chaos. Would order and peace never prevail?

Yes, for it was not for nothing that Mazzini had labored in exile, nor that Cavour as prime minister had thrown himself into the struggle to make Italy one people, one nation. Now again, in 1859, came the determination to oust the foreign aggressor, Austria, even from Venice. Victor Emmanuel, having learned the lesson of 1849, called upon Napoleon III of France to help him. For in spite of her violent revolution of 1789, France had returned once more to hereditary monarchy.

So again Turin was overrun with volunteer soldiers.

Don Bosco had his hands full with his boys. For they straggled home after the treaty between Franz Joseph and Napoleon, or rushed after Garibaldi who had just been made dictator of rebellious Naples and Palermo.

When, in the wake of the army, the dread cholera broke out in Turin, with twenty-five hundred cases and fourteen hundred deaths, with the nobles and city fathers fleeing to the hills, it was Don Bosco who came to the rescue. He quarantined the younger boys, but called for volunteers among the older ones to help him fight.

Of those who rushed forward, Don Bosco chose forty boys. For three hot months that summer, they worked in the arcaded streets of the lower town, taking the sick to hospitals, carrying food and wine, burying the dead that dropped in the streets. Not one of his boys was infected.

At last freed of Austria, except for Venice, King Victor Emmanuel called a parliament in Turin to which all the states of central Italy sent representatives. The unity of Italy must no longer be denied. The world state demanded it. The people demanded it. If Sicily and Rome, to which the Pope had again returned as temporal ruler, still held out, then they must be drawn into the union by force. Surely, at last, these mediæval principalities must concede their individual rights to govern for the well-being of the whole.

So a breach was made in the thick Vatican walls, and the King's soldiers poured into the Eternal City. The Pope was promised unlimited spiritual power but no voice in temporal affairs. When Naples and Sicily also succumbed in 1861, Victor Emmanuel II was proclaimed King of all Italy, the end of a fifty-year struggle. How the bells of Turin did peal, for its own House of Savoy had been destined to establish a constitutional monarchy. The union of Italy was accomplished.

The national capital, transferred from Turin to Florence, at last came to rest in Rome. The ideal of Mazzini, of Cavour, was made real: "A free church in a free state."

Now for Don Bosco there were many lessons in all these events to bring home to his boys. The ideal of liberty, of freedom, was glorious in the hands of the wise. But his flock could see for themselves what liberty became in the hands of brigands and adventurers. Had they not formed a bodyguard for their master on his errands of mercy to the dark courtyards behind the arcades? Even their stout clubs would have failed to save his life but for *Grigio*, the gray one, the mysterious giant wolf-hound who would appear from nowhere at the call of his master, to plant his fangs in a murderer until the man howled for mercy. Rebuked and often confessed, the brigands would make off in terror of the dog, who would bound along with the boys, licking their hands in delight, to disappear again in the darkness when they had safely reached their own gate.

A hundred boys Mother Margherita had managed in her dormitory up to the day of her death, giving them freedom to shout as they pleased, to trample even her garden in their mock-battles, so long as they were clean of speech and honest.

Then too, the national ideal of unity, of the many for one and one for the many, Don Bosco incorporated into his Order which was spreading so fast in Spain and in France that for many years he made a yearly pilgrimage among his Oratories.

Only once did he visit Paris, and for the very good reason that he was so mobbed, so celebrated, so fêted and dined, so burdened with fame, that he could never venture among that loving-hearted throng again.

For all these years, during which he had built Oratory after Oratory, including churches, playgrounds, workshops, school rooms, dormitories, and training colleges for young priests, he had managed to pay for his countless buildings. How? By gifts, either out of admiration for him and his "rascals," or in gratitude for his seemingly miraculous cures.

To others than his boys, it was quite true that Don Bosco was a saint, gifted with sight and hearing not granted to many men, with extraordinary insight or deep knowledge.

His boys could hide nothing from him. They used to laugh, the older ones, at how they had tried to hide thoughts and deeds from him. It was no use. He saw them as clearly as he saw the boy's face as he passed him on the playground, or bent his head to listen to a partial confession.

There was no limit to this gift of sight, nor to that of healing. Though he always said, "It is not I who heal—I have no power," but gave all the credit for his cures to Our Lady.

For all that, he was sought as eagerly by the rich to heal them of incurable ills as he was by the poor who came by the hundred to bring him their sons. And who had not heard about the powerful protection of *Grigio*, who saved his life countless times?

The noise of all this was blown about Paris, so that, to his discomfort, he must live through four months of weary fame. "The Italian St. Vincent de Paul," they called him, "the Saint of Turin." Marquises, countesses, baronesses, dukes and duchesses vied with one another to entertain him. He preached to thousands in St. Sulpice and the

Madeleine. The élite of France knelt at his feet, stood in line before his confessional, besought him to heal them. In vain did he tell them that his mission on earth was to the poor, to their sons and their daughters. For by this time, Don Bosco had had to open his heart to girls too, and to organize Oratories for them, with sisters to teach them. *Figlie di Maria*, he called them, Daughters of Mary.

Wherever he went in Paris, crowds pressed to see the holy man, to touch his black cape, borrowed for the journey, to kiss his hand, not hesitating even to pull out his hair or to cut off a lock. In fact, Don Bosco as an old man was accorded the same reception as a Charles A. Lindbergh.

Nor did he know how to protect or deny himself to these crowds, tormented as he was in his goings and comings, not even to the doubtings of an elderly man who waited for three hours to speak to him, an old man who acknowledged himself to be Victor Hugo. So he healed as many as touched him, and at last escaped them by leaving Paris forever.

As he sat in the railway carriage, an old man weary with fame and adulation, before his closed eyes came a picture. He could see the sun making a glow on Monte Rosa, and beneath it down among the blue hills of Piedmont, an old whitewashed farmhouse, dazzling white under a blue cerulean sky. The fields behind the house were waving with young corn. The hill slopes were fragrant with vines. He was a child again.

By accident he had broken a jar of olive oil. Carefully he swept the floor and quickly picked up the broken crock. Then he remembered his mother's adage: "God sees everywhere." So he ran out to the birch tree to cut a stout withe. With his knife he even carved notches in it. When he saw his mother coming up the hill he ran to meet her.

"Here, Mama, you will have to use a new birch rod, *la verga*, on me today."

But hearing the story of the accident, she shook her head and put the switch behind the kitchen door.

What a long way he had come, a long way from Becchi to Paris. And now he was going home to his noisy happy brood in the Via Collengo in the transformed Valdocco of Turin.

There was still work for him to do, work to the very end. It was not until his sixtieth year that he was invited to send his Salesians to Patagonia, at the very tip end of South America. And how eagerly they came forward to volunteer, to sail out across wide seas to teach savages at the ends of the earth.

Today, his boys and girls have organized Oratories like those of Turin in seventeen countries, on five continents. The institutions number some fourteen hundred and fifty. The numbers pile up to dizzy heights. Each year the twenty-eight thousand boys and girls who march out of day schools or night schools, out of trade and craft schools in which they have served a five-year apprenticeship, out of orphan homes and boarding schools and seminaries, will join that army of nearly two million who are still proud to call themselves sons and daughters of Don Bosco, of Our Lady. In countries where the need for healing has been greatest, they have established nineteen hospitals and seventy-five dispensaries.

Once Don Bosco had a curious dream in which he saw a large wheel turning noisily. The wheel seemed to symbolize his Oratories. Only Turin heard its first revolution. The second turn all of Italy heard. All Europe heard the third. Finally the whole world heard the song of its turning. So he himself watched his dreams come true, even to the world turn of the wheel. And still it keeps on revolving. Is it any wonder that he was canonized as a Saint in 1933?

In 1935, Italy made a moving picture about Don Bosco so that we might see him as he was fifty years ago among his busy, happy boys and girls. In their own printing presses they are shown printing the books he wrote. In their trade schools they are learning to handle tools and so go out into life equipped to earn their bread.

Don Bosco did not think of them as a mass, but as individuals. It was unimportant that they should give their hearts to him, but most essential that they give their hearts to those shining Ones in Heaven. He felt that the redemption of boys and girls, whom he took even out of prisons or reform schools, lay in their work and play and music, but above all in their individual relationship to the sacraments of the Church. She was the Great Mother. He taught them that everything in his own life was achieved through work and prayer and through conscious oneness with Divinity.

His children thought that he would romp with them always. But when he grew too feeble for their rough games, they would stop their play whenever he walked through the yard or along the streets, and rush up to kiss his hand or his robe. But he made them understand that even after his weary body lay down to rest, he would still be with them, just as he had been on earth, able to help each one to change the beast of his outer self into the lamb of peace.

Today we, like the host of Salesians, salute him as Saint.

LORD SHAFTESBURY
1801–1885

In the sixth century before our era, the young Prince Gautama, called now the Buddha, took a walk which changed his entire life. For he saw, beyond the shelter of his father's palace walls, men carrying a coffin, and so learned of death. He saw dirty, hungry children and so learned of poverty. Because of this the young prince escaped from his beautiful prison to spend his entire life in trying to free people from misery and make them happy.

At the beginning of the nineteenth century, Anthony Ashley Cooper, the fourteen-year-old son of the sixth Earl of Shaftesbury, had a similar experience which affected his whole life. He was walking just beyond the walls of his school, Yarrow, when he met a group of ruffians carrying a coffin. Swearing, shouting, jesting, they were followed by a noisy band of small ragged hoodlums. The sensitive young aristocrat was amazed that in merry Christian England, men so drunken and ribald could engage in an errand so solemn without benefit of clergy to help bury their dead. The boy made a swift vow to God then that if his own life were spared, he would dedicate it to bringing happiness to England's poor.

You may discover for yourself a bronze plate on the wall of Yarrow to mark the spot. For that boy grew up to do "more than any single man or any single government in English history" for the forgotten child and his father and mother. He became a world champion of lost causes.

After Oxford, Lord Ashley * went up for Parliament in time to help bring to an end Wilberforce's long struggle for the emancipation of West Indian slaves. For him this year of 1833 was memorable, not only for the passing of Wilberforce and Hannah More, and the freeing of seven hundred thousand slaves, but for the passage of his own first Factory Act forbidding child labor under nine years of age. The political struggle, begun this year and carried to partial victory in 1850 in the Ten Hour Act, had to be continued for forty years until its final victory in 1874. Why?

Because peaceful rural England had suddenly changed overnight into an industrial nation. The inventions of the fly-shuttle and the spinning jenny, of steamship and train and water-driven machinery, had caused the sudden springing up of cotton and silk factories, small and large, in the north of England. These demanded men and women to guide the looms, but also lilliputians to crawl beneath them. A mere babe would do. So orphanages and poorhouses were emptied and the children sent off to pour into factories as apprentices to the mill owners.

In reality they were slaves, these children, working from

* So-called until 1851 when, at his father's death, he succeeded to the title of Lord Shaftesbury.

thirteen to sixteen hours a day, beaten mercilessly if they fell asleep or got tangled in the machinery. Many factories owned long bunk houses whose beds were never empty, one relay of children dragging in to take the warm places of those driven out under the lash. The factory must be kept running night and day. Of what value the happiness or well-being of a scrawny chit of a child?

The one bright spot in the lives of these factory waifs was their hour of Sunday School. What satisfaction this would have given to Hannah More! Moreover it was the teachers of these schools who were the first rebels against the system. They appealed to Lord Ashley for help, since he was one of the great leaders of Evangelical Sunday Schools, an activity he was to continue for half a century.

So he journeyed to Leeds and to Manchester to see conditions for himself. Within the mills he found little people bobbing in and out from beneath the looms to pick up the waste cotton from the floor. The air reeked of oil and heat. Little tongues lagged out for want of a drink of water. Since the overseer was paid according to the amount of work done, his strap was in constant use. Toward evening, when sleep crept like a gray shroud over the children, and muscles refused to obey, the lashes fell regularly up and down the length of the room.

Lord Ashley looked at the men and women bending over the flying shuttles, their faces gray with strain and fear, their eyes dull with apathy.

He waited for nine o'clock closing time, and saw the line of older sisters or mothers waiting at the gate to pick up the sobbing weary mites and tote them home. He joined the silent procession and followed, tramping a mile down the road to a cottage where a father lay sleeping, his head buried on his arms at a table. Younger children slept on a mattress on the floor.

From the stove the mother dished out a bowl of hot porridge, gathered the already sleeping tot in her arms, propped back her head, and forced the warm gruel through her lips. Mechanically the child swallowed a little, then tumbled back in a dead sleep of exhaustion. The mother laid her down on the one bed.

"How old is she, your little Maggie?" whispered Lord Ashley, his face as white as the handkerchief he had used often that day.

"She's goin' on nine, sir," answered the mother. "I'd keep her home, but him gets only eight shillings the week, and how else shall we live? People talk of freeing the blacks of Jamaica. Let them look nearer home, I says."

Lord Ashley promised her freedom for her sleeping children, and went out into the night, back to the factory to visit the night shift. Aged as gnomes and dwarfs, the children were so stunted in growth that those of ten looked four or five. He found that their pay of five shillings a week was not all in cash but partly in tickets on the truck-shop, which sold food for the company, high priced and of poor quality.

He found that when a finger or hand was accidentally lopped off, or a child coughed too hard or burned with fever, the child was merely sent home or back to the bunk house. Neither medical care nor nursing was provided when an epidemic of childhood diseases swept these sheds.

Horrified at the cruelty, the needless crippling of hundreds of small bodies, Lord Ashley returned to Parliament with a bill limiting the hours of women and children to ten, and prohibiting labor of a child under nine years.

Bitter waged the fight against him. If the thirty thousand tiny girls at work in England were freed, the mill-owners said that the country would lose her industrial supremacy. And though Ashley fought hard, bringing up his bill again year after year, the little children he tried to rescue were grown men and women with children of their own before the bill was finally passed with power to enforce it.

But in the years since 1850 millions of workers have blessed his name. For this English Factory Act was the father of all others in all lands. Now, nearly a century later, we in America are carrying on the same fight for governmental prevention of children's labor, and have not yet won. For the same forces of greed and selfish interest, of tyranny of capital and power of money over human life, are still opponents of social justice.

Meanwhile, Lord Ashley faced the problem of the children working in the mines. Terrible as was the lot of the factory hands, these seemed to him ten times worse. For the small pit-slaves were kept toiling deep underground, away from the sun. They began at three years to pick up coal for father, going on at five years to haul the coal tubs by means of chains which circled their waists and then passed between their legs as they crawled like dogs on all fours through the long passages in water and mud.

But the Prime Minister of England was himself a mine-owner, and since the "Friend of the children" could not move the House by his own words, he demanded in 1842 that they send a commission to investigate for themselves. Thus they took down the stories from the children, word for word.

John Masden, eight and a half, told how he dragged heavy loads for fourteen hours a day. He showed the deep cuts on his legs from the chains. He bent his head to show

how the hair had been worn away by constant rubbing against the damp eighteen-inch roof of the passages. Of course John was undersized and weak, yet he should have kept his weight down to the boys of five to seven, explained the overseers.

Eleven-year-old Ellison Jones said she had worked for three years from two A.M. to two P.M. She had to carry a heavy coal bucket up four ladders. "I have the strap when I do not do Father's bidding," she explained. It was estimated that Ellison carried her coal sixteen to twenty trips a day, the distance of the height of St. Paul's tower.

Janet Cumming was eleven, too. "I gang wie the women at five at night, and work all night on Fridays and come up at twelve of the day. I carry the large bits of coal from the coal-face to the pit-bottom. Yes, I have to bend my back and legs. Oh, no, sir, I have no liking for the work, but Father makes me like it."

Agnes Kerr at fifteen said she had worked in the pits since nine. She made eighteen to twenty journeys a day, up and down many ladders, carrying her buckets a distance of two hundred and fifty fathoms.

At fourteen, Scottish Margaret Leveston carried fifty-six pounds of coal in her "wooden backit." "It is na guid," she admitted wearily, "the work is sair. We begin when it is gai dark. I dinna ken the hour."

After being put off for days to present his final plea based on the findings of this commission, Lord Ashley finally faced the House. For an instant he gripped the table edge and prayed "for the tongue of an angel." Then he felt courage and strength flow into him, and made an impassioned two-hour appeal against "the intolerable burden of industrial avarice."

He insisted that Parliament at last face the truth. Nor did he spare their feelings, but described the wounds on those small thin bodies inflicted by beatings with sticks bristling with rusty nails. He told of how they were hit with great chunks of coal, so that arms and ribs were broken, and still they must work on, since if they whimpered, they were only beaten more. When too crippled or diseased to be of further use, they were as callously dumped out of the mine as common slack.

Surely the heritage of an English child should be happiness, yet these mites grew old and shriveled, crippled with rheumatism from the dampness, never knowing play or sunshine.

"For twenty millions of money you purchased the liberty of the negro, a blessed deed," he reminded them. "You may this night, by a cheap and harmless vote, free thousands of small slaves."

Strong men wept. Even his opponents admitted that they had not been so moved in years. So what could they do but pass his bill? Would that the peers might have heard him, for he spent another two months' work persuading them before his bill protecting the children in mines passed into law on August 10, 1842. A great victory for him! But Lord Ashley saw in it no personal glory, but rather a glory for Britain and for the good of all mankind. He felt rightfully that one such act of mercy lifted the whole world.

WE MAY well wonder why reforms come so slowly. We may think that to see a need is all that is necessary to correct it. Yet there seems never a good force without an evil force to combat it. When the sorry despotism of George

III had been curbed by new parliamentary reforms, the struggle between Whigs and Tories had resolved in an issue between Liberals and Conservatives. When royal tyranny had succumbed to a constitutional monarchy, capital, or money "in a loomp," had become the new despot. The divine right of kings had shifted to the divine right of wealth over human beings.

And only one man in Britain seemed to care. On the flyleaves of a book on Factory Legislation, in after years, Lord Shaftesbury wrote:

"In *The Times* of Saturday, April 11th, 1868, there is a review of the *Life of Wilberforce*. There are many things said in it of him that might be said of me, but they never will be. He started with a Committee and a Prime Minister to back him. I started to assail home interests, with every one, save a few unimposing persons, against me." And he names his bitterest opponents: O'Connell, Gladstone, Brougham, Cobden, Sir Robert Peel.

Following his legislation for protection of children in mines, he now championed one of the most pitiful of all lost causes, the plight of the chimney sweeps. With huge stone and brick mansions to heat against the bitter penetrating fog of winter, all the nation's chimneys must be swept clean of the soot of soft coal at least once a year. Master sweepers used an army of apprenticed orphans, stolen or lost children, and those sold by poor parents. The masters promised much and broke every promise. They were to give the child a leather cap with a brass number on it, to wash him once a week, to send him to church on Sundays, to treat him with as much care as possible.

In exchange for these empty words plus a cash payment to the parents, the little boys and girls of four or five began their life of slavery as sweeps. First they were stripped of clothing and doused with strong salt water, then dried before a fire and doused again with the stinging brine. This was to harden the tender skin.

For flues were narrow – sometimes only eight or nine inches square – and apt to be hot. Elbows and knees were skinned oftener than not. Yet if a child refused to climb up, the soles of his feet were tickled with lighted straws. Whether he liked it or not, he must scramble up the chimney from inside, up to the very top where he could see the sky and the black face of the master above him. Then back he had to climb down again, sweeping the soot as he went.

The one hope of the climbing boys was to be sent into a great mansion, for then the kind-hearted maids in pity often gave them bits of mutton from the roast, and thick slices of bread and butter.

If the chimney narrowed so that the child, naked though he was, got stuck and called to the master to pull out bricks from the top, he got only a beating for his misery. Or if the dislodged soot dropped down on his face as he climbed, suffocating him until he perished for want of air, he was merely thrown out and a new sweep trained in his place.

At night the weary little people slept on their sacks of soot in a damp cellar, huddling together for warmth, crying themselves to sleep from the hurts of the soot in their sores. Then up before day to wander in small bands through the streets crying, "Sweep! Sweep!" more often abbreviated to "Weep! Weep!"

Again and again, Lord Shaftesbury brought in bills to protect or abolish this criminal use of "human brushes," but always the bill was defeated by "vested interests," the insurance companies and the master sweeps, conservative lords and even ladies.

Nor could he arouse public opinion. Indignant protests, tracts, articles, poems were written for the cause, all to no avail. Conservative British housewives had always had their chimneys swept, and custom was as infallible a rule as the law of the Medes and Persians. Besides, of what value were the grimy little "chimbly sweeps" anyhow? So the evil went on, resulting in terrible crippling, suffering, and often death.

Then the literary folk of the day began to champion the cause. Charles Kingsley wrote his immortal *Water Babies*, and English children wept over little black Tom who so longed to be white.

William Blake wrote his exquisite *Songs of Innocence*:

When my mother died I was very young,
And my father sold me, while yet my tongue
Could scarcely cry, "Weep! Weep! Weep!"
So your chimneys I sweep and in soot I sleep.

or this other poem to *The Chimney Sweeper*:

A little black thing, among the snow,
Crying "Weep! Weep!" in notes of woe!
"Where are thy father and mother? say?"
"They are gone up to the church to pray.

"Because I was happy upon the heath,
And smiled among the winter's snow,
They clothed me in the clothes of death,
And taught me to sing the notes of woe.

"And because I am happy & dance & sing,
They think they have done me no injury,
And are gone to praise God & His Priest & King,
Who make up a heaven of our misery."

In *Oliver Twist*, Dickens shows Oliver being bound to the villainous master sweep, Gamfield. Oliver stands trembling before the magistrate.

"Well, well," said the old gentleman, "I suppose he's fond of chimney-sweeping?"

"He dotes on it, your worship," replied Bundle, giving Oliver a sly pinch to intimate that he had better not say he didn't.

Poor Oliver is saved from his fate by accident, when the short sighted magistrate, in searching for his ink-bottle, catches sight of the boy's terrified face.

This was Dickens' sly satire on the only concession that Parliament had made to Lord Ashley's repeated attempts to put through a bill. As early as 1834, they passed a law prohibiting the master sweeps from forcing or stealing children. The little sweeps could be apprenticed only by their own consent. But of course poor parents continued to force their children to declare before a magistrate that they wanted nothing so much as a life of sweeping.

Not all the good Earl's valiant efforts during forty-five years could prevail, until with the help of Blake, Kingsley and Dickens, the public conscience of the English people, so long asleep, began to quicken. Finally in 1875, during the Russo-Turkish war and Disraeli's Ministry, the Earl and his friends determined to make a desperate attempt to end the terrible business once for all. If Vienna chimneys could be cleaned by means of a brush at the end of a long coil of heavy wire, why not substitute the same brush for English climbers?

"It is one hundred and two years," said the Earl, "since the good Jonas Hanway first brought this brutal iniquity before the public. Yet in many parts of England and Ireland it still prevails with the full consent of thousands of all classes."

But now the press took up the cudgels for the neglected children, *The Times* publishing story after story of actual cases such as that of Thomas Price, aged seven. Forced to go up a second time into the hot flue at a chemical works, the boy screamed and sobbed, but the master pushed him up, saying, "The young devil is foxing." Finally, half asphyxiated, he was taken out and thrown down on some straw to be beaten back into consciousness, the same treatment accorded the galley slaves in the time of St. Vincent de Paul. Soon after, the child died in convulsions. The master was prosecuted and given a sentence of ten years' deportation. *

Yet hundreds of similar cases went unpunished, and these reported over a period of years at last stirred sluggish apathy until all England cried out to put an end to it. The bill was finally passed in June, 1875.

"Had Shaftesbury done nothing else in his long life, he would have lived in history by this record alone," wrote his biographers, Mr. and Mrs. Hammond.

Whenever Lord Shaftesbury fought for a reform, it was because he himself had first made a personal investigation. He descended mine shafts and crawled on hands and knees to see for himself the tiny gate-openers sitting in water.

* Reported in *Lord Shaftesbury* by J. L. and Barbara Hammond, Longmans, Green & Co.

He visited mills in small factories and large, until their inhumanity seared his soul. Before pushing through his housing bills, he himself visited filthy houses in London, alive with fighting humans and insects, and later shook off the vermin from his coat at the door of his home in Grosvenor Square.

Yet it was not enough to see for himself. He must take powerful people with him. Often he and Charles Dickens prowled the streets through the night. The descriptions in Dickens' novels were so realistic that Baboushka, shut away in the Fortress of St. Peter and St. Paul, could not bear to read them. She had experienced them all in Siberia.

Another night-prowler with the Earl was his Grace, Albert, Consort of Queen Victoria. Albert, profoundly shocked by what he saw, told his Queen, and together they became life-long champions of Shaftesbury and his reforms. Yet their hands were as tied by the conservatives as his own. When we read of a modern king visiting the abandoned mining villages of Durham or Wales, or the overcrowded houses in congested London, we thought of these trips of Shaftesbury and Prince Albert, who was the first royal Englishman ever known to "go slumming."

One of the most engrossing of Lord Shaftesbury's enterprises, The Ragged Schools Union, was intimately connected with these teeming London streets. It is one of the few nineteenth-century philanthropies which he did not originate. Yet when he read of how Mr. Storey had extended his fourteen London Sunday Schools to night and day industrial schools for street urchins, Lord Shaftesbury promptly visited him and soon increased his fourteen schools to one hundred and forty.

The movement was similar to Hannah More's Mendip village schools, or Don Bosco's *ragazzi* Oratories.

It was the good Earl who suggested in 1844 a union of these schools, and who became its first president, continuing this service for forty-one years, to the day of his death. So great was his faith in the redemption of the boys and girls of London's poor, that he said, "I firmly believe that the Ragged School Movement is a most important episode in the history of mankind. I know of nothing which has been so stamped by the finger of God."

"Entirely supported by voluntary contributions," Charles Dickens maintained that this was "one of the noblest sentences in the English language." Having himself worked in a London blacking factory, he knew what an industrial school meant to these youngsters, and so became one of its most loyal sponsors, drawing many wealthy men to support it by the power of his pen.

When the first census of two hundred and sixty children was made in 1844, it was found that twenty-seven had served a term in prison, thirty-six had run away from home, nineteen slept in common lodging houses when they could earn their rent, forty-one lived by begging, twenty-nine never slept in beds, but in doorways or under arches, seventeen had no shoes, thirty-seven no hats or caps, and twelve no underwear.

Only this two hundred and sixty out of the one hundred thousand children in London were given schooling. They met, the Earl found, under embankment arches, in stables, lofts, old rooms, wherever they could find a niche. He describes them as "bold and pert, and dirty as London sparrows, but pale, feeble, and sadly inferior to them in plumpness of outline; squalid, half naked. They look not like the inhabitants of the earth, and yet are on it."

When the new president of the Union went to Drury Lane to search for one of his boys, he found eighty-four people, including twenty-three children, living in a house of nine small rooms. In common with other houses of the district, the cellar was also let to a nondescript lot of derelicts and thieves; the floor being covered with straw, the men reeled in from the twenty gin-palaces on the Lane, and slept where they fell.

How could people live decently in such conditions? Parliament must do something about housing. Each generation including our own faces the same problem. But in those days, no man had ever before taken the trouble to look into the housing of the poor, nor had connected it with the problem of crime.

Rightly, Lord Ashley felt he must begin to remedy matters with the children. Yet starting a new school was not easy. It took nothing short of a modern football hero for a teacher. Being engaged elsewhere one evening, the Earl sent a friend to see how a new school was doing. Arriving an hour after the opening, the friend found nearly all the lamps out, the windows broken, the teacher outside the door covered with mud, and inside, the master lying on his back, while six boys sat astride him singing lustily, "Pop goes the weasel."

It did not look like a propitious start for a school. However, by the fourth night, all was in order. The original group of boys were now monitors keeping down any signs of rowdyism in the newcomers.

Charles Dickens describes the Field Lane School as "a low-roofed den, with dirt, pestilence, sickening atmosphere.

The pupils were like fiends, howling, fighting, stealing from each other, dancing like a legion of devils, blowing out the lights, throwing books into the gutter. In two years the place had become orderly, gas-lighted, whitewashed, well attended, thoroughly established."

In ten years, this same Field Lane School was running one free nursery for babies, two evening industrial schools for youths and adults, and three for women, four industrial classes in tailoring and shoemaking, an employment agency, organized work in wood-chopping, a distribution of bread to the needy, a bath-house, a Bible class for ten thousand, and a school missionary to visit the sick.

Yet this was but one of dozens of such centers in London. And in each of these departments, "the good Earl had his hand."

It was due to one of his flashes of inspiration that he formed his boys into boot-black brigades. He wanted to test out character for a larger scheme of sending them as emigrants to the colonies, or enrolling them in the navy. Was a boy honest? Did he have integrity? Was he persevering and trustworthy? Would he make a first-class colonist and man? Boot-blacking would tell. So the boys were equipped with brushes and blacking and went out to Bond and Regent Streets.

Now an unlooked-for boon awaited them. For Prince Albert, organizing the first great industrial exposition in 1851, flooded the city with thousands of visitors, most of whom had need indeed to have their boots shined after tramping in muddy streets. So the new industry brought in thousands of pounds a year, besides weeding out the boys for colonies or naval training ships.

Lord Shaftesbury induced Parliament to grant him free

passage for one hundred and fifty boys a year to Australia, New Zealand or Canada. What keen competition it stirred up among the schools to make good.

One lad wrote back from Brisbane that he was engaged as a shepherd for two pounds (ten dollars) a year, "with my rations and washing. The blacks catch kangaroos and eat them," he added. "Parrots and cockatoos are very numerous. I am very happy here."

Now after a long struggle to establish his Ragged Schools with voluntary funds, their fame grew. The London police commissioner announced that crime had been reduced seventy-five per cent. Many believed that the movement had averted a revolution during the stirring days of 1848. Gifts flowed in: a check from Jenny Lind for a hundred pounds for the Liverpool branch; a check for one hundred and fifty thousand pounds from George Peabody to use for improved housing for the poor.

Now, too, came a host of friends and supporters, from the Duchess of Teck, mother of Queen Mary, and Victoria and Albert themselves, down to the humblest volunteer teacher. Among the latter was a sister of Elizabeth Barrett Browning. The poet herself wrote:

Do you hear the children weeping, O my brother,
'Ere the sorrow comes with years?
They are weeping in the playtime of the others—
In the country of the free.

At last the twenty-five thousand slum children who received instruction in the Ragged Schools shamed the Government in 1870 into taking responsibility for all its children, some million and a half who still had no schooling at all. Now all existing schools were to be subsidized and free education extended throughout the kingdom.

The enormous and obvious benefits to the nation from Lord Shaftesbury's schools helped more than a little to put through his economic reforms.

YET IT was not enough for the good Earl to befriend all the poor and the oppressed of England, Ireland, Scotland and Wales. No, he thought of England now as the mother of nations. Since 1876 Victoria had been Empress of India. But because Britain had seized the government of India, therefore Britain must take care to give the Indian people a just equivalent.

Although Lord Shaftesbury served as Commissioner to India for only two years during his political career, yet for the remaining fifty years he carried India in his heart. He believed that England must justify her rule of the country by placing all her own resources of science for India's use in order that this subject people might become self-supporting in agriculture and in industry.

To him, British rule meant stewardship. The people must not be exploited for selfish gain, but taught how to govern themselves, and above all they should be given Western resources to solve their problems of drought, famine and flood.

Now, almost eighty, Shaftesbury's last great industrial struggle was for a Factory Act in India. Englishmen alone were responsible for the terrible conditions in the Bombay cotton factories, where, in heat of ninety to ninety-five degrees, women and children worked under native overseers from eleven to sixteen hours a day, Sunday and weekday alike.

In spite of frail health, Lord Shaftesbury made one of the great pleas of his life in April, 1879. He had fought and won countless bills and reforms for the poor of his small island. During Victoria's reign more than a hundred acts were passed to safeguard children. But England was now an Empire, and the Earl demanded of his peers a principle of humanity, "sound and applicable from the north to the south, from the east to the west, to every spot on the earth, wherever Britain rules."

English merchants had no right, he maintained, to think only of the money to be made today. They must think, as well, of the country and the world of tomorrow, when this generation of stunted and overworked children should have grown to be men.

He described a visit he had made to Bradford early in his fight for factory reform, in 1838.

"I asked for a collection of cripples and deformities. In a short time more than eighty were gathered in a large courtyard. They were mere samples of the entire mass. I assert without exaggeration, that no power of language could describe the varieties, and I may say the cruelties, in all these degradations of the human form. They stood or squatted before me in the shapes of the letters of the alphabet. This was the effect of prolonged toil on the tender forms of children at early ages. When I visited Bradford under the limitation of hours, some years afterwards, I called for a similar exhibition of cripples; but, God be praised, there was not one to be found in that vast city."

By a curious coincidence, the son of the former Member from Bradford was now Secretary to India.

"Forty-six years ago," the Earl concluded, "I addressed the House of Commons in a kindred appeal [for the Ten

Hour Law of 1833] and they heard me. I now turn to your lordships and implore you in the same spirit, for God's sake and in His name, to have mercy on the children of India."

So in that April of 1879, his bill regulating the working hours of women and children in India won through.

And not only India did the Earl befriend. In 1863 he was speaking in Parliament on behalf of the Poles, following their insurrection against Russia. In 1882 he was defending the Jews who were being mercilessly persecuted throughout the Russian Empire. During the long struggle in America to free the slaves, he backed Lincoln and delighted in the friendship of Harriet Beecher Stowe.

Indeed, so vigorous was his championship of freedom for the blacks of America, that an indignant Southern editor wrote: "Who is this Earl of Shaftesbury? Some unknown lordling; one of your modern philanthropists suddenly started up to take part in a passing agitation. It is a pity he does not look about him at home. Where was he when Lord Ashley was so nobly fighting for the Factory Bill and pleading the cause of the English slaves? We never even heard of the name of this Lord Shaftesbury then."

Who is the Happy Warrior? Who is he
That every man in arms should wish to be?
It is the generous spirit, who, when brought
Among the tasks of real life, hath wrought
Upon the plan that pleased his boyish thought.

Who is Lord Shaftesbury? A man who, by sixty years of incessant sacrifice and labor for forgotten men, women and children, "rose above party and class to be the best known and most loved person in the British Empire, and an institution in himself." It was fitting, then, that his eightieth birthday should be celebrated with pomp and circumstance. The grand party was held in the London Guild Hall: its host, the Lord Mayor of London.

The guest of honor, erect and slender, with a face sensitive, austere, lonely, resembling that of our own Lincoln, must have been less touched by the Lord Mayor's gift of the key to London town than by the happy faces of the multitude of his children.

First there were the boys and girls of his Ragged Schools, over which he said he would rather preside as president than over the Royal Society. The chosen delegation of boys brought him a ship model they had made, and the girls an embroidered muffler. No longer did they sleep in doorways or under railroad arches. Someone had cared, and they had a home and good food, and new shoes for this great day.

Next came the London flower-girls. Had he not befriended them and established a trust fund in memory of his wife to tide them over the terrible winters when no one bought their "vilets"? Now they strewed roses and sweet lavender in his path, all the way from the carriage up the broad red-carpeted steps of the Guild Hall.

Here were stalwart lads representing the hundreds of boys, some of them thieves even, whom he had taken out of the gutter to send off to the colonies. And this smartly uniformed group from a training ship of the Queen's Navy stood at salute. Already they were proving to their great benefactor that they could make good.

Then along came his friends the pedlars, or costermongers, whom he had taught to treat their donkeys as their brothers. They formed long lines, both carts and donkeys decked out in ribbons and blossoms. Their birthday gift of a donkey became the adored playmate of the Earl's grandchildren.

And now came a group of blind people for whom he had worked for fifty years. Carved toys they brought him, and radiant faces.

Former chimney sweeps came, the climbing boys he had rescued; and the children saved from slavery in brick kilns, mines, factories, potteries, tobacco works. Grown now to men and women, they all hailed him as their liberator.

A delegation of Crimean war cripples pressed in, men saved by Florence Nightingale. It was Lord Shaftesbury's commission sent to her aid that saved the British Army, by giving her authority for her great work of organizing field hospitals.

Even Negroes came, to honor the friend who had helped Wilberforce free them.

What a birthday party that was!

Among the thousands of congratulations was one by Lord Tennyson, the poet laureate, to the Lord Mayor: "Allow me to assure you in plain prose how cordially I join with those who honor the Earl of Shaftesbury as the friend of the poor, and who wish him many years of health and strength in which to continue his good work. . ."

There must have been many at this birthday fête, among the lords and ladies of the realm, who marveled how one man came to be so beloved. Perhaps the secret was in his own giant capacity to love. The deep causes underlying his life work are plainly read in his diary.

For although he was born in St. Giles House with its great park, its garden, its stables and lake, yet throughout his childhood he knew only coldness, cruelty, hunger, bullying, misery. A poor little rich boy living in a castle, and yet less loved perhaps, at least by his family, than the littlest scrap of a factory child he had saved. One being there was who loved him, his old nurse, who, alas, died when he was eight, and whom he called his spiritual mother. Yet instead of embittering him, his childhood experiences gave him a boundless compassion for all who suffer, for the forgotten, the exploited in any land.

Then came the dedication of his life at fourteen, and hence his works—to the degree of his dedication.

Thirdly he had the adoration of his beautiful wife who was willing to sacrifice wealth and worldly honors with him, in order that the children of England might be fed and clothed, even to the making of ten thousand bowls of soup in her own kitchen in one winter.

And lastly, his hero.

For to the good Earl, John Wesley was a supreme hero, "the noblest character in modern history." It has been said that what Wesley was to the eighteenth century in rousing it from the sleep of death, Shaftesbury was to the nineteenth in applying his principles to the social and industrial problems of a new industrial era.

Certain it is that John Wesley's inner fire of living love kindled sparks that lit up the lives of Hannah More, William Wilberforce and Lord Shaftesbury, and through them changed misery into happiness for millions on four continents.

Now in turn the sparks from Lord Shaftesbury's Ragged Schools were to light countless torches as pupils and teachers caught a vision of how they, too, could serve humanity. Thus, Quinton Hogg developed his Polytechnic or continuation schools, and Dr. Bernardo his children's homes; Stanley the African explorer financed his work for cripples; Baroness Burdett-Coutts her schools and philanthropies all over the world.

After Lord Shaftesbury's death in 1885, an event which appeared to the world as an international tragedy, the Duke of Argyll addressed his fellow peers: "My Lords, the social reforms of the last century have not been due mainly to the Liberal Party, but to the influence, character and perseverance of one man—Lord Shaftesbury."

Spurgeon, the great preacher who was drawn into the Ragged Schools work through Dickens, said: "Among men I do not know whom I should place second, but I would certainly put Lord Shaftesbury first."

On the day of his funeral, inside Westminster Abbey the great of the realm and the representatives of his two hundred societies and organizations bowed to the solemn chanting of the choir and to the words of the Bishop of London as he said the last rites for "the greatest peer of English History." Outside Westminster pressed a silent multitude of thousands of his grateful poor. Sky rain fell on their heads, heart rain from their eyes. A working man was heard to exclaim: "Our Earl's gone: God a'mighty knowed how he loved us, and we loved him! We shan't look upon his like again."

It is of him that Blake might have written:

I will not cease from Mental Fight,
Nor shall the Sword sleep in my hand,
Till we have built Jerusalem
In England's green & pleasant land.

HANNAH MORE

1745–1833

One of the enjoyments of a biography is that through the eyes and life of our hero we may enter his own peculiar age, and may measure his work for humanity in the light of our twentieth century. With Hannah More, we go "back of the beyond," into the very England from which Thomas Paine freed himself; back into a form of humanitarianism which became one of the forces of progress for centuries to come.

Hannah was born the very year that the dashing pretender to the Stuart throne, Bonnie Prince Charlie, landed in the Hebrides and gathered his fiery Highlanders for those border wars that were so destructive to Scotland, throwing her people into a state of poverty which would take a century and more to heal. For even the canny Scots were no match against the methodical Hanoverian George II.

Her father being a stout Tory and strong supporter of the Church of England, Hannah was brought up straitly. But her mother was a Dissenter, sympathizing with the powerful John Wesley who went about advocating a warm, human, personal religious life, in opposition to the stiff formalism of the church. These two streams of religious expression were to be united in Hannah's life, even though they were to become two conflicting forces in eighteenth-century English life.

As a tiny child, Hannah would pretend that a chair was her horse and that she was riding away to London town to see "bishops and booksellers." A curious prophecy for a mite of four.

From childhood, too, she pored over books, longing for an education which was denied to "females." Yet she got one all the same, and a very good one, too, thanks to her father who was head of a boys' school in Stapleton, near Bristol. Hannah would sit spellbound to hear him recite Greek and Latin poetry. Though she understood not one word, the sonorous roll of Virgil or Æschylus fed her feeling for rhythm which played so large a rôle in her life.

Both she and her four sisters were brought up on the *Spectator* of Addison, and she later considered it a very good work to nurture a child's mind. Otherwise, her education had to be got from hearing the conversation of her elders. "Children must be seen and not heard." Surely the adage which all American children delight to disregard came from this very period. One can imagine a little child with big hazel eyes sitting close by her mother's ample skirts, listening to the conversation of the guests who came to their home. These included the rector of the parish, members of the gentry come to discuss the education of their children, visiting lecturers, scientists, men of letters.

That the flair for conversation became one of her own chief assets was proved by an amusing anecdote told of her.

At sixteen, during a summer vacation at home, she had one of the sudden illnesses which were to follow her all her life. Her father called the family physician, Dr. Woodward. The instant he sat down beside her bed, they began to converse, and the old doctor became so engrossed in his conversation with her that he stayed on for three hours. He forgot time and engagements, and even the errand he had come for. Indeed, he only remembered it as he was leaving the house. Then he hurried back upstairs, bent over the flushed face and brilliant eyes and asked, "How are you today, my poor child?"

After her mother's death, when Hannah was twelve, she entered the school taught by her two elder sisters, Mary and Elizabeth, a Select School for Young Ladies, in Bristol. Apt at languages, she easily mastered French, Italian, Spanish, and kept on with her Latin. These were happy years, for at sixteen she began teaching in the school. And since she had a flair for dramatics and for verse, her sisters encouraged her to dramatize Bible stories in verse and pastoral plays which the girls of the school acted out. Also for them she prepared a Shakespeare anthology. She loved to plan parties in which the talk was entirely in the language and meter of Shakespeare — a form of entertainment which would be as profitable to budding twentieth-century poets as it was to those of her day.

At seventeen, Hannah wrote her first full-length play, *A Search After Happiness*. Of course the school produced it for parents who generously applauded. But would a publisher in London be willing to accept it? the young author wondered. Would the booksellers sell it? How she longed to journey to London to see a real play, *Macbeth* or *Hamlet* or *King Lear*.

She wanted especially to see David Garrick, the greatest Shakespearean actor of the age. But Garrick was famous now, and never came to the provinces. She had an intense yearning to "know the great and hear the wise." She was all on tiptoe with life.

Now England was still at war with France over the colonies in the New World, and over possession of India. She gained ground in India but lost Canada to France. And the heralds went crying through the Bristol streets, "The King is dead: Long live the King." High time that George II be succeeded by his grandson, George III.

"The new George is a great Tory," said Hannah's father, "and a thorough Englishman." He was, to his cost, alas. All the five sisters, Patty, Hannah, Sally, Mary and Elizabeth, launched into a discussion of the royal House of Hanover.

But Hannah soon had other things to think about than politics. For being ill again, she was sent away to the country to rest, and there met a Mr. Turner who was most attentive to her. Now marriages in England at this time were usually arranged for by the parents. And usually the eldest sisters were provided for first. So the More family was electrified to have Hannah, next to Patty the youngest, actually proposed to, and by a man of means, a country gentleman living alone in his manor house.

What a flurry of excitement among the sisters as they helped to prepare Hannah's trousseau! The appointed wedding day came, but no bridegroom. Instead, he sent his servant to plead his excuse of a sudden indisposition, and postponing the date. Again, all arrangements were made at the church, with invitations, flowers, the kindly old rector and the boys' choir. And again, at the last moment his servant came with an apology.

Hannah's face turned white, then scarlet. Whatever had she done? What had happened to kind Mr. Turner, always so shy, so correct, so solicitous of her?

Her father and sisters were indignant. They put Hannah to bed with one of her burning headaches, and held a conclave. A family friend offered to act as mediator. Mr. Turner, it seemed, meant no disrespect, but was entirely too shy to make up his mind definitely to bring a young bride to his ancestral home. Instead, he settled upon her an income of two hundred pounds a year, in slight recompense for the cost of her trousseau and her humiliation.

At first, the bride-to-be refused any such unthinkable arrangement. She had poured upon this elderly suitor all her girlish affection. If she must give up the marriage, she must also give up any thought of his support. Her father wept for her. But there were other avenues open, she told him, with her chin up-tilted. She longed to write. In order to earn her living, she could go on teaching. And she hid herself away among her books, reading Latin all day long. She would master Cicero now, and learn Virgil by heart.

Yet as months passed, her friends and family alike began begging her to reconsider and to accept the money waiting for her in the bank. It would free her of teaching. She could go up to London, see Garrick in *Hamlet*, find a publisher perhaps for her play. Her sister Sally offered to go with her.

Who could refuse? So she let the family pack them off

in the London coach. The wish of her childhood was at last to be realized. This was in 1772, and Hannah was twenty-seven years old.

The first play she saw was *King Lear*. She was just in time. For David Garrick, having already lionized the stage for a quarter of a century, was considering retiring in the heyday of his fame. Why not? He had transformed the technique of acting; had repudiated the old, stiff, chanting declamation by "returning to nature," reading lines as he would naturally speak them, suiting a thousand changes of mood with facial expression and gesture. In fact, David Garrick was to the stage what John Wesley was to the Church, and what Wordsworth would become to poetry.

No wonder, then, that Hannah was electrified at his Lear. She wept with Cordelia as she was led away to prison with her poor tortured father:

Lear. . . . *Come, let's away to prison;*
We two alone will sing like birds i' the cage:
When thou dost ask me blessing, I'll kneel down,
And ask of thee forgiveness: so we'll live,
And pray, and sing, and tell old tales, and laugh
At gilded butterflies, and hear poor rogues
Talk of court news; . . .
And take upon's the mystery of things,
As if we were God's spies: . . .

That night Hannah could not sleep, but wrote some verses on Garrick's Lear and shyly sent them to him. To her surprise, she was asked to call. That was the beginning of a life-long friendship. For soon she went to stay with the Garricks, and even after his death, continued for thirty winters to live with Mrs. Garrick.

It was his praise of her Lear verses that gave Hannah the courage to show Garrick her plays. One tragedy he singled out, wrote both prologue and epilogue for it, and produced it at Covent Garden. To Hannah's surprise the play was acclaimed a success.

The Garricks were so charmed with Hannah that they introduced her to their wide circle of friends, who promptly appropriated this slender provincial with her dark eyes sparkling with enthusiasm, her simplicity, her vivacity and wit, her quick and sunny repartee.

At home, her father had talked over everything of world interest with his five daughters. Now she found that her conversation was enjoyed by no other than Lady Elizabeth Montague; by Samuel Johnson, and Sir Joshua Reynolds. The talented girl was invited to dine with lords and ladies, with members of the court circle. Older men—Zachary Macaulay, Horace Walpole—delighted in her, as did the younger men, brilliant members of Parliament like William Wilberforce and Pitt.

For all this rich and interesting life which so stimulated her writing she could thank Mr. Turner who had freed her from earning her living as well as from becoming mistress of a country house, hidden away from the London she so loved.

From her own letters, and those of Sally, written to the family at home, we have fascinating glimpses of this London life. Of her first meeting with Garrick, Sally wrote: "After an hour passed together, they parted reciprocally pleased, having discovered in each other what was gratifying to both, a natural manner, original powers, and wit in union with good nature."

The very next day Hannah was asked to visit the Garrick home, where she met Mrs. Elizabeth Montague, who began at once inviting her to her famous blue-stocking breakfast parties and evening conversations with the élite of London literary society. Slight as was Hannah's output at this time, she could yet hold her own with young or old by the wealth of her mind stored with the greatness of the classics, and by her wit and natural charm. She herself later describes Mrs. Montague, Queen of the Blues, in her magnificent home in Mayfair:

"Her form (for she has no body) is delicate even to fragility; her countenance the most animated in the world; the spritely vivacity of fifteen, with the judgment and experience of a Nestor. But I fear she is hastening to decay very fast; her spirits are so active that they must soon wear out the little frail receptacle that holds them."

Mrs. Montague was then fifty-six and lived to be eighty, so that Hannah had still many years of her parties.

Through the Garricks, too, Hannah met Sir Joshua Reynolds; and it was at his home that she first met Dr. Johnson. She was as rapturous as a school girl at being introduced to a living author. She knew all about his eccentric ways, and expected him to make faces at her, and to sit in a corner sunk in melancholy. Instead, he came to meet her, his eyes twinkling, holding on his finger Sir Joshua's pet South American parrot. Before he had spoken a word to her, he began reciting a verse from her own *Morning Hymn*.

Fancy that! The greatest author in England, twice her age, quoting her own verses!

Sally wrote home: "Hannah has been introduced by Miss Reynolds (sister of Sir Joshua) to Edmund Burke—the sublime and beautiful Edmund Burke. From a large party of literary persons assembled at Sir Joshua's she received the most encouraging compliments. Miss Reynolds repeats her little poem by heart, with which also the great Johnson is much pleased."

How eagerly the three sisters at home with their father must have waited for these weekly epistles. Another day, Sally wrote: "Miss Reynolds ordered the coach to take us to Dr. Johnson's *very own house*. Yes, Abyssinia Johnson! Dictionary Johnson! Rambler's, Idler's and Irene's Johnson! Can you picture to yourselves the palpitations of our hearts as we approached his mansion? Once inside, the conversation turned upon a new work of his just going to the press—*Tour of the Hebrides*; and then he spoke about his old friend Richardson, author of *Clarissa*."

Sally goes on to tell of how Hannah sat down in a big armchair hoping that a ray of the great man's genius would enter her. But Dr. Johnson laughed and admitted that he never sat in the chair. Yet all the same, he was naïvely delighted at her enthusiasm over this visit to him.

With the manners of a chevalier, he saw them down the long passage to their coach—that famous coach which Sir Joshua had painted outside with the four seasons in allegorical figures, and whose wheels were ornamented with carved foliage, while its liveried servants "were laced with silver." No wonder the two sisters were nearly overcome with all this splendor.

Yet Hannah kept a steady head, quite unturned by adulation or the magnificence of her new friends.

It was in 1775—the very year of the battles of Lexington

and Bunker Hill, the year of the desperate resolve of the colonies, goaded by Thomas Paine, to declare their independence from despotic George III and his equally despotic Parliament—that Hannah wrote a most amusing letter home:

"I am going today to a great dinner. Nothing can be conceived so absurd, extravagant and fantastical, as the present mode of dressing the head. . . I have just escaped from one of the most fashionable disfigurers, and though I charged him to dress me with the greatest simplicity, and to have only a very distant eye upon the fashion, just enough to avoid the pride of singularity, without running into ridiculous excess, yet in spite of all these sage didactics, I absolutely blush at myself, and turn to the glass with as much caution as a vain beauty just risen from the small-pox; which cannot be a more disfiguring disease than the present mode of dress."

This same year, Sally regaled the family with: "Tuesday evening we drank tea at Sir Joshua's with Dr. Johnson. Hannah is certainly a great favorite. She was placed next him, and they had the entire conversation to themselves. They were both in remarkably high spirits; it was certainly her lucky night! I overheard her say so many good things. The old genius was extremely jocular, and the young one very pleasant. You would have judged we had been at some comedy, had you heard our peals of laughter. They, indeed, tried which could 'pepper the highest,' and it is not clear to me that the lexicographer was really the highest seasoner."

Dr. Johnson was then sixty-seven, and Hannah thirty-one. He evidently shared Sally's high admiration of her sister, which was without a taint of envy. And fortunate it was for the family that Sally could describe these happy triumphs for their Hannah. Yet after the first few seasons, Hannah went up to London alone, because the Garricks insisted that she make her home with them, whether at Adelphi House in town, or at Lambeth in the country.

What a home that was for her! The largest Shakespearean library in the world, with a wealth of all great literature besides.

Hannah herself describes the garden of the villa: "The situation of this garden pleases me infinitely. It is on the banks of the Thames; the temple in Shakespeare's memory about thirty or forty rods from it. Here is the famous chair, curiously wrought out of a cherry-tree which really grew in the garden of Shakespeare at Stratford. I sat in it, but caught no ray of inspiration. But what drew and deserved my attention was a most noble statue of this great original man, in an attitude strikingly pensive, his limbs strongly muscular, his countenance expressive of some vast conception, and his whole form seemingly the bigger from some universal idea. . . The statue cost five hundred pounds."

Here, in this ideal retreat, Hannah plunged into reading and writing. The house was always full of guests, coming and going: the great ones of the century, musicians, actors, poets, writers, artists. One evening was given to distinguished French men and women, with Gibbon as the only other English guest. He had just published his *Decline and Fall of the Roman Empire,* and though not a word of English was spoken, Hannah had a delightful conversation with the great historian.

During this time, Garrick made his farewell bow to the theater by reënacting all his old favorites: Macbeth, Lear, Hamlet, the Richards, Ben Jonson's *Alchemist* and *Every*

Man in His Humour. Sitting beside Mrs. Garrick, Hannah saw him twenty-seven times in one season; his last Lear, his last Hamlet. She was writing her tragedy, *Percy*, and profited much from his invaluable criticisms.

She told her family of intermissions at the theater in which she could chat with young Sheridan and with Edmund Burke, who as a Whig was working passionately to avoid further civil war with the American colonies. But the King was stiff with Tory prejudice, and Parliament as obdurate.

At the very time that General Howe was capturing Philadelphia and Burgoyne was surrendering at Saratoga, Garrick was putting on Hannah's *Percy* to full houses and thundering appreciation. So now, his young protégée was acclaimed by literary London, and dined with Mrs. Siddons who appeared in her play.

Now the American war was going badly for England. Whigs and Tories were at loggerheads over it. The repeated attempts at parliamentary reform came to nothing. George must first be forced to his knees by defeats on land and sea. America must first write her constitution.

Overworked with his farewell performances, also by the annual festivals he had organized at Stratford-on-Avon, Garrick succumbed to an illness, and Hannah rushed up from Bristol to comfort Mrs. Garrick.

She wrote her *Sacred Dramas* soon after this, and met the Prince of Wales, the George IV to be.

She saw a good deal, also, of Horace Walpole who had upheld the French Revolution until the beginning of the Terror of 1792. Now all the upper classes in England rose up at the tales of ferocious cruelty to king and nobles.

Burke, terrified for England, wrote his *Reflections on the French Revolution.* Walpole commended him for it, while Thomas Paine answered him with his thunderous *Rights of Man,* and Mary Wollstonecraft with her *Rights of Women.*

Now Hannah's pen, too, was called to the service of her country. When the speech of citizen Duport, denouncing to the Assembly all religious education of youth in France, was reported in England in December, 1792, Hannah indignantly refuted it.

"Nature and reason – these ought to be the new gods of men – these are my gods!" cried Duport.

To which Hannah replied that "frenzy can demolish faster than wisdom can build." Ably she proved that "atheists are not without their own bigotry, even though most loudly they decry the bigotry of others."

It was to refute this very tendency in the young Republic toward the overthrow of religion as well as kingly despotism, that Thomas Paine, thrown into prison, wrote his famous defense of religion, *The Age of Reason,* which was to discredit him for two hundred years in the very America he had helped to free. Yet his treatise to combat French atheism, so bitterly branded as godless in his own age is considered but a mild form of Unitarianism in our own. So it is that a hero denounced by one age is lauded by the next.

It seems to be a habit of revolutions to create new gods: nature and reason, work and the state, Aryan blood and the hammer of Thor.

But there was another call for Hannah's pen. In this same momentous year of 1792, she was asked to write a tract for the poor which would counteract those written by Paine and his followers inciting the people to overthrow outworn tyrannies of king and government and church alike. These tracts were being distributed broadcast in shops, cottages, newly opened factories, even in the pits of mines.

So Hannah wrote *Village Politics*. She admitted afterwards that "it was a vulgar little piece, scribbled on one sick day." Being heartily ashamed of it, she did not sign it. Yet it made her famous.

It was in the form of a dialogue between Jack Anvil, the blacksmith, and Tom Hod, the mason. It begins like this:

Jack. *What's the matter, Tom, why dost look so dismal?*

Tom. *Dismal, indeed! Well enough I may.*

Jack. *What! Is the old mare dead? Or work scarce?*

Tom. *No, no, work's plenty enough, if a man had the heart to go to it.*

Jack. *What book art reading? Why dost look so like a hang-dog?*

Tom. (Looking at the book). *Cause enough. Why, I find here that I'm very unhappy, and very miserable, which I should never have known if I had not had the good luck to meet with this book. O, 'tis a precious book!*

Jack. *A good sign, though, that you can't find out you're unhappy without looking into a book first. What is the matter?*

Tom. *Matter? Why, I want liberty.*

Jack. *Liberty! That's bad, indeed! What, has anyone fetched a warrant for thee? Come, man, cheer up, I'll be bound for thee.*

Tom. *No, no. I want a new constitution.*

Jack. *Indeed! Why, I thought thou hadst been a des-*

perate healthy fellow. Send for the Doctor immediately.

Tom. *I'm not sick. I want liberty and equality and the rights of man!*

Jack. *O, now I understand thee. What! Thou art a leveler and a republican, I warrant!*

Tom. *I'm a friend of the people. I want a reform.*

Jack. *Then the shortest way is to mend thyself.*

Tom. *But I want a general reform.*

Well, well, there are always two sides to a question. Perhaps Paine himself laughed at it, for it was clever, though he knew only too well that England was sadly in need of a general reform. Yet not even Paine would have wanted it followed by such a reign of terror as that in France. Better that reform come slowly; better that Jack and Tom joke a bit over demanding liberty and equality.

At any rate, the tract took London by storm. The first issue exhausted, it was ordered printed by the thousand by delighted Tories who wanted England to stay as it was, and wanted above all that the people should be kept in ignorance of their rights, in order to respect their time-honored customs of law and order, of prejudice and privilege.

Poor Hannah, hiding away, was astonished to be discovered by internal evidence in the piece, sought out, overwhelmed. The Bishop of London wrote to congratulate her, to tell her how the tract was praised at Windsor, and that he had given it to the Attorney-General to disperse throughout the country. Already it had been put into the hands of every man in His Majesty's Army and Navy.

The peers of the realm breathed a sigh of relief. A revolution three thousand miles away was bad enough: but that bloody one across the channel was dangerously near. Hannah More's satire, "every bit as good as Swift," would restore the people to good English-mutton-and-dumpling common sense.

No wonder Hannah was glad to escape from all this adulation, to the safe harbor of Cowslip Green.

Four years before, she had searched about the country near Bristol till she had found the house of her dreams, a thatched cottage in a meadow shining with cowslips, and a hedge-walled garden with rose trees nearly as tall as the eaves. A sweet paradise in which to spend her summers, even though she continued to come up to London for winters with Mrs. Garrick.

Here the four sisters had joined her, delighted to have at last a country home of their own, since not one of them had married. Here, in their peaceful, happy household, within sight of the towering Mendip Hills, Hannah had settled down to her life-work of writing novels, dramas, verse.

Here to Cowslip Green came a constant stream of visitors, among whom, during the summer of 1789, was William Wilberforce who drove up in his carriage to spend his thirtieth birthday. A momentous visit, for he became the second man in Hannah's life to change her whole future.

Among the younger members of Parliament whom she had met—Pitt, Fox, Canning, Burke—Hannah had been much drawn to William Wilberforce and his concern to free England of the curse of slave traffic. Although well aware of the unpopularity of his cause among fashionable London society, she had herself made a bold plea for the abolition of the slave trade in her book called *Religion of the Fashionable World*.

"Such abolition," she wrote, "will restore the luster of

the British name, and cut off, at a single stroke, as large and disgraceful a portion of national guilt as ever impaired the nature, or dishonored the councils of a Christian country."

Hannah had often been asked to dine with Lady Midleton in order to talk with Wilberforce, who was her special protégé.

In 1789, Hannah was present at "the opening of the great cause of abolition in the House of Commons, in which Pitt and Fox are united with Wilberforce." It was after this session that she had a chat with Mr. Raikes, the Gloucester editor who had organized Sunday Schools for the poor children of the parish, the first in the world. Afterwards, on this same evening, Hannah dined with a party of peers, and "found not one friend to the humane bill."

So all the five sisters welcomed the young reformer to Cowslip Green, the more so, since he was accounted one of the most brilliant conversationalists of his day.

It was Patty who urged their guest to visit the famous caves and cliffs of Cheddar ten miles away. It was Elizabeth who packed a lunch and sent him off in his carriage for the day's outing. It was Hannah who gayly waved him good-by.

When he returned, Patty ran to meet him. "How did you like our Mendip cliffs?" she asked him.

"To speak truth, Miss Patty," he replied, "I was so overcome by the misery and poverty of the people that I could hardly look at the rocks." And bowing, he went up to his room, dismissing his secretary.

Patty, alarmed, held a consultation among the sisters. Was their guest ill? Whatever did he mean by the misery of the people? A few miners and colliers, she supposed, dirty and unkempt, but one should take no notice of them. Whereas the cliffs, a limestone ridge, rich in minerals, stretching away from Wells to Bristol Channel, formed the most curious natural landmark in their vicinity.

The sisters gathered around the supper table with a good deal of concealed curiosity about their guest who already, as they knew, was beginning to spend his large fortune in many hidden ways.

When the supper was served, he asked Hannah to dismiss the servant. Then he leaned forward, a curious radiance lighting his sensitive face.

"Miss Hannah More, something must be done for Cheddar."

It was quite as startling as if he had said, "Something must be done for the West Indies."

Then he described to his astonished hostesses the character of their neighbors at Cheddar. Half savage, lawless, miserably poor, living in hovels or in the clefts of the rocks, they had tried to rob him under pretext of selling bits of broken rock.

Mr. Wilberforce had sat down among them, opened his wallet and distributed his money. That having won them, he learned the full extent of their ignorant wretchedness. Almost abandoned by the Church, able to earn but a pittance in the mines, they were forced to live by stealing.

Now perhaps any other guest at Cowslip Green would have gone his way with scarcely another thought about Cheddar. There must have been hundreds of villages in England, Scotland, Ireland and Wales nearly as badly off. After all, what could a gentlewoman writer of the eighteenth century do about her lawless neighbors ten miles away, in an age without either telephones or automobiles?

But during that evening, William Wilberforce laid upon their very souls the plight of Cheddar, and both Hannah and Patty thrilled to the cause "as if God had spoken to their hearts." Wilberforce promised to stand behind them with his wealth, but they must undertake the work themselves.

"If you will be at the trouble, I will be at the expense," he told them.

THAT was the beginning of forty years' labor among the mining villages of the Mendip Hills. That was why, after Wilberforce had gone, that Hannah and Patty mounted their horses and splashed along the muddy roads to see what could be done.

Perhaps it was John and Charles Wesley who determined the character of their work. For Hannah and Wilberforce had both caught fire from their enthusiasm about the power of the Bible to work strange miracles in human hearts and lives. Or, perhaps it was Mr. Raikes whose Sunday Schools were attracting so much comment. At any rate, since all the hope of the future lay in the children, they determined to begin with them.

Such a thing as free schools was unheard of in the England of 1789. Noblemen's sons, or even those of landed gentry, could go to Eton or Harrow or Exeter, and thence up to Oxford and Cambridge. But the poor went uneducated. Few could read or write. "Better so," said the gentry, "else they may get out of hand."

So the children of the poor ran wild. With the coming of factories and mines, running wild was to be substituted with grilling labor of twelve hours a day and more.

Patty and Hannah both wrote accounts of this first visit

to Cheddar. Along the road, they met a Quaker out rabbit-hunting. When they had proposed their errand of establishing a Sunday School with the Bible as textbook, his eyes filled with tears.

"You will have much difficulty," he warned them, "but let not the enemy tempt you to go back, and God bless the work!" So he directed them to a rich farmer whom they must first placate.

Hannah wrote to Wilberforce: "You would have been shocked could you have seen the petty tyrant whose insolence we stroked and tamed, the ugly children we fondled, the poulets and spaniels we caressed, the cider we consumed, and the wine we swallowed."

After these attentions on the part of the two sisters, the farmer was finally mollified but thought it a pity they should take any trouble since the two thousand poor and destitute of Cheddar were well off, "having a large legacy to be given them in times of distress; though to be sure, for the last thirty-seven years it had been tied up in chancery court."

They then visited twelve well-to-do farmer families, "all hard, brutal, ignorant," who yet conceded that it might be a good thing to shut up the children in school so they couldn't rob their orchards. But even among these families, Hannah wrote: "There is as much knowledge of Christ as in the wilds of Africa. For they are as ignorant as beasts, intoxicated every day before dinner, and plunged into such vice that I begin to think London is a virtuous place. We are sending missionaries to distant lands, and yet our own villages are perishing for want of instruction."

As for the poor of the village, they seemed to Hannah

an incredible multitude of wretches. No wonder Wilberforce was distressed.

So much for a picture of English country life. But when we remember that England had been more in wars than out for longer than her people could remember, and that her king had as great a prejudice against educating the poor as had Russia, it is not so strange after all. Perhaps the greater wonder is that only three people in England seemed to care.

"Would you like to learn to read the Bible?" Hannah asked the dirty hoodlums that pressed wonderingly about the sisters, fingering their voluminous silk skirts.

"Wot's it like, laidy?"

"Did you never hear of God, my poor child?"

"Bet cher life, every time me old bloke beats me."

Hannah looked at Patty, and Patty looked at Hannah!

One by one the obstacles against their wild plan of a school were beaten down. By writing to the larger towns in the shire, they were able to secure a spinning mistress, and, for the day and Sunday School, a widow, Mrs. Baker, and her daughter Betty, who were willing to come to Cheddar to live. They leased an empty house for seven years, ordered partitions to be knocked out and a window put in. The large garden of an acre they had set in order.

Then they invited the children to come—any children over six who liked. On the first Sunday appointed for the opening, the two sisters again rode over to find one hundred and forty children enrolled. After a Bible story, a hymn, and a promise of prizes for those who would memorize a Psalm, Hannah formed them in a procession and marched them all to church, to the astonishment of the curate who rode over from Wells, twelve miles away, for a short weekly service. For congregation, eight in the morning and twenty in the afternoon was thought a good attendance. There was scarcely an instance of a poor person being visited, Hannah found.

Now, to her chagrin, in spite of her magnificent audience of children, the curate preached exactly twelve minutes, on the laws of the land and the glory of the divine right of kings.

No wonder that Thomas Paine's wicked sedition and John Wesley's gospel were so needed in this fair land of England. For the Church had grown formal and stiff and aloof, taking no interest or care for its poor. No rector had lived in Cheddar for the past forty years.

After service, Hannah was surrounded by a group of glowering farmers who had come in from miles about at the strange and disturbing news of a Bible School for children. "Reading never did good to anyone," they argued. Others angrily declared that "religion would ruin agriculture."

One wealthy farmer said he did not want saints but workmen, and he didn't fancy his plowman being wiser than himself. "The lower class are fated to be poor, ignorant and wicked."

But when it was announced that no subscription would be asked for the new school, "every heart was cheered, and every eye brightened."

Hannah did not argue. She patted the heads of their dogs and laughingly told them to wait and see whether the crops would suffer, promising that this year fewer apples would be stolen from their orchards.

Five weeks later, the school had become so popular that the children were proudly reading "The Lord is my shepherd" to their mothers, for whom Mrs. Baker had opened the house one evening a week to teach sewing and knitting. Since Hannah wished the school to become as nearly self-supporting as possible, the older girls too were being taught to knit stockings, and to spin flax and wool, while the boys were taught carpentry and gardening.

Meanwhile the More sisters had pressed on to three other villages in the Mendip Hills, finding the people even more savage and vicious than at Cheddar. The men spent their days in the mines, emerging grimy and weary to drink in the tavern and quarrel and sleep. They never saw the sun. The children were taught thievery from infancy. No constable dared serve a summons for fear of being thrown off the cliffs.

Hannah wrote Wilberforce: "I was told I must first propitiate the chief despot of the village who is very rich and very brutal; so I ventured into the den of this monster, in a country as savage as himself. He begged that I would not think of bringing any religion into the country, as it was the worst thing in the world for the poor: it made them lazy and useless.

"I pleaded with each of the better families that I had a little plan which I hoped would secure their orchards from being robbed, their rabbits from being stolen, their game from being shot, and might lower the poor rates."

In reply to this letter, her backer replied: "Your labors can only be equaled by Spenser's Lady-Knights, and they seem to be much of the same kind too. I mean you have all sorts of monsters to contend with. . . I trust you will speak freely when the money is exhausted."

At Shipham, Hannah found that the vicarage had not been inhabited for a hundred years. For the last forty the vicar had not preached or even visited the village. So she claimed the old vicarage, and had it repaired at the vicar's expense. But where to find a teacher?

Someone told her of a young girl, a farmer's daughter, who took time from her Cheddar cheese-making to gather about her a group of thirty children to tell them Bible stories. As a reward for their diligence, this girl gave them homemade gingerbread and Bibles bought with her own small earnings.

Hannah mounted her horse and rode straight off to see the girl. Yes, Patience could read and write a little, and was humbly thrilled at the idea of helping with the school. Might she bring her sister who was in service with a farmer's family a mile away?

Thus it was that the two girls, Patience and Flower, were engaged as mistresses of the new school in the old vicarage. Two young men were found to teach the boys. The opening of the school was an unforgettable experience to Hannah. Of the eager throng of ragamuffins, she was told that three boys had been sentenced to serve a term in jail, and that this white-faced group had a mother condemned to hang. And yet of these "banditti" as Hannah called them, one hundred and seventy came crowding in to learn. Many of the older men and women stood about the walls and wept. At last someone cared. The children need not grow up like themselves.

Here also Hannah started a weekly class of thirty older girls to read, sew, knit and spin.

Back in Cheddar, the school and mothers' clubs were flourishing. Hannah had found a factory in a larger town to buy the knitted work. For the first time in their lives the mothers and older girls could earn a bit for themselves.

Now Hannah had her hands full, training teachers, writing textbooks, organizing schools in more and more villages: Yalton and Axhedge, a stocking town, with a hundred little dirty, half-starved children.

On the first anniversary Hannah arranged for a feast, a dinner for the children, followed by a tea for the mothers, at which the clothing they had made was distributed. The party was a startling success.

Indeed, as the years passed, this annual event in July became of such importance that it made the Mendip Hills famous and quite transformed the district. It was perhaps the first big Sunday School picnic, this "Mendip Feast."

Having selected a high meadow equidistant from the villages, within sight of the Irish Sea, everyone prayed for a sunny day. Very early the long line of carts filled with food left Cowslip Green, followed by carriages of gentry and clergy and riders on horseback, sometimes a mile long. At a fixed spot beside the tents, the procession formed, headed by village drums and fiddlers playing *God Save the King*. Behind the band came Hannah and Patty, then Mrs. Baker and Betty shepherding the two hundred children of Cheddar. Then each village in turn, all swinging into line two and two. The boys carried green branches as for May Day, and the girls held bunches of flowers, late roses and white daisies and blue canterbury bells.

After the children were seated in circles at movable tables, often nine hundred at once, they sang grace and fell upon the feast of good English beef, plum pudding and cider; a feast which took days to prepare, and a half hour to consume.

Then came the examination by villages of the Catechism, the chanting in unison of psalms or passages of the Bible, followed by the cherished prizes of a Bible or hymn book given to each of the hundreds of children by Hannah.

After the children, the new brides came up to receive each a new Bible, a pair of white stockings, and five shillings in money, almost a fortune to them, since they could buy a new spinning wheel for three and sixpence.

Then all together, the whole company sang *God Save the King*, the fresh young voices ardent and joyous on this grand feast-day. The eight thousand people who came from the whole countryside to see the great sight, expecting signs of rowdiness, were amazed and deeply touched. "For the children were as quiet as the lambs grazing in the meadows beside us," wrote Hannah to their friend and benefactor in London.

After a prayer of dismissal by a curate for each group, the children marched away by villages, singing as they went, until their voices died away down the valleys, and many of the bystanders wept. The only other songs known in these villages were the ribald ballads of the tap room, and their only play the rough gang wars between villages. So the order and decorum of these gatherings were considered the more remarkable.

Gradually the work extended over an area of twenty-eight miles. Every Sunday of summer, Hannah and Patty would set out early on horseback from Cowslip Green to visit two or three villages, where each taught classes and encouraged the young teachers. There was much executive work to be done in so large an undertaking, and many problems to settle. Cheddar became a normal school where teachers were trained for the opening of new schools.

All this hard riding on dry or muddy roads, through frequent showers, was very hard on the delicate Hannah. Often she was ill, and Patty must press on alone. Yet on each New Year's Day, Hannah could not help making a resolution to start fresh schools in spite of all the difficulties involved. She said she could not come to Judgment Day with all these people still untaught. Such hundreds of ignorant little savages to be gathered into the big fold!

Nailsea had a glass factory and collieries with many of the worst characters in the country, but even Nailsea begged for a school. Hannah wrote to Wilberforce of her first visit:

"The colliers are more human than the people of the glass-houses. The work there is irregular; the furnaces cannot be allowed to cool, so that Sunday brings no rest. The cottages face the glass-houses, with their great furnaces roaring, and a mass of swearing, eating and drinking human beings, half-dressed, with black faces, in a most horrible and infernal appearance."

The few better class families had never insisted on a curate "for fear their tithes would be raised! I blush for my species."

Yet this ancient law of paying a tithe to the church was to be bitterly disputed by the country people in England as late as 1937.

As usual, she called on every single family, and came away unharmed; she was welcomed to Little Hell or Botany Bay, as they called their fiery village.

"We found a large ox-house. This we roofed and floored, and by putting in a couple of windows, it made a good school-room," she writes. Mothers crowded in with the children, though the mothers' reading club had to be abandoned because not one of them could read.

If it had not been for the kindly sisters, backed by the ever generous Wilberforce, these villages would have suffered indeed, for now came hard times. First a fever pestilence, then a fuel famine. Their young teachers became nurse, supply station, friend. One of them wrote Miss Hannah: "No words can describe the sensations of this poor village of Shipham at seeing a wagon-load of coal you sent enter."

Here, the people burned their chairs and tables to keep from perishing of cold.

Hannah wrote to Wilberforce that she felt indignant with herself for any sums she had wasted in her life, so great now was the need for even a little barley broth. "We lost seven in two days, many of them children."

Again in 1817 came an intense period of depression among the villages, with eleven hundred men out of work, and all the mills, mines and factories lying idle. To lose even the wage of one shilling, twelve cents a day, spelled tragedy. So Hannah courageously bought up a quantity of copper each week, had it stored in warehouses, hoping to resell it by the time the depression was ended. After her twenty-six years of work, the mothers and fathers no longer drank in the taverns during the hard times. The children had wrought this miracle, plus the Bible and human kindness.

Now came a period of persecution for Hannah More. It began at Wedmore where the farmers had lived in terror of the miners. But the chief landlord would not agree to Hannah's plan for a school. His way was to shout and swear at the boys if they came near his own house. His wife upheld him. "The poor in a loomp are bad," she argued. "Providence intended them to be servants and slaves. Let them be. We don't need your school here."

Nothing daunted, though lacking a house, and even the church closed to her, Hannah met her children under an apple tree. But at the first singing of a hymn by Watt, a farmer ran up crying, "Oh, I'm afraid this must be *Methody*." For it seems that John Wesley had once preached under an apple tree of his mother's farm. The apple tree had soon died, so the farmer was afraid this orchard, too, would be destroyed.

So, the apple tree failing, and a rain finding them with no shelter, Hannah decided to build a little cottage with thatched roof. But this did not end the matter. In all the villages, now, men stirred up evil reports; these were largely curates, it is sad to relate. They accused the young teachers of being Calvinists and Methodists because they made up prayers of their own. They considered the slightest enthusiasm about religion a crime.

Now the Dissenters accused Hannah herself of adhering too strictly to the Church of England, while the High Church group thought her entirely too liberal toward the hated Methodists, and advised her solemnly to publish a confession of her faith.

She made no defense. But her heart bled. For many weeks she was ill because of all this dissension and trouble. She could not sleep for thinking of her children, still needing so much. It seemed as if her whole life's work were being undermined and eaten away from her. She was accused even of political and international intrigue, because it was known that Wilberforce, who backed her work, was trying to bring about the abolition of the slave trade, and was working for peace between England and France. Every anti-abolitionist was hostile to religious instruction at home.

In 1800 some farmers went so far as to consult a fortune-teller to know if Hannah More's schools were really Methodist. The fortune-teller asked why they thought so. "Because they sing Watt's hymns," answered the men. "But Watt is a good churchman," objected the woman. "Oh, then, it must be the tunes that are likely Methodist!"

Eight years later, when brought to court because her teachers had no licenses, she at last wrote a letter of appeal to the Bishop of Bath and Wells.

"I have been accused of spreading French principles of defiance to king and to church. Instead I plead guilty of having written an answer to citizen Duport and devoted the two hundred pounds it brought to the relief of French emigrant clergy.

"I am charged with delighting in war. I am accused of being with Hadfield in his attack on the King's life! That I am in the pay of Mr. Pitt! That I was concerned with Charlotte Corday in the murder of Marat!

"My Lord, when I settled here, many years ago, I found the poor in a deplorable state, with no Sunday School in the district except in my own village which necessitated long and tedious rides on horseback. My plan for schools is limited. They learn on week-days such coarse work as may fit them for servants. My object is not to make fanatics but to train up the lower classes to habits of industry and piety. I know no way of teaching morals but by teaching principles; or of inculcating Christian principles without a knowledge of Scripture.

"We use in teaching two little tracts of Questions for the Mendip Schools, a Church Catechism, Spelling Book, Psalter, Common Prayer, Testament and Bible.

"Because the poor have an enthusiasm for expressing their new religious life, should they be condemned and left destitute of instruction?

"I am told that my writings ought to be burned by the hands of the common hangman."

Yet the tracts for the poor which Hannah had written with the help of her sisters, following the success of her Jack and Tom tract, sold up into millions of copies, the poor reading them avidly, since through fear of a revolution, George III taxed working men's magazines and periodicals so that they could no longer afford them.

Moreover all her books had an extraordinary vogue. Her *Sacred Dramas* ran into nineteen editions, her novel *Cœleb* into thirty, while her book on the education of a princess, written for Princess Charlotte, must have been read by every young girl of the upper classes in England.

At last, with her bishops and booksellers behind her, the intense and ridiculous opposition to her work blew over. Sooner or later, all of her accusers were themselves condemned. And now all England knew of her schools on the Mendip Hills.

ONE DAY a country gentleman, on in years, looked wistfully over the hedge at the foxglove and mignonette nodding in Hannah's garden. A maid was cutting roses.

"I have often admired this garden," he said. "Can you tell me to whom it belongs?"

"That I can, sir. To Miss Hannah More, sir," said the maid, dropping him a curtsy.

"Can it be!" exclaimed the gentleman, opening the gate. "My compliments to your mistress, and say to her that Mr. Turner is calling."

"Mr. Turner," murmured Hannah to Patty. "Not *the* Mr. Turner?"

But so it was, a most agreeable old gentleman who was delighted to renew a friendship after twenty years. Delighted, also, to receive copies of all of Hannah's books, and to bequeath to her at his death one thousand pounds.

So money poured into Hannah's lap for her schools, from friends, from her book sales, from Wilberforce.

In reply to her first letter about the Cheddar school, he wrote: "Your plan is a very good one. As for expense, the best proof you can give me that you believe me heartily in the cause is to call on me for money without reserve. I shall take the liberty of enclosing a draft for forty pounds. But this is only meant for a beginning."

During the remainder of his life, he kept this promise. Once he wrote that he had more money than he thought, and begged her to get a carriage as the long horseback rides through the rain were too hard on her. But this she refused for many years.

In 1802, the Cowslip Green house being outgrown, the sisters bought a piece of land called Barley Wood a mile away and built a roomy, comfortable house. It was full of people from morning to night, as teachers and even parents came from the Mendip parishes to consult Mrs. Hannah, as they called her.

In 1808, after two years of illness over the persecution affair, Hannah was preparing for the twentieth reunion of Cheddar. She wrote Wilberforce:

"Do you remember John Hill, our first scholar, whose

gentle and good manners you used to notice? He afterwards became one of our teachers, but war tore him from us. Judge of our pleasure to see him in full regimentals, acting as paymaster and sergeant-major!

"There was a sort of review. Everybody praised the training of eight hundred men so well disciplined. One of the officers said to me: 'All this is owing to the great abilities and industry of Sergeant Hill. He is the greatest master of military tactics we have. At first, he was so religious we thought him a Methodist; but we find him so fine a soldier and so correct in his morals that we do not trouble ourselves about his religion. He will probably be adjutant at the next vacancy.'"

At seventy-four, all of her dear sisters had passed away, but Hannah still carried on alone, and for that year's feast on her own wide lawns, she prepared thirteen hundred prizes: a far cry from that first little group in Cheddar.

More than anything else she wanted her children to carry the simple religion they were taught into their daily lives, to live it. Amid all the conflict of her age between different sects, she wrote:

"Bible Christianity is what I love, that does not insist upon opinions. A Christianity practical and pure, which teaches holiness, humility, repentance, and faith, and which, after summing up all the evangelical gifts, declares that the greatest of these is charity."

You may ask: What, after all, is the significance or importance of this work of Hannah More? Perhaps our Sunday Schools, our Girl Scouts and Campfire Girls, our 4-H Clubs, even our trade schools, all owe more than we dream to this far-away beginning a century and a half ago. Perhaps Cheddar was the first settlement house.

Her work prepared the way for the great reforms of Lord Shaftesbury who introduced in Parliament his first Factory Act the very year of her death. It proved to England, in her own lifetime, the necessity for education even of the poor.

In 1823, at the age of seventy-eight, she wrote a long letter to Wilberforce:

"If I know a little of anything in the world, it is about the poor. When I set up our schools, I was considered by the farmers, and even by their betters, as the greatest enemy of my country.

"'We shan't have a boy to plow, or a wench to dress a shoulder of mutton,' was the general cry. One of them pointed to Glastonbury Tor, saying we should make things as bad and much worse, as when the monks first brought religion and learning there.

"I have not, after thirty-six years, altered my opinion. But our instructions have been, and still are, confined to the Scriptures, and such books as are preparatory to, and connected with them. At Blagdon, we attempted something one step higher, and employed a man who, in addition to his large Sunday School, taught farmers' sons on a week-end. I planned under the guise of arithmetic to teach them such principles as to fit them to become church wardens, jurymen, constables, and to teach them the solemnities of an oath. These sinister designs were promptly quashed and the class had to be dissolved.

"But now the tide turns! Our poor are now to be made scholars and philosophers. I am the champion of ignorance and the poor must not only read English but ancient history, and even the sciences are to be laid open to them.

"Not only in the great National Schools * but in the little paltry cottage seminaries of three-pence a week, I hear the most audacious instances of the affectation of literature. A poor little girl of this stamp was in my room one day when a gentleman was sitting with me. He asked her what she was reading at school.

"'Oh, sir, the whole circle of the sciences!'

"'Indeed,' said he, 'that must be a very large work.'

"'No, sir, it is a very little book. It cost half a crown.'

"My friend smiled and lamented that what was such easy attainment had cost him so much time and money.

"The misfortune is, that the growing ultra-ism on the side of learning, falsely so-called, will irritate and inflame the old bigotry, which hugged absolute ignorance as hidden treasure, not to be parted with, while that sober measure of Christian instruction which lies between the two extremes, will be regretted by both parties.

"Many a child is brought to me in my room for a little reward of a tract. Since I began this scrawl, a sharp little girl was brought in for this purpose. She repeated a short poem extremely well. I then said, 'Now I must examine what you know of the Bible. Who was Abraham?'

"After some hesitation she answered, 'I think he was an Exeter man!'

"Happily my own schools go on in their old-fashioned way. I taught the teachers their alphabets thirty years ago. They continue pious, faithful, and sober-minded."

Yet for all of this new learning, by the year 1832, the year before her death at the age of eighty-eight, only one-

* Bell's National Society for promoting the education of the poor in the principles of the Established Church, organized in 1809 by voluntary subscription. It was not until the twentieth century that the government completed its system of free elementary and secondary school education.

fourth of the children in England were being educated by philanthropic groups. A French historian wrote that "England had the lowest place among Protestant countries in education."

It was not until 1838, five years after her death, that Lord Melbourne's Government voted twenty thousand pounds to aid the schools already started among various church groups. The following year, they increased the sum and appointed a board of inspectors to help spend it, the forerunners of the Boards of Education, and of the free school law of 1870.

So it was that Wilberforce and Hannah More led the Government by nearly a century, even if they did use the Bible as their textbook. At seventy-five, all the philanthropists who visited England came to sit at her feet. They found her dark hazel eyes as brilliant beneath her quaint white ruffled bonnet as they had been at eighteen, and her wit as sparkling. Lords and ladies came, Wordsworth and Southey, humble folk and proud. One and all she regaled with stories of her Mendip Hills.

In order that the work might continue after her death, Hannah left it in the hands of a devoted committee empowered to spend the various trust funds, that of her mothers' clubs alone being two thousand pounds, the accumulation of their small club dues of sixpence a month!

Some day when you visit lovely Gloucestershire and motor among the villages of the Mendip Hills, and peep over the hedge at Cowslip Green on the road from Bristol to Exeter, you will think of Hannah More splashing through the rain to her forgotten villages. Or you will see her, a charming old lady at Barley Wood, dispensing wit and wisdom to the humanitarians of her age.

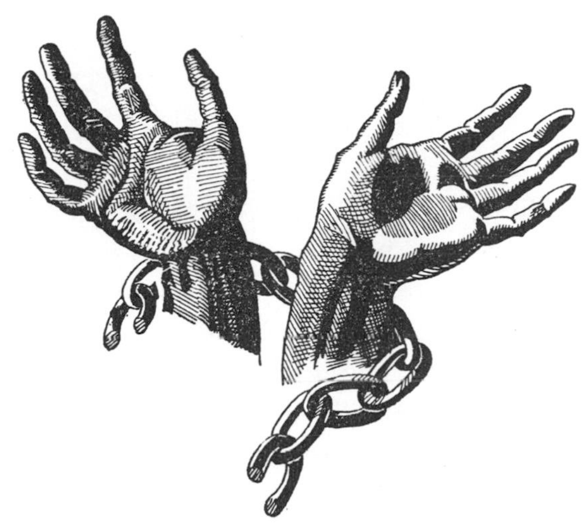

WILLIAM WILBERFORCE
1759–1833

To THE lasting joy of millions of black people, William Wilberforce was seized with what the Quakers call a "concern" — a concern for the slaves of the West Indies. Interested from childhood in the slave market of Bristol, it was not until during the years of 1785 to 1787 that he investigated for himself the whole sorry business of English merchant trade.

For a hundred years and more, he learned that their chief cargoes had been, not spices or gold or corn or wheat, but human beings, black folks snatched by force from their homes in Africa. If the trade was hazardous, it was also exceedingly profitable. The English West Indies Company had only to hire Arabs or enemy blacks to surround an African village at night, set fire to all the huts, kill off the old people and little children, herd the able-bodied men and women together, tether them neck to neck, and drive them on foot to the sea coast, often as far as seven hundred miles.

Arrived at a port, those who did not faint or die by the way were crowded into a rude fortress prison, often with no food other than weeds or roots, until the arrival of a ship.

Then began a sea voyage of days and weeks during which the prisoners were still kept chained together in the dark hold, without air or sufficient food or water.

Those who survived the diseases and illnesses of this voyage were then sold in a slave market in England or Spain. The sick ones might be bought for five dollars a head, while the more hardy blacks brought from one to three hundred dollars each. Families were, of course, separated; a wife from her husband, children from their parents. Then followed another long voyage in filth and stench to the West Indies where the slaves were herded on plantations and made to do the work of sugar-cane growing. Being weak and unused to such labor, or stubborn or lazy, they were driven and lashed with whips as though they were mules or worn-out horses.

All these gruesome details and more made young Wilberforce's heart bleed for pity. But he found that eighteenth-century England took them for granted. It was not that people had no feeling, but rather a strong prejudice against meddling with another man's property. Besides, the cotton and sugar plantations of the colonies must be worked, since they formed a large proportion of the national revenue. Nor could English prisons and poorhouses furnish the laborers required. To place a former convict as overseer in charge of hundreds of black slaves, and under him other convicts in charge of ten, each provided with a short and a long whip kept in constant motion, proved of the greatest economic value. Sugar production required this system. And neither the Church of England nor Parliament felt it encumbent upon them to interfere.

But Wilberforce did. A brilliant young member of the House, with wealth and social position behind him, with a peculiar gift of swaying men's minds and hearts by means of his eloquence, he had determined to dedicate his life to this cause of the abolition of slave trade, and finally, of slavery itself. It was not a popular cause. He must expect to fight many enemies, even among the best people. Yet several circumstances contributed to make Wilberforce determine to carry the fight through to victory.

Of his friends, Lady Midleton was one of the very few who upheld him. She it was of whom Hannah More wrote: "Lady Midleton lavishes so much thought on the blacks that it is a marvel she has any strength left, yet she cares even for suffering animals."

Another friend was Thomas Clarkson who had won a prize for his Latin essay in Cambridge on this very subject: *An liceat invitos in servitutem dare*. After college he translated his essay into English and had it published. A group of Quakers, who had long been much exercised over England's treatment of slaves, invited Clarkson to join their Society of Anti-Slavery, organized in 1783. Now, in 1787, Clarkson took Wilberforce to one of their meetings. In all England, here was a little group of twelve people on a little so-called Christian island deeply concerned about the unChristian treatment of thousands of blacks on a group of small pagan islands.

After visiting together the slave markets of London and Liverpool, Bristol and Lancaster, the two young men were fired to dedicate their whole lives to the cause, and united,

Wilberforce to work within Parliament, and Clarkson outside. Only death separated them.

Always frail in health, in 1788 Wilberforce had a desperate illness. Given up as incurable by his physicians, he was told that he had only a few days to live. He sent for his friend Pitt, one of the most powerful young leaders of the House.

"You must carry on for me," Wilberforce said to him. "They tell me I've got to die. You'll have to take over my fight for the anti-slave trade bill."

And Pitt promised.

But by some miracle Wilberforce did not die. When, due to his own system of medical treatment, he crept back out of the shadows, he knew that it was for the cause of slavery that he had been given his life. His "concern" now became a "mission."

A further influence determining this mission was that of the Wesleys. When, three years before, Wilberforce had left his London clubs, his gaming tables, and his wealthy society friends for a long trip abroad, he had unknowingly chosen as his secretary-reader a young Wesleyan. Wilberforce was skeptical and prejudiced at first, yet out of their talks together grew an inner light, so that he returned to England a Methodist at heart.

Hearing alarming rumors about her son, his mother wrote to him in indignant protest.

"It is quite true," he replied to her. "But don't let it trouble you, Mother. I shall not give up my seat in Parliament nor take to a cell. Come and visit me and see for yourself."

And she saw that her son's "change of heart" had only made him more considerate of her, kinder to his servants, and indeed to all in need of his help, but more than ever determined that the system of a white master owning a black slave whom he could beat or not as he chose must be abolished. So he never left the Church of England, but instead, won over numbers of the clergy to his cause. Yet he had a peculiar veneration for both Charles and John Wesley.

It was in Hannah More's home that Wilberforce first met Charles Wesley.

"When I came into the room," he wrote to a friend, "Charles Wesley rose from the tea table, and, coming forward to meet me, gave me solemnly his blessing. Such was the effect of his manner and appearance that it altogether upset me, and I burst into tears, unable to restrain myself."

It was in deference to this evangelist and hymn writer who had so touched his heart that, after his death, Wilberforce made a liberal allowance to Mrs. Wesley as long as she lived.

Just before he introduced his first abolition bill into Parliament, Wilberforce received a letter from John Wesley:

"Unless God has raised you up for this very thing, you will be worn out by the opposition of men and devils: but if God be for you, who can be against you? Are all of them together stronger than God? Oh! be not weary of well-doing. Go on in the name of God and in the power of His might, till even American slavery, the vilest thing that ever saw the sun, shall vanish away before it.

"That He who has guided you from your youth up may continue to strengthen you in this and in all things, is the prayer of

Your affectionate servant,

"February 24, 1791

John Wesley."

What a blessing that was, written just three days before his death, the last words of his pen. Small wonder that the heart of William Wilberforce was strangely strengthened in spite of the failure, two months later, of his bill "to prevent further importation of slaves into the West Indies."

"Wilberforce made an eloquent speech," writes Mr. Giliat,* "describing the horrors of the carrying trade, the suffocation of the slaves, their being forced to dance in fetters to keep fit, the insanity, their throwing themselves into the sea, preferring drowning to slavery, their being compelled to eat vile food by putting live coals to their mouths.

"Never," cried Wilberforce, "never will we desist till we have wiped away this scandal from the load of guilt under which we at present labor, and until we have extinguished every trace of this bloody traffic which our posterity will scarcely believe had been suffered to exist so long, a disgrace and a dishonor to our country."

Thus he took his stand, in the face of an overwhelming majority against him. For it was evident that he and his cause had many enemies: admirals and captains of slave ships, plantation owners and importers. These maintained that the slaves were far better off than in their native villages, that they would never work without being lashed, and that sugar could not be produced without slaves. They were supported by most of the monied men of the country. Did not the wealth of the Southern colonies of America depend entirely upon the same slave labor?

Now Wilberforce turned his face toward America and began to make inquiries. He found that when, as early as 1774, Thomas Jefferson had protested vehemently against

* *Heroes of Modern Crusades.*

further importation of slaves to the American colonies, Lord Dartmouth, president of the British Board of Trade, declared, "We cannot allow the colonies to check or discourage in any degree a traffic so beneficial to the nation." And yet this same lord was a prominent Evangelical whom his conservative friends nicknamed "the praying Psalm-singer." Such a word as humanity had probably never entered the good gentleman's head.

Yet the Quakers of the colonies knew the word well, and had sternly forbade any of their members to own slaves. It was into their midst that Thomas Paine arrived in time to publish a protest against slavery in his *Pennsylvania Magazine*, before plunging into the Revolution. Five years later, in 1780, as secretary of the Pennsylvania Assembly, Paine again championed the cause.

The Assembly, composed largely of Quakers, determined to put through a bill of abolition, and delegated Paine to draw up its preamble. This Wilberforce now read:

"1. When we contemplate our abhorrence of that condition, to which the arms and tyranny of Great Britain were exerted to reduce us, when we look back on the variety of dangers to which we have been exposed, and how miraculously our wants have been supplied . . . we are . . . led to a grateful sense of the manifold blessings, which we have undeservedly received from the hand of that Being. . .

"Therefore we rejoice to extend a portion of that freedom to others, which hath been extended to us, and release them from the state of thralldom, to which we ourselves were tyrannously doomed.

"We esteem it a peculiar blessing granted to us, that we are enabled this day to add one more step to universal civilization, by removing as much as possible the groans of those who have lived in undeserved bondage, and from which, by the assumed authority of the Kings of Great Britain, no effectual legal relief could be obtained. . . We find our hearts enlarged with kindness and benevolence toward men of all conditions and nations; and we conceive ourselves called upon by the blessings which we have received to manifest the sincerity of our profession, and to give a substantial proof of our gratitude.

"2. And whereas the condition of those persons, who have been denominated negro and mulatto slaves, has been attended with circumstances, which not only deprived them of the common blessings that they were by nature entitled to, but has cast them into deepest affliction, by an unnatural separation and sale of husband and wife from each other and from their children, an injury, the greatness of which can only be conceived by supposing that we were in the same unhappy case. . .

"3. Be it enacted that . . ." *

Thus the act abolishing slavery in Pennsylvania was passed on October 1, 1780. Likewise every Northern state had passed a similar law. But Wilberforce found that so prejudiced was Britain against any act of the rebellious colonies, that their example was ineffective.

Upon inquiry he found that for the Christian trade one hundred and fifty thousand negroes were taken annually out of Africa, and fifty thousand for the Mohammedan trade.

As Wilberforce studied the problem he found that throughout the known history of the world, slavery had existed. Ancient records of Babylonian conquests of neigh-

* *Life and Writings of Thomas Paine*, Vol. 8, p. 117. V. Parke & Co.

boring peoples told of killing off the unfit but of keeping the fit as captives. The able-bodied became the slaves of the king and his captains. Artisans were set to work in their own handicrafts of pottery or weaving, at beating gold or setting precious gems. The rest were used in gang-slavery to build roads or canals or palaces, to work mines of gold or turquoise, as soldiers, or to till the land.

Egypt followed the same practices. Did not Pharaoh carry off the Israelites bodily to do his hard menial labor, even to the making of bricks without straw?

Wilberforce read stories of the appalling cruelty of Rome toward her conquered peoples, of the happier fate of the six thousand crucified by Crassus than of those thrown into the arena to fight wild beasts in the gladiatorial games. He learned that this horrible sport, which flourished in Rome for more than two centuries, was but a revival of an old Etruscan sport, which in turn grew out of the prehistoric custom in West Africa of a massacre of captives at the burial of a fallen chief. All Rome went to shout at these games, and not until the first century was there a single recorded voice of protest. Had Seneca caught the note of love and pity from the gentle Nazarene?

Greece too had her slaves; every household of any importance had its own. They were never so cruelly treated as in Rome, but often became trusted and loved members of the family, or continued on in service long after they were freed.

The great Plato would have abolished slavery entirely. The Stoics and Epicureans, many of whom were slaves, condemned it, but since they could not alter it, they decided that it could not affect the soul, and so ignored it. Certain slaves, like Epictetus and Plotinus, left enduring and immortal writings to prove that a slave's soul could rise to the heights of great literary achievement.

"Why," mused Wilberforce, "should one nation glory in cruelty to its slaves, while its nearest neighbor abhorred this practice and even argued in favor of emancipation?" Was not the Greek sense of beauty of greater lasting power than the Roman sense of might? The first bred pity and justice, and the second inhumanity and lust for greater power.

Turning farther east, Wilberforce searched the writings of Mohammed to find the attitude of Islam on the burning question of slavery. To his amazement he read in the last sermon of Mohammed, still accepted as the Islamic code of conduct, this verse:

"And your slaves, see that ye feed them with such food as ye eat yourselves, and clothe them with the stuff ye wear. And if they commit a fault which ye are not inclined to forgive, then sell them, for they are the servants of the Lord, and are not to be tormented."

Did not England pride itself upon being a Christian nation, and her king a defender of the Faith? Were not all men children of one Father? Yet all Europe seemed to be engaged in this same inhuman traffic. However had it started?

With Portugal, he found. It was in 1442 that Prince Henry of Portugal set sail on a cruise of exploration and trade, and brought back the first cargo of living black folk from Africa. They must have found a ready market, for by 1480 the hardy Portuguese were bringing in slaves regularly and had established a trade in Europe, with slave markets in Lisbon and Seville. Fifty years later, they sold from ten to twelve thousand slaves annually in the Lisbon market alone.

It was but natural that Spain should follow. In 1511, King Ferdinand authorized a slave trade to his West Indian Islands to work in the mines of Hispaniola, discovered by Christopher Columbus. Four years later, Charles V gave a monopoly of slave-trading to a Flemish courtier, who passed it on to Genoese merchants, and they in turn to a Portuguese trader for an annual importation of four thousand blacks. Thus the Holy Roman Empire entered the game.

Now it was England's turn to step into this lucrative business. And it was none other than a woman, Queen Elizabeth, who not only permitted the sailor Hawkins to engage in the trade but "personally took a share in it."

With the later acquisition of the West Indies from Holland, Spain and France, and the development of cotton and sugar, slaves became to England an economic necessity.

The American colonies had long become involved. The first shipment of blacks from Guinea were landed by a Dutch ship at Jamestown, Virginia, in 1620, the same year as the landing of the Pilgrims. Soon all the work of the Southern colonies, as of Jamaica and the West Indies, was done by slaves, in spite of the prickings of conscience and the protests of a few humane leaders.

In the journal of a Scotch lady who visited the West Indies at the time of our own Revolution, we have her account of the blacks:

"The negroes who are all in troops are sorted so as to match each other in size and strength. Every ten has a driver, who walks behind them, holding in his hand a short whip and a long one. You will easily guess the use of these weapons, a circumstance of all others the most horrid. They are naked, male and female, down to the girdle, and you constantly observe where the application has been made. But however dreadful this must appear to a humane European, I will do the creoles the justice to say, they would be averse to it as we are, could it be avoided, which has often been tried to no purpose. They go up the hill at a trot and return at a gallop, and did you not know the cruel necessity of this alertness, you would believe them the merriest people in the world." *

Yet Wilberforce's opponents argued that slaves were far better off even under the lash than in their free native villages; that the new industrial supremacy of England could not be maintained without them.

From the West Indies themselves came a storm of protest. "You employ slaves in your own mines and mills," wrote the plantation owners. "Why not turn your thoughts to reforming conditions for them, and leave us alone to manage our own affairs?"

Moreover a rebellion of blacks in the French colony of San Domingo, on the wake of the French Reign of Terror, so frightened King George that he ever after opposed Wilberforce. Naturally, the Tories all followed suit.

Wilberforce was considered by them nothing more than a fanatic for wishing to stop the trade and so bring ruin upon all British colonial islands.

Just as his enemies predicted, the slaves got wind of all this agitation on their behalf, and decided to rebel against Britain and rule themselves.

* From *Journal of a Lady of Quality from Scotland to the West Indies, 1775–1776*, by courtesy of Yale University Press.

Wilberforce admitted readily enough that the whole problem was complicated, but never could he concede that it was insoluble. Had the consciousness of mankind made no progress during these twenty centuries? So he worked harder than ever to lift this scourge from England. He wrote a book, and paid to have his friends' books published. He talked constantly to the clergy to stir up the Church to assume responsibility. He tried to appeal to the masses, to the peers, to stir up sluggish British conscience. Personally he never left a kindness undone. He gave as liberally to Hannah More's villages as to his anti-slavery campaign, during a period of twenty years.

He asked Hannah More to write him a poem on this burning question, something that would appeal to all classes of people.

The resultant verses were translated into many languages, and set to music by Charles Wesley. In the last verse she writes as a scribe of the slaves:

Then let our masters gladly find
A free man works the faster;
Who serves his God with heart and mind
Will better serve his Master.

This proved a sound prophecy, and a group of Wesleyan missionaries went out to the West Indies to teach the black man to serve his master without stealing or lying, to prepare him for the freedom to come.

Meanwhile in Parliament, Wilberforce carried on his fight. Year after year he introduced bill after bill. If it passed the Commons, it was defeated by the Lords. If it passed the second reading, it was certain to be thrown out at the third, or tabled, or delayed in committee until the session ended.

At last in 1806, he felt that the time of victory had come. In spite of bitter opposition he said with deep faith, "God can turn the hearts of men." As he looked about the House a strange exaltation seized him. Pitt and Fox were gone, but others had taken their places: Canning, Buxton, Macaulay. During the last debate he felt more and more certain that this time the bill would pass. Six or eight young noblemen sprang to their feet to speak for it at the same time. At last, slavery had become a popular issue. His heart was so nearly bursting with joy and thanksgiving that he could not hear the plaudits showered on himself.

"Such applause as was scarcely ever before given to any man in either House," wrote Bishop Portens.

When the vote was announced it stood two hundred and eighty-three to sixteen. Amid the thundering cheers and the shower of congratulations upon him, someone proposed that they make out a list of the names of the sixteen.

Wilberforce protested quickly. "Never mind the miserable sixteen," he cried, his face radiant. "Let us think only of our glorious two hundred and eighty-three."

So it was that after twenty-two years of labor, his fight was won. The bill for the abolition of slave-trading became a law of Britain affecting all her colonies from the year 1807.

The whole world acclaimed England. All England acclaimed William Wilberforce. Sir James Mackintosh wrote from the West Indies a long letter of rejoicing and congratulation.

"The wonder is that a short period in the short life of

one man is, well and wisely directed, sufficient to remedy the miseries of millions for ages," he wrote.

There now remained a long further struggle to perfect the law, and to prosecute those traders who continued to break it, with more horrible cruelty than before. The trade was lucrative to them, even if two out of three ships were captured. But new restrictions were added, and Wilberforce set as his goal the complete emancipation of all slaves, a goal which would forever abolish the trade.

Now he imagined the redeemed captives as William Blake expressed it:

. . . when their hands and bars are burst
Let the slave grinding at the mill run out into fields,
Let him look up into the heavens & laugh in the bright air;
Let the enchained soul, shut up in darkness and in sighing,
Whose face has never seen a smile in thirty weary years,
Rise and look out; his chains are loose, his dungeon doors are open;
And let his wife and children return from the oppressor's scourge.
They look behind at every step, & believe it is a dream,
Singing; "The sun has left his blackness & has found a fresher morning."

"God will bless this country for it," Wilberforce would say, and his prophecy seemed to come true, for the navy had a series of victories ending in 1815 with the defeat of Napoleon. And the very year of his death, 1833, the year of complete emancipation, brought in also far-sweeping changes in British life which had been demanded since the American Revolution; namely, the Factory Acts, the taking over of secondary education, the amendment of the Poor Laws, a reform of the Church of Ireland, and the beneficial effects of the reforms of Parliament granted the year before.

It was as if, having at last taken the step of humanity toward its black peoples, England could then forge its own freedom.

Wilberforce died on July 20, 1833. Great memorial mass meetings of negroes were held in New York and Philadelphia and in the West Indies. One month after his passing, on August 30, 1833, just forty-two years after his first bill was introduced, both Houses voted to free seven hundred thousand slaves over a period of several years, with a payment from the exchequer of twenty million pounds to compensate the slave-owners.

Thirty years later, President Lincoln signed the bill emancipating the three million slaves in America.

Denmark, which in 1792 had led all nations in the abolition of slave trade, was followed by France, and finally by Spain and Portugal. Truly, the way was paved for the twentieth century to abolish slavery completely from the face of the earth, for the first time in its known history. Without respect of creed or color or race, all men must at last be declared free and equal in the sight of government, of international law, and brothers of one another.

So the concern of the English and American Quakers was at rest.

So the mission of William Wilberforce was accomplished.

SARAH JOSEPHA HALE
1788–1879

FOR FORTY years Sarah Hale, who was herself a beautiful and gifted woman, molded the tastes and characters of American girls and women. She told them how to be beautiful, how to succeed as wives and mothers. She told them what to wear, what to embroider, what good things to make in their kitchens for their men, what to read, what to think, whom to appreciate and whom to praise. For them she opened the doors of the nineteenth century into education, into industry, into the professions.

If you were to plan a party of questions and answers on the origin of our American institutions, Sarah Hale would be the answer to a score of them:

Questions: WHO

organized the first Seamen's Institute?

is responsible for Thanksgiving Day as a national holiday?

suggested the first playground?
started the first Day Nursery?
raised money to finish Bunker Hill Monument, and to preserve Mt. Vernon as a national monument?
was the first woman champion of higher education for girls?
founded the first society to secure higher wages and better working conditions for women and children?
sent out the first medical women missionaries?
took the word "Female" out of Vassar College?
wrote "Mary had a little lamb?"

Answer: SARAH JOSEPHA HALE.

Just as intense as Wilberforce's concern to emancipate slaves, was Sarah Hale's passion to liberate women. She felt that the whole future not only of men and boys but of America itself lay in their hands. She insisted that they be placed in a position of equality with men as far as their mental and spiritual equipment for life.

Her strong convictions about women and girls came out of her own experience. Born in a hamlet of New Hampshire, she and her brother were taught their lessons by their mother. But when the time came for her brother to go off to college, Sarah had to stay at home. There was no college for girls in America in 1806. Of course Dartmouth refused to admit her. Sarah rebelled. She felt she had just as much right to an education as her brother. Had she not kept up with him in everything, Latin and mathematics and logic?

Her one consolation was that he agreed with her. So he brought home his books at vacation time and patiently went over with her all his notes, thus sharing with her his Latin and Greek, his science and French.

For seven winters, Sarah taught the children in the village school, until her marriage to Dr. David Hale.

And now for nine years her life was a paradise. She adored her husband, and her little home, and each of her five children. Every evening from eight to ten, her husband read with her. As her brother had, he believed her mind to be as good as his. They studied together French and botany, geology and mineralogy, and took turns reading the classics: Tacitus, Ovid, Cicero, Virgil. They discussed politics and world affairs.

Suddenly her paradise was shattered by her husband's death. There followed six years of tragedy, of stark grappling with reality. How, with five young children, was she to earn a living? So few avenues were open to her. Some kindly Masonic friends of her husband financed a millinery shop, but somehow Sarah couldn't make a go of that. They published her first book of poems, and then her first novel. This latter caught on quickly, running into five printings during the first month.

A Boston publishing house wrote to offer her the editorship of the new *Ladies' Magazine* they were starting. Thankfully, tremblingly, at forty Sarah Hale moved her family to Boston and began her life-job. In the very first issue she started her campaign for the progress of female improvement.

Eight years later, Mr. Louis A. Godey of Philadelphia, who published *Godey's Lady's Book*, offered to buy the *Boston Ladies' Magazine*, and asked Mrs. Hale to be its editor. She continued until she was ninety.

Now Mrs. Hale might well have spent all her time at her

desk, for hers was a pioneer venture. When before had contributions by women ever been accepted by a magazine? When had there ever before been a champion for women's causes? She found herself immersed in correspondence, foreign and domestic, in the reading of many manuscripts, in rallying to the concerns of her contemporaries: Lucretia Mott, Susan Anthony, Emma Willard, Mary Lyon, Margaret Fuller, Lucy Stone, Elizabeth Blackwell, Harriet Beecher Stowe. Yes, she might well have been glued to her desk.

Yet she found time for her own practical contribution to humanity outside her editorial office. While in Boston her attention was called to the sad condition of seamen's families. In the year 1830, Boston's chief industry was cod fishing and shipping. A seaman was paid ten shillings eighteen pence a month as wage, but it took two months' wages to pay for his outfit at company stores. His heavy drinking ate up more, so that he could leave little enough with his wife, often barely sufficient for rent and fuel. How, then, was she to provide food for her children during the months of the fishing?

Mrs. Hale had faced the problem herself of how to earn. Now she found that hundreds of young wives and mothers were facing the same problem. Most of them were thrifty and self-respecting, but quite untaught in the classics. Washing clothes or simple needlework were the only avenues open to them. So Mrs. Hale started sewing groups, cutting out for them shirts and blue jeans, so that they could supply their men with part of the necessary outfits.

Next, she opened a store to sell the surplus, and stocked it with other articles so that the seamen could buy their outfits more cheaply than before and so leave a larger sum for their wives.

Of course she faced sharp and ugly opposition from boarding-house keepers along the waterfront, who made a percentage on all outfits, and from manufacturers who had paid starvation wages for making shirts and jeans while Mrs. Hale paid an honest wage and yet underbid them in price.

In order to fight these early New England grafters, Mrs. Hale organized a Society for Seamen, or a Seamen's Institute with a boarding house of its own called *Mariner's House,* furnished out of Beacon Street attics, through her editorial appeals. Out of this first small beginning have sprung up all the Sailors Snug Harbors which have meant so much to seamen the world over.

But she did not stop there. The problem was many sided. For the older children of seamen, Mrs. Hale opened the first industrial or trade school for girls so that they might learn sewing, cutting and fitting. Thus they could learn to make their own clothes and also help their mothers with the outfit-sewing for their fathers.

Now while the mothers and older sisters sewed, Mrs. Hale wondered what to do with the tiny tots. So for them she arranged the first day nursery, looked after in turn by the older girls of the sewing school.

At that time in our American life, men thought women good for nothing but to mother babies. Mrs. Hale disagreed, but she did think that women should do their task of mothering superlatively well. And what was more practical than for girls to start out learning the art in their teens?

But she remembered her own passionate desire for an

education. She wouldn't regiment these seamen's daughters to sewing and baby culture alone. No, someone must read aloud a story book while they sewed. Naturally the girls were delighted. They begged for more. Again, in answer to her editorials, the women of Boston ransacked their libraries, and there grew up so popular a library for girls that Mrs. Hale extended it later to the men also.

When the fleet came sailing home, some men might find that a good book and a clay pipe in their own cozy warm kitchen was more inviting, than lounging all day and night in the taverns along the waterfront.

So this first library for seamen has grown to thousands of libraries for coast guards, lighthouses, sailors on land and on sea.

When Mrs. Hale visited the mothers in their homes, she was heartsick at the damp, musty, tumble-down houses—the only homes they could afford. She framed a bill and took it to the Massachusetts State Legislature—a bill for better housing, with low rents. The bill failed.

That was more than a century ago. Today, in nearly every great city in our fair land, the same bad housing conditions still prevail. And today, staunch friends of the poor are still coming forward with housing bills, though few of such bills have carried. During the last year, tremendous projects have been undertaken by our own government in tearing down old slums and replacing them with clean, cheap, sanitary and really beautiful houses. The relation of bad housing to crime is now recognized.

Mrs. Hale was a wise woman. She felt deeply, intensely, about the needs of the seamen's families. But neither then in her early career, nor during the long years in her editor's chair, did she invite hatred and unpopularity as so many fanatics are willing to do for their causes. Her way was to state a need, or to champion a cause, and in a few months to restate it, and in another few months to restate it again from another angle. This she had to keep on doing, for years.

HER campaign for a national Thanksgiving Day well illustrates her method. She worked for seventeen years to bring this to pass. She was just one year old when Thanksgiving Day was first proclaimed by Washington in 1789. Of course he wished to revive the day set apart by our Pilgrim fathers in 1621—to make it forever a part of the heritage of our republic. But in the years since, each state had grown accustomed to fixing its own Thanksgiving Day.

Beginning in November, 1846, with the suggestion that all the states adopt the last Thursday in November of that year, Mrs. Hale repeated it patiently each year. In her editorial for October, 1851, she added: "Some states appoint the time just after harvests are gathered, others after the public canals are closed." Out on Long Island, it was after the cows were driven home from the sea pastures. She thought it was too bad that the six million American families could not sit down to dinner together.

"It matters much religiously and nationally," she answered her opponents, "that all observe the same day . . . from the St. John's to the Rio Grande, from the Atlantic to the Pacific border, the telegraph * of human happiness would move every heart to gladden . . . and to render thanks to God for the blessings showered on our beloved country.

* Only two years before, in 1844, Morse organized his first private company to operate a telegraph line between New York, Washington and Baltimore. Thus Mrs. Hale extended the principle of the telegraph to a flash of human happiness over the length and breadth of the land.

"We have been urging it for several years. If the last Thursday in November were fixed there would be two great national festivals, Independence Day . . . and Thanksgiving Day. . .

"Will not every state governor in our republic lend a favorable ear to our petition and name the last Thursday the Thanksgiving Day of 1851?"

But "vested interests" or owners of cows still objected. By 1853 she had caught a world vision as she so often did about her pet plans. Again she put the question: "Shall it be the last Thursday in November this year? If the state governors will this year unite on this day, there is little doubt but a precedent will be established which will become a fixed custom forever. Then our nation will have a holiday worthy of republican Christians . . . and as other nations attain to the political and religious privileges we enjoy, their people would adopt the same day for a public thanksgiving, till the tide of rejoicing rolls round the globe." Alas how few nations have joined us!

She listed the twenty states and territories that had united the previous year, and hoped that with Virginia and Vermont added this year, 1853, "twenty-three millions of people might be sitting down . . . together to a feast of joy and thankfulness."

Yet even then her dream was not realized. She carried on a voluminous correspondence on the subject with every Governor, many officials and literally thousands of individuals. Finally, she appealed directly to President Lincoln. And he heard her cry. On October 3, 1863, he issued the first National proclamation since the time of Washington.

". . . It is a time peculiarly fitting to give thanks since in the midst of Civil War peace has been preserved with all nations, order has been maintained, the laws have been respected, and harmony has prevailed except in the field of military conflict."

Then Mr. Lincoln enumerated all the good things that had come to the nation: mining, extension of the boundaries of states, increase of population. So he said it was fit that the whole American people acknowledge these gifts of God.

"I do, therefore, invite my fellow citizens in every part of the United States and also those who are at sea or who are sojourning in foreign lands to set apart and observe the last Thursday of November next as a Day of Thanksgiving and praise to our Beneficent Father who dwelleth in the heavens . . . and fervently implore the interposition of the Almighty . . . to heal the wounds of the nation to the full enjoyment of peace, harmony, tranquillity and Union."

How grateful Sarah Hale must have been as she sat down with her children to her turkey dinner that year of 1863. Yet she seemed less certain of Lincoln's successor, President Johnson, for again in her editorial of November, three years later, she made a plea for a presidential proclamation. "Shall 1866 be the glorious year that establishes the custom forever, by the union now of every state and territory on this twenty-ninth of November?"

And again the President heard her cry, for the following month she rejoiced that "all the people of the country have been bidden and united on the same day in this festival of public rejoicing giving thanks to Almighty God our Heavenly Father for His blessings on us."

Since when, thanks to her, each successive President has proclaimed a common Thanksgiving Day.

Her outstanding contribution to her age, continued over

her entire professional life of forty years, was her liberation of girls and women from their restricted domestic life to that of the larger life of community and world.

Godey's Lady's Book set the fashions, it is true, for hoop skirts or basques or poke bonnets, for Dutch rarebit and tea rusks, Tudor cake and stewed rabbits, yet its editor deplored the fact that girls could talk of nothing but food or clothes. Nor did she want them to spend the best years of youth in sitting down to wait for a lover, or to grasp at a suitor instead of waiting for a truly great love.

"Every woman has a mission on earth," she affirmed. "There is something to do for each one; a household to put in order, a child to attend to, some degraded and homeless humanity to befriend."

But her greatest weapon in the emancipation of women was that of education. "We are the advocate of a thorough and comprehensive system of female education as the only means by which woman can be qualified to wield her universal moral influence for the best good of the world." This she wrote in the issue of May, 1845.

So she began begging for high schools for girls. Why provide schools only for boys? Year by year she hammered on this need. In 1853 she reminded her readers that there was still only one high school for girls in the United States; this was in Roger Williams' state, in Providence, Rhode Island. To be sure, Massachusetts had started one, but it was promptly so overrun with girls that there was neither room nor teachers enough and so they closed it!

"And why not throw open the profession of teaching children to girls and women?" Surely they were far more fitted for it by nature than men. She told stories of little children's hands struck with rulers until the nails turned black and dropped off. Was not this sure proof of the need of girls as teachers?

Fortunately, the gold rush of '49 came to her aid, and hundreds of young men teachers trekked westward. How Sarah Hale rejoiced! Now at last, girls could creep into their places.

But again the crying need of training teachers filled her heart and her pen. She sent bill after bill to Congress asking for free normal schools for teachers. Her editorials in the 1850s are filled with pleas.

"To advocate this great object of education among women, and placing in their hands the profession of teachers for all the children in the nation, has been our cherished aim for this year [1850]. This has given distinction to this journal and kept it far in advance of all other literary publications in our land. We have sought to elevate the character of women . . . " not to push them forward into the realm of men, but to be better mothers of men, she explains.

It is quite true that it gave her fashion-story magazine distinction. It enlarged her correspondence all over the world. To her desk came educators, judges, senators, all who were interested in the development of the youth of America.

Remembering her own necessity to earn, she was ever alert for new ways and means for other girls and women. In 1853 she listed all the employments then open. She exulted that the author of the *Day Book* in New York employed six women compositors. What an innovation in the printing world to allow girl typesetters! In their own establishment in Philadelphia, she rejoiced that Mr. Godey "employed eighty-eight females, not counting his editor and her female contributors." Not counting either the one hundred and fifty women and girls of the city who earned money in their own homes by hand-coloring the beautiful plates for each issue of the *Lady's Book*.

Mrs. Hale had suggested years before that girls might wait on table in restaurants instead of doing the heavy dish-washing. And she wrote to Mr. A. T. Stewart in New York asking that he try girls as clerks in his elegant store. He did try and he liked them. Other stores followed his lead.

There were many young authors whom she befriended, "females" as well as geniuses like Poe who were poverty stricken and ill. How eagerly they must have turned to her Editor's Page at the back of the book to scan the list of titles of accepted stories. How heartbroken when they read: "We have no room for the following."

In an editorial of November, 1850, Mrs. Hale writes directly to young authors. "It is not the money we get, but the wisdom we gain, which makes authorship desirable for a woman." She advises all would-be writers to keep a diary, and to write in it every day for half an hour. At the end of a year, the author will find that it will be worth more than all her scribbling for periodicals during a lifetime. "For keeping a diary is the best corrective for the fault of the age, which is reading without reflection, and will compel her to think. If the young lady will reread it, she will find her actions, thoughts, hopes and resolutions, and will correct her own faults, will become ashamed of writing on trifles, and will find out and pursue a course of self-training, the only mode of education which makes one really enjoy what is learned."

Well, even if Mrs. Hale does discourage would-be writers, many another sage had advised the keeping of a diary. And many of those published long years after their writing are among our most precious treasures of literature.

ANOTHER of Mrs. Hale's pet hobbies was the opening of the medical profession to women, and the training of medical missionaries.

This came about first through her championship of Elizabeth Blackwell who startled the world by wanting to become a doctor. The mortality of infants was frightful, and Elizabeth felt a "concern" to lower it, and to save both mothers and babies. But not a medical college in the country would admit her. She was denounced in the press and in pulpits as either mad or bad. Only *Godey's* praised her courage and urged her to go on. Even if Harvard Medical refused her, someone ought to take her in.

Finally, the Geneva Medical School of New York accepted the courageous girl and she was graduated in 1849, the first woman to receive a medical degree.

How quick was Sarah Hale to see the worth and power of women physicians. She set about helping to found the Female Medical College of Philadelphia the following year.

Why not train women to go out as medical missionaries? The idea was scouted by the men. Mrs. Hale founded the Ladies' Missionary Society of Philadelphia in 1851. And what a struggle they had for eighteen years to educate the men to the idea of sending out lone females to care for the "heathen."

All during the years of the 1850s, Mrs. Hale's editorials bristled with her campaign to educate the public to this startling new idea. She published telling letters from missionary wives in far-away Turkey or China, in which they described the acute need for women as doctors, since for lack of them, the native women must resort to their witch doctors or to charms.

Nor was Mrs. Hale shy about asking for contributions to her numerous causes. She made her pleas friendly but strong, and put them on the dignified foundation of memberships, from one dollar up.

She never failed to mention large gifts or bequests of women to educational institutions or causes, nor did she ever fail to mention the founding of a new school.

She kept her readers informed of every advance gained for women in England, and quoted large sections of Ruskin's lecture called *Sesame and Lilies*, in which she delighted.

The exact moment when she herself became emancipated from the word "female" seems unrecorded, but once convinced that it should be discarded, she waged a vigorous warfare against the word. On this war she spent eleven years!

In the 1860s her happy warfare was directed especially against "Vassar Female College." She rejoiced when she first heard of Mr. Matthew Vassar's plan to found a college for girls which would be on an equal footing intellectually with Harvard and Dartmouth. Now at last, girls could have what Mrs. Hale herself had so passionately longed for. So she wrote at once to praise his plan and to offer her magazine as his friend.

What a gift that was to Mr. Vassar — not only the hundreds of dollars' worth of free advertising, but the counsel and help of the one woman in America best fitted to advise him.

His first prospectus she vetoed thoroughly. A college for

women without a single one on its faculty? She wrote a stirring editorial. Surely the many seminaries and small colleges had discovered women of the caliber necessary for college teaching. The men at the head of the new college had but to find them.

So the men set about it and finally managed to discover Maria Mitchell for astronomy, a woman as resident physician, and eighteen women under-teachers. What a triumph for Mrs. Hale!

In her issue of August, 1866, Mrs. Hale speaks enthusiastically of receiving the first Annual Catalogue of the new college, with a list of twenty-two ladies on its faculty against eight men, to teach three hundred and fifty-three students. She rejoices greatly at its high aim, and hopes that it may raise women intellectually and morally. "Thus she will be enabled to perceive her true work and the best means to reach it and to do it."

"We look to the graduates of Vassar Female College to elevate woman by showing how she can by the best cultivation and best use of all her faculties, bring about the elevation of home, society and of the world."

A very large mission but a glorious one for the graduates of any school.

For many months she had been carrying on a bright and vivacious correspondence with Mr. Vassar on the deletion of the odious word "female" from his college.

Now she carried her campaign into her issue of August, 1866. "We have fallen into the evil habit of classifying American women with the animal tribe, by using the term female as a sign of the *human feminine*. . . Let this odium be corrected. Not Vassar Female College, but Vassar College for Young Women."

The moment the magazine came into his hands, Mr. Vassar penned her a letter:

"My dear Mrs. Hale:

"I hasten to inform you that the great agony is over—your long cherished wishes realized. Woman stands redeemed, at least so far as Vassar College is concerned, from the vulgarism in the associated name of 'female' . . . "

The September issue carried her shout of victory. "On June twenty-fifth last, the Trustees of Vassar College voted unanimously to drop Female from the title."

You may see for yourselves today the space over the door of the main hall where the stone-carved FEMALE has been replaced by a blank stone.

Mrs. Hale gave three cheers and hearty thanks to the Trustees and hoped that all other institutions in America would "soon follow the good example of Vassar College."

No wonder Sarah Hale made such a place for her magazine in the nineteenth century. No wonder she was so beloved by a multitude of men and women in every walk of life; by writers, women in lonely posts in foreign lands, seamen, teachers, every girl in America who was trying to earn her living. Rich and poor, high and lowly, looked to her as an arbiter of good judgment and taste and a staunch supporter in any trial. How often had she not begged her readers to "aid young teachers and all those struggling to redeem the world from the bonds of ignorance and evil." For forty years she had held up to girls the highest ideals of womanhood: beauty of character, of intellect, of face and of form.

She herself was exquisitely small, with large sparkling

eyes. Her hair parted in the middle fell in curls on either side of her lovely face. No wonder her friends called her "the duchess of fiction."

Her last editorial to her one hundred thousand readers, she wrote in 1878. "And now, having reached my ninetieth year, I must bid farewell to my countrywomen, with the hope that this work of half a century may be blessed to the furtherance of their happiness and usefulness in their Divinely appointed sphere. New avenues for higher culture and for good works are opening before them, which fifty years ago were unknown. That they may improve these opportunities, and be faithful to their high vocation, is my heartfelt prayer."

Not even at ninety was her hair gray, nor her eyes less bright, nor her face wrinkled. Her biographer, Ruth E. Finley, tells us her secret for keeping beautiful—more potent than all the myriad aids to beauty today. It is whispered that in her top bureau drawer she always kept strips of brown wrapping paper, which, moistened with vinegar and applied to her temples and chin, were a sure antidote against wrinkles.

She made her own hand lotion of lard, rose-water and cocoanut milk, and never washed her hands without using it.

She had made her mind distinguished by storing it with great ideas. She sought out in individual men and women their greatness and celebrated it. No wonder her anthologies of distinguished women went into many editions.

She enlarged her heart by a compassion which was world wide in its dimensions. Yet she was not a mere theoretician, but a practical philanthropist; she took time away from her busy desk to go out into life and act wherever she felt the need, whether in seamen's homes, or on committees of children's hospitals, missionary medical societies, or educational institutions.

And yet, ironically enough, like Lewis Carroll, she is known chiefly for her nonsense rhyme, "Mary had a little lamb." Many others have claimed its authorship, but you will find it included in her first book of poems for children, treasured in the Boston Public Library. The hundreds of parodies it called forth were often laughed over by Mary's editor-author.

Also included in this first little volume of her child poems, which she had written for her own dear five, was this familiar prayer set in verse:

Our Father in heaven,
We hallow Thy name!
May Thy kingdom be hold,
On earth be the same—
O, give to us, daily,
Our portion of bread!
It is from Thy bounty
That all must be fed.

Forgive our transgressions,
And teach us to know
That humble compassion
That pardons each foe—
Keep us from temptation,
From weakness and sin—
And Thine be the glory
Forever—Amen!

THOMAS PAINE
1737–1809

LIKE MOST English boys born on a farm, Tom Paine lived close to nature. Among his pets, snakes, ants, robins, rabbits, was a crow who got killed by a hawk. Tom buried him in the garden under a sheltering beech tree. Tom was eight years old then. He caught up a bit of paper and a pencil, put his tongue in his cheek, and wrote:

Here lies the body of John Crow,
Who once was high but now is low;
Ye brother crows take warning all,
For as you rise, so must you fall.

There is calm reason in this, and philosophy and sage advice, which he himself was to need much later in life. It was as if Tom were writing an epitaph for himself in place of John Crow.

In August, when all the hedges bloomed overnight with spider webs, Tom ran out to find a big fly caught in one. When he had broken the gossamer threads and liberated the insect, he sat down to write another verse. He felt strangely happy. To set free a fly—a winged thing imprisoned—to watch it hesitate for an instant, as if it could scarcely believe its good fortune, and then suddenly take to its wings and go zooming off. . . What a thing it was, this freedom. Tom felt as if he had wings himself. But then his mother called him sharply to stop day-dreaming and go off on the errand she had sent him. And he came back to earth.

That night he dreamed about finding a whole garden full of spider webs, each full of flies, and of setting them all free. He would be a kind of hero then, to the fly kingdom at least, a liberator; but the spiders might not look upon him kindly if he deprived them of dinner. What if they all decided to march in and bite him? Well then, he would put on knightly armor, that was all.

When his friends set snares to catch a hare, Tom went round and sprang them, though not because it was against the law. And woe betide the boy whose trap worked. For he was sure of a beating from Tom Paine's fists which he wouldn't soon forget.

"Well," Tom would pant, "just think how you would feel if you were the hare, *caught*."

And when crisp fall days brought the sound of the horn, and the scarlet-coated riders and the dogs in leash, the boys would run to the edge of the road to see them pass; lords and ladies, huntsmen, "whippers in" and all. Only Tom would stick out his tongue at them. And all that day Tom's face would scowl as he kept thinking to the fox, "Run, old thing . . . run for your life . . . use your four swift feet . . . don't let them catch you. Use your cunning head. Stay free!"

Now Tom went to the grammar school of Thetford to learn the three Rs, and much about the history of England, with kings and wars and rebellions. His heart would burn at the sense of injustice suffered by the English people at the hands of arrogant and selfish kings.

It made him restless, full of dreams. He longed to be a hero. Thetford of Norfolk seemed very small. His father's work of farming and stay-making (corset-making, we call it) had no poetry, no glory, nothing at all to recommend it. And though at thirteen he left school with a longing to dash off to be the hero he dreamed, yet life held much of discipline for him, with years of apprenticeship in learning that odious stay-making.

Often he heard in his heart the call of America.

"I happened, when a school boy," he tells us, "to pick up a pleasant natural history of Virginia, and my inclination from that day of seeing the western side of the Atlantic never left me."

At sixteen he could stand it no longer, so he slipped away to a seaport, Great Yarmouth, perhaps, and looked longingly from the wharf at the trim little sloop with sails all ready to lift. An old salt pointed out her owner who rejoiced in the cheerful name of Captain Death. All the better, as it had the tang of a pirate or a jolly rover smuggler.

"Will you take me on, sir? I am strong and not afraid of anything."

"Time will tell," was the laconic reply.

But he was a likely lad with his broad shoulders and his snapping black eyes. So Tom and his bundle soon clambered aboard. How his heart pounded as he watched the sails billowing out! Free. Off to begin life.

Yet not for long, for his Quaker father haled him home when they touched port again, and set him sternly down to his stays, stitching in the long steels that would make an eighteenth-century lady's back as straight as her prejudices.

Once again the sea called, and the boy went off on a brig, this time into an actual sea-fight against the French.

But again it was too soon. He was not yet to cross the high seas. He found he could not rush his destiny. There was more discipline ahead for him, many years of floundering about, of failing in one thing or another. But he dreamed and he thought; he saw how people suffered. He caught the temper of King George and his parliament—their oppressive despotism. He heard lectures on science. He and his friends held debates on world politics.

It was much like a college debating society today, except that Tom Paine was set apart in the minds of his friends. They might never leave the small island on which they lived, but Tom would. He would go to far places—be somebody, they felt.

> *"Immortal Paine," one of them eulogized him,*
> *"Thy soul of fire must sure ascend the sky."*

He felt it himself and was impatient to begin, not realizing that he needed to be toughened by struggle, needed to learn compassion from failure, needed to collect taxes for the government in order to know how hard it was for the poor in England to meet them, and how little they got in return.

He indulged in much talk about the colonies in America —about their repeated requests for representation in government. He heard much about their stubbornness against a sugar tax and a stamp tax. Three thousand miles was a long distance, yet Thomas Paine bridged it in his imagination because his sympathies were all for the colonists, and his indignation stirred against the arrogance and injustice of the King. He could tell the king what to do. He would set America free to live her own life. He felt rebellious and out of joint with his times, out of sorts with life in England.

He lost his job. The sheriff put his furniture in the street. He went up to London. Like many other young people in trouble, he sought a great city, hoping that there lay his fortune and his destiny.

And so it did, for in London he met a great American called Benjamin Franklin, still engaged in a futile attempt to hold intact the British Empire and yet advance the cause of the just rights of her American colonies. Thomas Paine did not seek out Franklin to tell him his personal troubles, but to express to him his belief in the future of America.

It must have been an electric meeting, with sparks flying from one to the other. Franklin, beset on every hand by difficulties, about to be impeached from his high office of Postmaster-General, must have been warmed indeed by the ardor of the younger man.

Yet to Thomas Paine, the grand thing about their meeting was that Franklin knew him at once as a fellow patriot.

Washington, Franklin, Paine and Warren, Gates, Han-

cock and Greene—their names were to be linked inseparably in Blake's *Prophecy of America*. What matter now that in England Paine was considered a failure?

"America has need of you," Franklin told him. "If you are free, why not leave at once by the next sailing vessel? Go to my own city of Philadelphia. In serving the Commonwealth, you will find yourself."

Somehow Thomas Paine got together his passage fee and set out on his adventures. He felt that he would never again be what he was, that in America a new life awaited him, a life of victory, of glory.

To how many thousands has America not been the Promised Land, dreamed of, saved for, looked forward to for years? Peasants and students from Italy or from Lithuania, from Finland or from Greece, have found freedom to work and to save, have known happiness beyond their wildest hopes. And they have contributed much to America: they have built her railroads, dug her coal and mined her gold; they have erected her skyscrapers and managed her banks; they have turned the wheels that make her the leading industrial nation of the world.

Yet not one immigrant has given to America what Thomas Paine gave, not in brawn but in ideas and in ideals: precious, priceless, imperishable gifts. And to Thomas Paine America gave the opportunity that comes not once in a lifetime, not once in a century perhaps, but once in an age of time, an opportunity to become the Elder Brother to a nation, one of the Immortals.

It came about in this way. When, in November, 1774, Thomas landed in Philadelphia, he presented his letter of introduction to Franklin's son-in-law, William Bache. Mr. Bache did not size him up as a failure, but liked him and found a post for him, as editor of the new *Pennsylvania Magazine*. So at once Thomas Paine had a tool, a pen and a voice. And he had something to say to Pennsylvanians that they liked to hear, so that the subscription list soon increased from three hundred to fifteen hundred.

Paine had an unshakable conviction about the high destiny of America, for since the country was divinely discovered, divinely set going, it must be meant for some far-off divine end, he thought.

"The degree of improvement which America has already arrived at is unparalleled and astonishing," he wrote in his magazine, "but 'tis miniature to what it will one day boast of, if Heaven continue her happiness."

As he had suspected while still in England, justice was all on the side of the colonies. Now he pointed out that England had been trying to rule them, as she had India and Africa, without any humanity or justice. But these colonists were men of another temper; many of them were former rebels of Europe, the revolters against the tyranny of despots, whether temporal or spiritual.

No wonder, then, that they threw their tea to the fishes rather than submit to unjust taxation. To them, King George's whole theory of government was autocratic and despotic. Of course the colonies should have a voice in making their own laws. Of course they should have trial by jury.

Thomas Paine knew well enough the temper of England. Was not William Wilberforce engaging in a life struggle to free her black slaves in the West Indies? Instead, he could not yet secure even a measure of control over the atrocious and barbarous traffic in human lives.

Was not Hannah More struggling to bring education and

humanity to her Mendip villages, long neglected by the superficial snobbery of churchly aristocracy?

Was not John Wesley thundering at hearts hardened by smugness and prejudice?

Were not men and women still hanged for pilfering game to eat? And dissenters still sat in the pillory at the marketplace to be jeered at by small ruffians; while the poor still bent their backs to toil for the gentry.

Well he knew that neither George III nor Lord North nor the Bedfords could grant liberty to the colonists because they had it not in their own minds or souls. Instead, they were used to resorting to cruelty in order to force a people to its knees. America could never find peace or justice under such a system.

Thomas smarted under the atrocities committed by the English garrisons in Boston, as if they had been done in Philadelphia. Consequently, he wrote in his issue of January, 1775, the first plea for independence published in the country. "When I reflect . . . on all this . . . I hesitate not for a moment to believe that the Almighty will finally separate America from Britain. Call it Independency or what you will, if it is the cause of God and Humanity it will go on."

Hundreds had dared to think this very thought, but no one before had dared to voice it. Thomas Paine dared. He had not a drop of coward's blood, he was made of the stuff of heroes.

Scarcely four months later, English soldiers fired on the Minutemen of Lexington who had refused to give up their store of ammunition. That was "the shot heard round the world." Thomas Paine thrilled to it, and applauded the brave New Englanders for defending their rights.

And Boston's angel cried aloud. . .

But he saw clearly that it was a larger issue than that of repulsing British troops from Boston. It was not a small rebellion to be easily crushed as George III had crushed other rebellions in India or in Scotland or in Wales. Thomas Paine had a vision of what America could mean to the world, if she were free, independent from this source of constant friction, able to make her own laws, to build her own ships, to regulate her own trade.

Fired to white heat by his thoughts, he wrote a pamphlet which he signed "Common Sense."

"Rush it through," he begged a Philadelphia printer, "for I want it to come out as soon as the King's speech arrives on the next packet."

By the fortune of heaven, as he thought, the two actually did come out on the same day.

The first printing of *Common Sense* was snapped up like firecrackers and made as much noise as a cannon shot. With the proceeds, Paine bought mittens for the colonial troops who were starting off for Quebec. "I did this to do honor to the cause," he explained.

When the first printing was exhausted, he enlarged it and arranged for six thousand more to be struck off, again at his own expense.

Men thought it had been written by Franklin or by Samuel Adams or John Adams. It was caught up by everyone who could read, until some hundred and twenty thousand copies had been sold, flying as if on wings east and west, north and south, through the thirteen colonies.

The effect was electric. People said, "It's just what I myself think."

General Washington found it full of "sound logic and unanswerable reasoning."

Now whatever was in these two documents, that of George III and that of Thomas Paine? The first was in answer to the demands of the First Congress meeting in New York, for a settlement of grievances: no more unjust taxes; no more destruction of charters; no more substitution of laws made by a Parliament at a distance of three thousand miles in space and of three or four months in time; no more attacks of British troops on defenseless women and children . . . a long list.

Disregarding these, the King asserted that his Parliament had the right to bind the colonies in all cases whatever, and denounced them soundly as rebels and traitors, punishable accordingly.

And the pamphlet called *Common Sense?* * It reviewed the whole relationship with England in order to show why any reconciliation or future trust was impossible, why the colonies ought to unite and to separate from England, and to declare themselves independent and free. No wonder it rocked the colonies from end to end.

For a master hand wrote this great pamphlet which began with calm, clear, large reasoning:

"The cause of America is, in a great measure, the cause of all mankind."

It lifted the colonists from the small quarrel with England to think on larger issues. They had grown nearsighted from staring at their grievances. Now they were invited to put on world spectacles with which to view themselves.

* cf. *Complete Works of Thomas Paine,* Vol. 2. V. Parke & Co. 1908.

"Many circumstances have, and will arise, which are not local, but universal, and through which the principles of all lovers of mankind are affected. . . The laying of a country desolate with fire and sword, declaring war against the natural rights of all mankind, and extirpating the defenders thereof from the face of the earth, is the concern of every man to whom nature hath given the power of feeling." Thus the introduction.

In Part I, Paine shows that government is made necessary by our own lack of moral virtue. That is, if every man were just and honest and kindly, we would have no need of government. But at least we, a free people, need not submit either to the tyranny of an English despot or to that of his aristocratic pawns. While "the Commons, on whose virtue the freedom of England depends, have no voice whatever in our behalf."

In Part II, he levels to the dust the whole principle of the divine right of kings, and of the law of hereditary succession. From the Bible story of Gideon, he draws the conclusion that men were never meant to be governed except by the Lord.

Then the men of Israel said unto Gideon,
Rule thou over us, both thou, and thy son,
and thy son's son also: for thou hast
delivered us from the hand of Midian.

And Gideon said unto them,
I will not rule over you, neither shall my
son rule over you:
the Lord shall rule over you.

Judges 8: 22,23

Moreover, Paine asserts, it is falacious and ridiculous to trace proudly the line of English kings back to William the Conqueror, who was no more than a pirate and a French robber, "landing with an armed banditti, and establishing himself king of England against the consent of the natives. It is in plain terms a very paltry, rascally origin. In fact, it certainly hath no divinity in it."

In proof of the fact that a king is no guarantor of peace to his people, he states that since the Conquest, thirty kings and two minors have reigned, "in which time there have been eight civil wars and nineteen rebellions," not to mention the foreign wars in which other lands were ravaged.

In Part III, he strikes again the note of prophecy, his vision of the grandeur and world scope of this struggle of the colonies.

"This is not the affair of a city, a county, a province, a kingdom, but of a continent, of at least one-eighth part of the habitable globe. Nor is it the concern of a day, a year, or an age. All posterity will be more or less affected even to the end of time, by the proceedings now."

Whence came his authority for this? What master mind used his pen?

"Would a mother devour her own children?" he asks. But England is not even the only mother of America, since "this new world hath been the asylum for the present lovers of civil and religious liberty from every part of Europe." Moreover, since they were driven from England by tyranny, why own allegiance to such a mother?

He reviews the involvement of Spain and France in our difficulties. "What have we to do with setting the world at defiance?" he demands. "Our plan is commerce, and that, well attended to, will secure us the peace and friendship of all Europe; because it is the interest of Europe to have America a free port. Her trade will always be her protection."

How far-seeing were his eyes. How wisely tolerant and yet how unequivocal is his stand against becoming a party to contentions and quarrels not our own. In this he gave an ideal and an idea later to be caught up by Monroe, an ideal which has served us well these two hundred years and more.

"As Europe is our market for trade, we ought to form no partial connection with any part of it. It is the true interest of America to steer clear of European contentions, which she can never do, while, by her dependence on Britain, she is made the make-weight [that is, with Spain and France] in the scale of British politics."

So he marshals his arguments, clear, calm, unhurried, and urges separation and independence. But he senses also the urgency for acting now. "The present winter is worth an age if rightly employed, but if lost or neglected, the whole continent will partake of the misfortune." This is a grave warning. Paine had the boldness of a seer, of a sage-king, of a prophet of Israel.

But he goes further still. He outlines a plan for a Congress of the united colonies, which, with equal representation, must elect a president and sit in annual assembly. He suggests, to avoid favoritism, that the president be elected from each of the thirteen colonies in turn.

The first proceeding would be to send two representatives from each colony to a Continental Conference in order to draw up a Charter, a sort of Magna Carta of the united colonies. "Remembering that our strength is continental, not provincial, securing to all men freedom, property rights, free exercise of religion, a vote, just taxation."

He quotes Dragonetti: *

"'The science of the politician consists in fixing the true point of happiness and freedom. Those men would deserve the gratitude of ages who should discover a mode of government that contained the greatest sum of individual happiness, with the least national expense.'"

How we should hail such a politician today. Would that a Thomas Paine might rise up to show us how to purge our whole political system of its graft and greed and love of personal enrichment.

Then, remembering the many Tories in the colonies, and the groups still in favor of temporizing with England and remaining loyal at any price, he cries:

"But where, say some, is the king in America? I'll tell you, friends, He reigns above, and doth not make havoc of mankind, like the royal brute of Britain." Strong language, but it was true that the King had authorized despotic and cruel measures to put down this rebellious people, thinking thus to frighten the many by extreme measures to the few.

In Part IV, he goes a step further. "All men now believe that the time will come when the colonies ought to separate from England, but they know not how to find that time." No need to wait. For "the time hath found us."

One is reminded of Rupert Brooke:

Now God be praised who matched me for this hour. . .

So might Thomas Paine have cried out for himself, during the twenty years of his public life. So did he cry out now

* *On Virtue and Rewards.*

for the new democracy: "The hour hath found us—let us match the hour."

And for this event, the colonies must unite. "It is not in numbers, but in unity, that our great strength lies," he affirms.

"Youth is the seed time of good habits, as well in nations as in individuals. So it is wisest to form a union of colonies now, before trade can pit one against another. Moreover, we are already drawn together now, by adversity and trouble. A union is easier today than it will ever be again."

He advises that the common charter of government be formed first, and the choice of men to execute it later. "Nations have let slip this very chance that is ours today. Our opportunity is to begin government at the right end.

"The independence of America should have been considered as dating from and published by, the first musket that was fired against her." (That very shot of April 19, 1775.)

"We have every opportunity and every encouragement before us, to form the noblest, purest constitution on the face of the earth. We have it in our power to begin the world over again."

And now with the spirit of an Isaiah of old he predicts: "The birthday of a new world is at hand, and a race of men, perhaps as numerous as all Europe contains, are to receive their portion of freedom . . . from the events of a few months. The reflection is awful. . . How trifling, how ridiculous, do the little paltry covetings of a few weak men appear when weighed against the business of a world."

So he calls upon all men to unite, to forget differences of Whig and Tory and be each a good citizen, socially minded, and with sympathy for each other, a virtuous supporter of the rights of mankind, of the free and independent United States of America.

No wonder that thousands of copies of his *Common Sense* were read and reread. No wonder it fired men's souls and minds, and united the colonies into one mind and spirit. No wonder that, four months later, in July, 1776, the Declaration of Independence was actually adopted.

Although Thomas Jefferson has always been credited with drawing up this masterly document, The Thomas Paine National Association has made out a very good case for Paine as the author of the original draft from which Jefferson wrote the accepted form. The use of that small word "hath," so common to all of Paine's writings, the plea for the abolition of slaves, which he had written for his magazine, the wording of the phrases, and the repetition of many of the same ideas as those of *Common Sense*—all this, they maintain, points to a very close and intimate collaboration by the two life-long friends.

Four years later the proposed Constitution was written. Twenty-one years later came the Monroe Doctrine of non-interference with other nations and of closing the American continent to further establishment by any European power.

But the immediate effect of Paine's pamphlet was to unify the army, to give it a rallying cry of independence—something to fight hard for. The author might have cleared hundreds of pounds from its sale, but he felt too keenly the sense of a mission, and dedicated all gains from the work to serve the cause of freedom. Actually, he came out thirty-nine pounds in debt, though this was made right later by a purse given him by generous and grateful friends in Philadelphia.

AND now, since the army was greatly in need of volunteers, in spite of his Quaker upbringing Paine offered himself as aide-de-camp to General Greene. Perhaps this was not without a pricking of conscience, but he says, "I am thus far a Quaker, that I would gladly agree with all the world to lay aside the use of arms and settle matters by negotiation; but unless the whole will, the matter ends, and I take up my musket and thank Heaven He has put it in my power."

Moreover, when the good Quakers in the Penn colony protested, believing still in nonresistance and in loyalty to the Crown, he replied: "Would you stand and turn your backs if your wives and children were set upon by thieves and murderers? What difference, then, if they be New England wives and children, and the thief and murderer be the British nation? To arms!"

George III had retaliated for this impudence of arming by proclaiming the colonies in rebellion and hiring mercenary soldiers from Hesse. Nor did he hesitate to enlist the red men and negro slaves to help him subdue the rebels, though the red men knew no law but that of the tomahawk, and no warfare but that of ambush and surprise attack.

So, all that summer and fall and early winter, Thomas Paine lived among the soldiers, sharing their scant rations, their thin equipment. The war went badly. General Washington was defeated . . . New York fell into the hands of General Howe . . . Fort Washington could scarcely hold out another month . . . the army became discouraged. Thomas Paine did what he could to hearten his own regiment. But he could touch so few. At the darkest moment, using his drum for a desk, he sat down in camp and wrote *The Crisis*, signing the pamphlet "Common Sense."

Professor David Muzzey quotes the French Revolutionary general, Kellermann, as saying that "the *Marseillaise* was worth one hundred thousand men." And that "Paine's *Crisis* made a new army." *

"These are the times that try men's souls," Paine began. "The summer soldier and the sunshine patriot will, in this crisis, shrink from the service of his country; but he that stands it NOW, deserves the love and thanks of man and woman. Tyranny, like hell, is not easily conquered, yet we have this consolation with us, that the darker the conflict, the more glorious the triumph. . .

"Heaven knows how to put a proper price upon its good, and it would be strange indeed, if so celestial an article as FREEDOM should not be highly rated."

Great, calm, unhurried words again to fire the men with something greater to think on than bodily discomforts and loss of battles.

How the men must have glowed at Paine's tribute to George Washington, their General-in-Chief.

"There is a natural firmness in some minds, which cannot be unlocked by trifles, but which, when unlocked, discovers a cabinet of fortitude; and I reckon it among those kind of public blessings which we do not immediately see, that God hath blest him with uninterrupted health, and given him a mind that can even flourish upon care."

Again he calls upon the colonies to unite, since none can escape the hurt of each.

Again, too, he reiterates his belief in the high destiny of America. "God is surely watching over this land, and will

* cf. Bibliography.

not let her be destroyed by force, since she has ever striven for peace."

During these months with the army, he had seen men of every sort. Now he tells which he can admire.

"I love the man that can smile in trouble, that can gather strength from distress, and grow brave by reflection. 'Tis the business of little minds to shrink; but he whose heart is firm, and whose conscience approves his conduct, will pursue his principles unto death."

Nor were these but vain and rhetorical words. Thomas Paine was prepared to show men in three countries that he could not be bought, that his heart could remain firm, and that he could pursue his principles even unto death.

Later, Daniel Webster was to catch up Paine's cry of Union of the Colonies, in his Union of the States. And Lincoln at twenty was to pore over Paine's writings by the light of his wood fire, until into his soul too entered the same great principle of union.

Now the whole army caught up the cry, "These are the times that try men's souls . . . " and marched on under Washington, through ice and snow, crossing the Delaware to rout the Hessians at Trenton, finally defeating Cornwallis at Princeton.

Thus it was that at every dark hour during the whole of that seven-years' struggle, the people as well as the army grew to expect another of these timely editions of *The Crisis*, until, in his last one, the fifteenth, on the anniversary of the Battle of Lexington, in 1783, Paine rejoices that, " 'The times that tried men's souls' . . . are over, and that the greatest and completest revolution the world ever knew is gloriously and happily accomplished."

The Declaration stands like a rock, the Constitution is

written in the stars, we are Americans living in the United States of America—he was the first to use this term—and a great and universal destiny still awaits us. We have only to grow and to keep true to our ideals of justice and liberty, of happiness for all men.

So he spoke to his generation, and so equally he speaks to ours. Through his writing, Thomas Paine became a national and international figure. Appointed by Congress virtual Foreign Secretary, all letters and documents for foreign powers passed through his hands. He went to France at the close of the war, to ask for a loan of francs, and returned with a large gift of silver as well. He had found Louis XVI generous and sympathetic beyond his dream.

At last Thomas Paine returned home to Thetford in Norfolk, a famous man, to find his father dead, and his mother in her ninety-first year. He had long supported her, and now settled upon her a sum for life. How proud she must have been of him, this son who had become so celebrated in the New World.

The artist Romney begged to paint his portrait; his was a sensitive face, wistful and appealing. His friend Rickman describes him at this time as "about five foot ten in height, rather athletic, broad-shouldered and a little stooped. His eye, of which the painter could not convey the exquisite meaning, was full, brilliant and piercing; it had in it the muse of fire. In his dress and person he was cleanly; he wore his hair cued, with side curls powdered so that he looked altogether like a gentleman of the old French school. His manners were easy and gracious: his knowledge universal and boundless. In private company and among friends, his conversation had every fascination that anecdote, novelty and truth could give it. In most company and among strangers he said little. . ." *

Would he settle down now, his mother wondered, tend the farm, and go back to stay-making?

No, he had work to do, an old hobby, iron bridges. For he was the first ever to attempt a single iron span. And where did he get the idea? From the spider, the one who used to stretch her web in the garden.

So off he went to have cast a giant span of two hundred and ten feet. When it was ready he had it sent by ship to London and set up in a field at Paddington. It became the marvel and the wonder of the country, and Paine was happy as a boy over it, even if the English were slow to accept the startling idea. He dreamed of spanning the Thames and the Seine and the Hudson and the Schuylkill. Why, it would open a whole new era of commerce to the world, this single span iron bridge. Now that he had finished with revolutions, he had any number of things in the back of his head to work out for humanity: a ship run by steam, a smokeless candle, to discover the cause of Yellow Fever, the investigation of fixed stars. Like Franklin, the genius of his odd moments ran to science.

But just then he had to stop his bridge-building after all, and only because Edmund Burke had brought out a scathing criticism of the French Revolution and the whole system of representative government. So what could Thomas Paine do but sit down to answer his nonsense about the glory of hereditary succession? Didn't Burke know that it was impossible to hand down wisdom from father to son? Didn't he read history enough to know that not all the wisdom of Solomon could keep his son from becoming a

* Biography of Paine by Thomas Richman in *Works*, Vol. I.

tyrant? And did not even Pericles, the wisest ruler of Greece, despair of making a wise man of his own son?

So that was why he wrote *The Rights of Man,* as an answer to Burke.

James Madison said of it: "It is the exposition of the principles on which the government of the United States is based."

Perhaps to Thomas Paine it was simple enough, this statement of liberty, of security, of happiness for a people. It is based on Kant's ethical principle of a test of the good for one being the good for all. It is to safeguard a nation from allowing, through the form of democracy, the very same tyranny it had rebelled against. In a changing world, he would caution the generation of today from making laws which might be wholly unfit for a generation of tomorrow, or a hundred years hence. "Dead men have no right to legislate for living men," he insists. It is the wise provision of a man who thinks in terms of centuries.

The pamphlet stirred up deep whirlpools in three nations. In America it was hailed with joy by Thomas Jefferson, but despised by John Adams. For already, money, power, family were beginning to crowd out the rights and needs of the middle-class man. How would the new republic go? Would the new Federalism be but another form of royalty of privilege, of the divine rights of the gentry, the Whigs? *The Rights of Man* began to work in men's minds. Even though Paine was three thousand miles away, he yet wielded the power to make men think, to weigh issues and to plan for that America of the future, in which he had such unbounded faith. And nine years later, he was able to write a letter of warm congratulation to his friend Thomas Jefferson, who had just been elected to the presidency. The side of democracy had won. *The Rights* were to be respected.

The pamphlet stirred up more than a whirlpool in England. It swept the land like a flood. Paine became the popular hero of the hour, whom the people hailed as "deliverer." For they saw clearly enough that they must demand a transference of power from the Peers to the House of Commons whom they themselves must elect by wider suffrage. Then Government might rule the Crown.

But when the Government learned the cause of this wind of revolt, they suppressed the issues, clapped the printers into prison, and tried Paine for sedition. Fortunately, he sailed from Dover just twenty minutes in advance of the king's officers who arrived with a warrant for his arrest. A fateful day that, in September, 1792.

In France, his *Rights of Man* had been translated and snatched up by all the revolutionists who had made their desperate assault against the Bastille three years before. The previous month, the title of French Citizen was conferred upon Paine, among eighteen illustrious foreigners including Washington, Wilberforce and Schiller, "for having prepared the enfranchisement of peoples." A citizen had been sent to England to escort Paine to the French Assembly.

So now, in a little space of seven hours, Thomas Paine was to experience the sharpest contrasts of his life. Having been branded a traitor by England, hooted and harried, he had had to flee for his life, aided by that blessed poet and artist, William Blake. It was an ignominious and anxious flight, knowing that his friends might be imprisoned in his stead.

A seven hours' tossing in a little vessel upon the Channel

brought him to Calais. To his amazement he landed in a blare of trumpets and a roll of drums. He was received by the mayor of the city and by citizen officials of the new Republic, to the shouting of the people and the salute of troops. He was the center of admiring eyes at the grand banquet tendered him in the town hall.

And all this because of his pen, because of these writings of his head and his heart striving to make men free.

If you can meet with triumph and disaster,
And treat those two imposters just the same. . .

He learned that he had been elected as deputy from four departments to the new Convention which was to write a Constitution. Accepting that of Calais, he journeyed to Paris to take his seat—an honor which had not been offered him in America. At his hotel he was so beset and besieged with visitors that he could find no time for his writing, and so had to hold levees two mornings a week until he could retire to the country.

He learned that his *Common Sense* had been bound with Rousseau's *Contrat Social* into one edition. Bonaparte rushed to assure him that he kept his *Rights (Droits de l'Homme)* under his pillow at night, hoping that its wisdom might impress his mind while he slept. (Alas, he showed too well later that he had profited but little from the practice.) Danton said to Paine, "What you have done for the happiness and liberty of your country, I have in vain tried to do for mine."

Now Paine might have become a tower of strength and of homely wisdom to the new Republic of France, even as he had to America, but for an unforeseen battle over the person of poor Louis XVI. Paine had worked steadfastly against the party that desired to restore the monarchy, seeking to stabilize the form of government with equal representation by the people.

But a new party called the Jacobins had grown to power within the Assembly, a party advocating violence and repudiating all Paine's idealism. The cry grew stronger and stronger against the king. Alarmed, Paine tried to stem it with reason and with compassion.

It must have taken great moral courage to defy his colleagues. But he prepared as strong a defense for Louis Capet as he could pen. The king as a private citizen might have been a charming and lovable man. It was not the man but his office that ought to be made an end of. Paine plead with them in the name of humanity, of decency, to spare Louis' life, substituting imprisonment and then exile.

But Marat and Robespierre were in no temper for compassion, and refused to listen longer to his translated speech. "That's not by Thomas Paine," they shouted.

"Yes, it is correct, every word," Paine himself protested, hurrying down from his seat to the floor. "Louis Capet helped as no other foreigner to bring freedom from tyranny for America. Liberty and humanity have ever been the words that have expressed my thoughts, and it is my conviction that the union of these two principles, in all cases, tends more than anything else to insure the grandeur of a nation."

Danton and the plaudits of his group were smothered by the impatient booing at Paine. For the party in power were not concerned about the grandeur of a future nation at that moment, so much as in wreaking vengeance on a system of despotism, the symbol of which was a royal king and his royal family.

They trampled underfoot Paine's justice and moral reasoning, just as later they trampled upon the man himself. Having entered upon a reign of terror, they marked for the guillotine not only the royal family and all the noblemen and women they could lay hands on, but threw Paine himself into prison. Here the much hailed, much lauded liberator lay, ill and half starved, for nearly a year. They marked him too, for the guillotine, or thought they did. By some strange twist of fate, the white mark was chalked, instead, on the door of his neighbor.

Paine had tried hard to teach the revolutionists the difference between liberty and license, and the importance, the necessity of preserving society from the latter. Now it was too late. In the second revolution all the terrible hatred, long suppressed, rose to the surface. In the great boiling cauldron, the scum covered the top. In their delirium of liberty, men and women lost their reason, their humanity.

It was this that ate into Thomas Paine's very soul, for it was one of the major issues of his life.

"I defend the cause of the poor," he declared, "of the tradesmen, of the farmer, and of all those on whom the real burden of taxes fall, but above all, I defend the cause of humanity."

Nor was it an easy defense. In England, it branded him as a traitor and put a price on his head. In France, it all but cost him his life, and denied him the very liberty for which he had worked for twenty years. In America, it seared his last seven years with persecution, calumny, mental crucifixion.

To the one whom he called "A little corner in the world," he wrote of his yearning to return to America, to see his friends, and his good horse "Button" once more. Then he lifted his eyes to the far future, like a Hebrew seer.

"A thousand years hence," he wrote, "perhaps in less, America may be what Europe now is. The innocence of her character that won the hearts of all nations in her favor may sound like a romance and her inimitable virtue as if it had never been.

"The ruins of that liberty for which thousands bled may just furnish material for a village tale, or exhort a sigh from rustics, while the fashionable of that day, enveloped in dissipation, shall deride the principles and deny the fact.

"When we contemplate the fall of empires and the extinction of nations of the ancient world we see but little more to excite our regret than the moldering ruins of pompous palaces, magnificent universities, walls and towers of the most costly workmanship; but when the empire of America shall fall, the subject for contemplative sorrow will be infinitely greater than crumbling brass or marble. It will not then be said, here stood a temple of lost antiquity, here rose a babel of invisible heights, or there a palace of sumptuous extravagance; but here (ah painful thought!) the noblest work of human wisdom, the grandest scene of human glory, and the fair cause of freedom rose and fell."

Very impersonally, now, he could view his own unique share in this freedom. But during those troubled years in France, there came to him the consciousness of the cyclic rise and fall of governments in their varied forms: a monarchy of despotism overturned by a democracy, which would in turn allow the tyranny of an oligarchy within its own republic, to be followed in time by a dictatorship, and, as the great wheel turned, would lead back to monarchy, then finally to the kingdom of the prophets and the sibyls.

Now his eyes could travel beyond Europe, beyond America, to view that kingdom prophesied by the Grecian Sibyl: *

"The kingdom of God shall come upon good men; for the earth, which is the producer of all things, shall yield to men the best and infinite fruits; and the cities shall be full of good men, and there shall be no war in the earth, nor tumult: nor shall the earth groan by an earthquake; no wars, nor drought, nor famine, nor flood; nor hail to waste the fruits; but there shall be great peace in all the earth, and one king shall live in friendship with the other, to the end of the Age. And the Immortal, who lives in the heavens adorned with stars, shall give a common law to all men in all the earth, and instruct miserable men what things must be done; for he is the only God, and there is no other."

Judging from recent anniversary celebrations, from the widespread revival of interest in Thomas Paine, his work for America is not yet ended. In company with John Brown, "his soul goes marching on."

* Prophecy of the Greek Sibyllæ quoted by the Abbé de Mont-faucon de Villars.

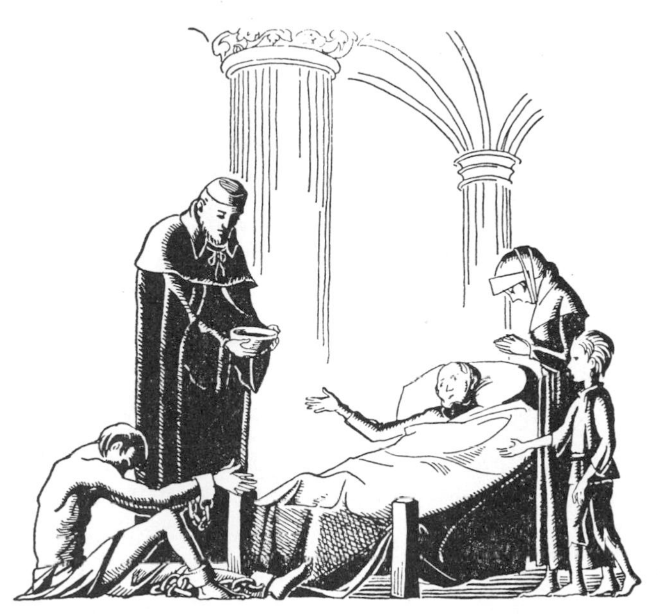

ST. VINCENT DE PAUL
1576–1660

EXPERIENCE is a golden key to unlock the secrets of that vast mass of humanity outside of ourselves. By it we are shown contrasts of poverty and riches, ignorance and wisdom, misery and happiness. Because of it we reach out into the universe to heal the hurt we ourselves have suffered.

Franklin Delano Roosevelt's pet charity is caring for crippled children, because he himself knows the meaning of being bound by paralysis and of training each painful muscle and tendon to obey his will.

Charles Dickens spent two years of childhood hardships in a London blacking warehouse. He had long hours and little pay. His only companions were rough street boys who could neither read nor write. He had to sleep in a garret. His father was in prison for debts. He suffered intense humility because he had to give up his few beloved books to grub among the blacking pots. The degradation ate into his very soul. But all his life long he drew on this material—these experiences gained during this short period. Out of his own heart and life came *David Copperfield.* And all his life he helped Lord Shaftesbury to lift the London poor.

So it was, too, with Vincent de Paul. Born a peasant, near Dax in southern France, he struggled up through poverty to study for the priesthood. His father had to sell a pair of oxen to pay his fees. Then came years during which he lived a series of Arabian Nights adventures. For after being ordained as a priest in 1600, he took ship to travel from Toulouse to Narbonne, since the waterway was cheaper than overland. His ship was captured by Turkish pirates who promptly clapped their prisoners into chains and made haste to the Barbary Coast.

Once in Tunis, the young priest was driven through the streets so that slave-dealers could judge of the white prisoners. He had to open his mouth to show his teeth; he was probed for possible wounds; he had to run, to wrestle, to lift heavy weights. Finally, on the public auction block he was sold to a fisherman.

But his master soon tired of his bargain, as his slave's constant seasickness interfered with his fishing. So he was sold again to an alchemist, and resold to an Italian turned Mussulman.

As the months dragged on, there seemed to Vincent no possible way either to gain his liberty or to earn enough to pay for his freedom. A sorry way to begin his priesthood! Yet his very priestly habits gained him his freedom after all. For hearing him sing at his work, the Mussulman's young Turkish wife became curious about the slave's faith. What manner of man was he? She followed him to the fields to beg him to sing his songs.

And though he had no book of Psalms, he chanted those he remembered, with canticles and hymns, and he told her the story of Bethlehem. The young Turk, caught by the compelling sweetness of his tale, finally persuaded her husband to return to France with his slave.

Thus it came about that after these many months, the young priest had the pleasure of restoring both the Mussulman and his pretty wife to the arms of the Mother Church at Avignon. His own freedom being bought by a prelate, he was thankful indeed to make his way up through France to Paris, a priest in search of a parish.

Once arrived, another adventure befell him. To his chagrin he was falsely accused of stealing a sum of money, and though he was not thrown into prison, he lived under a cloud of humiliation and distrust. So, because he believed it a sin to defend himself at the expense of another, and since he was unwanted in any parish, he sought out the place of greatest misery in the city, the hospital or Hôtel Dieu, which Catherine de' Medici had founded as a peace offering to God. Here he found outcasts and sufferers with troubles far greater than his own; here were the poor and the wretched in need of a friend. He was shocked at the condition of the hospital, understaffed, dirty and pestilence-ridden. Patiently he went up and down the long wards trying to minister to body and soul alike.

With his quick mind and genius for detail, he could see a thousand matters to remedy, but unfortunately the wealthy old Queen-dowager had not seen fit to appoint him her almoner.

Yet it was not to be the destiny of this priest to live always among outcasts. He was to know the contrasting life of the rich. After six years in Paris, still under a cloud of guilt, the real culprit confessed his theft, freeing Vincent of even the shadow of accusation. Yet ever after he had a feeling for debtors thrown into prison, and those guilty of no crime at all.

Now he was sent as tutor and resident family priest to the château of the Count and Countess de Gondi at Folleville, in the district of Amiens. He must teach the two young sons, become the beloved confidant and confessor of the Countess, and the respected and loved companion of the Count who, appointed Admiral of the French fleet by Henri IV, must ply his galleys up and down the Mediterranean to protect French merchant ships from the raids of Turkish and Moorish pirates.

Père Vincent might now have lived a life of ease, with his Gothic private chapel, his great library, the freedom of the château. He might have become a scholar drinking in the culture of the Renaissance. But he was a practical man with a great heart, and he could not shut his eyes to the wants of the eight thousand peasants on the estate, so he rode or walked about among the thirty or forty villages trying to minister to their needs.

He saw for himself how lax had grown the local clergy, hurrying through their services with mumbled prayers, paying scant attention to the home needs of their peasants.

In one parish where Père Vincent found a family sick and in extreme want, he preached a sermon telling of their need. That Sunday afternoon when he went to visit the family, he found that already half a dozen kindly women had preceded him with baskets, while others soon arrived with more. All this bounty poured out for one family, but what of others perhaps in even greater need?

So he invited the women to meet with him, and established the first known Charity Organization Society in France. Now peasants for miles about could declare their necessities to this group, who apportioned their baskets and provisions according to the need. Madame de Gondi was delighted with the plan, and at once gave the organization a sum of money to be used. From this simple beginning has spread the vast modern network of St. Vincent de Paul Societies all over the Catholic world. In his practical solution of needs, Père Vincent began his lifework.

You will remember Tennyson's creed of the Perfect Knight:

Speak true,
Live pure,
Right the wrong . . .
Else wherefore born.

The Middle Ages called forth Sir Launcelot as the knight of fair damsels in distress. The nineteenth century produced its Lord Shaftesbury. The seventeenth century called forth its knight of the poor; and Vincent de Paul rose up to answer. One man in the century. Yet how was he to achieve anything in the face of such poverty and intense distress as he found wherever he looked? Only by multiplying himself. This he did in three major organizations. First he had to go back to Paris, feeling rightly that only in the capital itself could he find the real theater for his work.

Here he organized another group of women along the lines of the group on the De Gondi estate. *La Confrérie de Charité,* he called it, the Fraternity of Charity. Its members included noblewomen, court ladies, and the wealthy upper class; and to them he made the service to humanity so attractive that they gave generously both of money and time to his hospitals and children's homes during the forty years of his Paris labors, and beyond.

But he needed another group who would give their whole lives to this service, who could plunge into the menial work of hospital and home because they loved it. So, under the care of his great friend Mlle. de Gras, was formed his *Filles de la Charité,* Daughters of Charity.

Also he needed men, a group of sons, and for their home and training school he was given the large palace of Saint Lazare. From this, his men came to be called Lazarites. Their mission was to go out, two together, among the poor villages, preaching simplicity and faith and living in practical kindliness. They were men tested and tried, refusing to take gifts or thanks, content as were the Daughters, or the Sisters as they came to be called, to be content without comforts or necessities even, but to serve and to live, as nearly as they could, the life of a saint upon earth.

Whereas in his first group, the *Confrérie,* anyone who wished might enter without vows of any kind, for his other two orders, his *filles* and his *fils,* there was one infallible rule of admission. No one could dedicate himself for life without a probationary or testing period.

For the good Père Vincent had to make certain that each one had what he called a "vocation." The impelling desire to join the groups must come from within, never from without. It was no light thing they were entering, indeed, for even if the order were not within the Church, even if they never became monks or nuns, yet the discipline was perhaps even more rigorous. Few seem to find it easy to become selfless in any age. Père Vincent made them search their hearts and root out every bad habit, every smallest fault. "For," he said, "the life or death of a sick child or a mother or an old man might depend upon just this." Only a complete and utter dedication could insure their humility.

David Garrick laughingly said, when he laid down his management of Drury Lane and of Covent Garden, that he had labored better than the Israelites for the Egyptians. They had to make bricks without straw, but he had to make actors and actresses without genius.

So might Père Vincent have said that he had to make saints out of simple country and town boys and girls without education or culture.

As truly as Socrates was a spiritual father to the young philosophers of Athens, so also was St. Vincent to his two hard-working orders. It seems extraordinary that he found the time to train them, and later, when they were sent to distant provinces, to keep in such close contact with them through letters. The most intimate difficulties of their lives were poured out to him, and they never found him wanting in practical kindly suggestion and advice.

How troublesome they found it, this having to work and live with one another. How irritated they must have been by their discomforts, such as the rigid rule of rising at four in the morning. No self-indulgence for them, but oftener than not hunger and cold.

Their father wrote to one sister: "The moment you feel antagonism toward another sister, say to her quickly with all the warmth that is in you, 'Sister, if you only knew how I love you!' No matter if you do not feel it, say it. And if she does not respond, say it again. Remember that if she annoys you, you may annoy her equally."

To another he wrote: "If you ever want to know why you have failed in any undertaking, you will find it is because you relied upon yourself. However much you work, there will be no real result until you see your own uselessness and understand that all your experience and cleverness are nothing unless God is working with you."

To one who had confessed a sin, he wrote: "When you touch reality you will make the fullest possible reparation for your sin."

In all their undertakings, whenever work was badly done or a failure, they were to say, "It is Père Vincent who did it." For since he had chosen them, allowed them to call themselves his Lazarites, or his Daughters of Charity, then he was henceforth responsible for their mistakes. However, when they accomplished their seeming miracles of healing and rehabilitation of whole villages, then they must give all the credit to God.

In the early days of the organization, he formed the habit of holding "conferences," friendly chats with the whole group, whether at his own home at Saint Lazare or at the Mother House of Mlle. de Gras. Then it was that the results of his intimate talks and letters could be discussed quite impersonally and openly, and the difficulties aired and solved.

During one such "conference" with his *filles*, he explained to them the reason for suffering—an attribute

common to them all, men and girls, widows and orphans, composing his two orders—and perhaps to a saint what straw was to bricks or genius to an actor.

"It is because we are each like a block of stone," he explained, "which is to be transformed into a statue. What must the sculptor do to carry out his design? First of all he must take the hammer, and chip off all he does not need. For this purpose he strikes the stone so violently that if you were watching him you would say he intended to break it to pieces. When he has got rid of the rougher parts, he takes a smaller hammer, and afterwards a chisel, to begin the face with its features. When that has taken form, he uses other and finer tools to bring it to that perfection which he has intended for his statue.

"Do you see, my daughters, that God treats us in just this way? Look at any poor sister of charity, any poor Mission priest, when God drew them out of the world they were still as rough and shapeless as unhewn stone. Nevertheless, it was from them He intended to form something beautiful, and He took hammer in hand, and struck great blows upon them."

Well his children knew that he, their Founder had had these blows: slavery, captivity, disappointments. He admitted to them his own inner cry: "*Ruinez en moi, Seigneur, tout ce qui vous y deplait.*"—Destroy in me, O Lord, all that You please—that is, hammer me as much as you like.

Moreover, his training consisted in the sharing of one of his own intense inner realities with them. Out of a profound contemplation of Divinity plus a boundless compassion, Père Vincent was able to see a shining spark of divinity in every human being whom he touched. This gift he set himself to communicate. How else could his daughters go into plague and pestilence, onto battlefields, into foul dens? So he radiated and communicated this sense of divinity in any and every human being. He anticipated William Blake's poem called *The Divine Image*:

For Mercy has a human heart,
Pity a human face,
And love, the human form divine,
And Peace, the human dress.

And all must love the human form,
In heathen, Turk or Jew,
Where Mercy, Love and Pity dwell,
There God is dwelling too.

So Père Vincent taught his groups to regard the poor, not as they looked or seemed, but as if they were lords and ladies whom it was a privilege to serve. He himself saw the poor as God in man.

THIS POINT of view seems the more remarkable when we realize the terrible hammer blows on the French peasants, their struggle even for food and shelter, caught as they were between the groups determined to gain despotic power; Catholics against Protestants, king against nobles. Their homes and their fields were trampled first by one side, then another, as civil wars, religious wars, foreign wars rolled over them. At the distant sound of marching feet, they would rush from their homes to hide in the woods. When the tide of battle swept on, they were fortunate to find their house standing or to escape death or mutilation.

Barns, granaries, sheds were gaping and empty of cows or hens, pigs or goats or rabbits or grain to make bread. It was enough to make of the peasants brutes rather than saints. How could they help but hate their tyrants? It was a hate that would brood for two generations and more, held in leash during the half century of absolute monarchy of Louis XIV to break forth in a torrent no man could stay in the Terror of the Revolution.

Yet it was to these very poor ones that St. Vincent sent out his orders, and went himself, to see them only as divine! For this work in outlying villages, anywhere in the country where a cry had come for help, Père Vincent insisted upon four main works: First, in order to feed the starving they must set up a soup kitchen, perhaps the first of its kind in France. The good father himself had made gallons of soup from the following recipe: For every one hundred persons, fill a large vessel with five cans of water, twenty-five pounds of bread cut up, two pounds of dripping, four pints of peas, and other vegetables in season, certainly onions or leeks.

Secondly, they must bury the dead. For he himself had seen the danger from the bodies lying unburied and fly-bitten in towns and villages, from which came the infections that spread pestilence. His workers must disinfect themselves and their houses. A startling command in the face of the storm of protest raised about the head of Louis Pasteur, two hundred years later.

Thirdly, they were to collect seeds for replanting of field and garden. This was one of his pet hobbies, as by means of seeds, the poor could help themselves. In two months during 1650 he spent forty thousand francs for seeds.

Fourthly, they were to attend to the welfare of souls.

Rightly this was placed last instead of first, because a starving man cared not at all for his soul's good. But the terror and mental anguish of peasants whose village had been overrun with rough soldiery needed merciful and gentle healing.

More than anyone else, Père Vincent lavished his training on Mlle. de Gras, as head of the women's order. She had longed as a child to take the vows of a nun, but shrank from hiding herself away from the world. She loved nothing so much as to be allowed to carry a basket of eggs and wine and bread to the poor family living in a hovel behind the cobbler's shop. She was never allowed to go alone on Paris streets except with her maid, of course, but all the same her heart was glad.

As a young girl she was presented at court and married a young secretary to Catherine de' Medici, who was then nearly at the end of her long and arrogant life.

When her husband died, Madame de Gras came to consult Père Vincent as to what to do with her life. Enter a convent? For answer he took her to visit one of his poor families in a dark court near Saint Geneviève. Here was her answer. So she bought a house in a poor neighborhood and gathered in as companions a small group of her friends, or of those sent to her by Père Vincent, to help nurse the sick and visit the poor.

"Your monastery is the houses of the poor," Father Vincent told her. "The dirty streets are your cloisters."

So there grew, out of this beginning, the order of *Filles de la Charité*. The sisters must adopt the same rigorous training as the men, must rise at four in the morning winter and summer, eat sparingly of plain food, must learn to take rebuke without self-defense, and must accept no gifts.

As head of the order, Père Vincent taught Mademoiselle, as she liked to be called, to assume no arrogance, no crystallized or hard acceptance of herself as head, but constantly to think of herself as the servant of all. She must have infinite tolerance with the human failings of the sisters under her. As her power grew, she assumed less and less of personal prominence; more and more was she hidden in her manifold works.

Actually, she became the first woman public speaker of her age, addressing groups of women on how they too might serve. She became a power in the city of Paris.

So within her order there grew a sense of corporate life. The three Franciscan laws of humility, poverty and obedience, the voluntary individual dedication, must be renewed each year. These bound together a body of women to a selfless service of humanity. Without them and his Lazarites, Père Vincent could never have accomplished his great work.

To Mlle. de Gras and her gray-frocked sisters, he gave the management of the large hospitals, the two children's homes, the day school, all the nursing.

Now that Père Vincent could multiply his hands and his feet, he turned to meet those needs which he himself had experienced. With the death of Catherine de' Medici, there was opportunity to reorganize the hospital, the God-hostel he had visited so often during his period of disgrace. Here was work both for his Ladies and Daughters of Charity, to call on the sick, to furnish new linen, to ventilate the reeking corridors, to segregate infectious diseases, to train new nurses.

For all visiting of the sick in hospitals or at home, he made a set of practical rules: "Cheerfully and kindly salute the patient. Arrange the tray, spread a clean napkin, wash the sick person's hands, say Grace, pour out his soup, cut up his meat, feed the patient if too sick. Do all cheerfully and in a spirit of love as if to your own child."

Then remembering that he himself had narrowly escaped prison, he visited the Paris dungeons into which men were thrown for stealing a loaf of bread, for debt, for being a member of a party temporarily or permanently out of power. Here indeed was work for his sons: evils of dampness, disease, foul air, filth which not forty years could rectify. But at least he eased much misery.

Next he remembered his experience as a slave, and sent volunteers as missionaries to the Barbary Coast empowered to buy up slaves when necessary, but at least to do what they could for them.

Then he applied to his former patron and friend, Count de Gondi, for permission to visit the slave prison in Paris where desperate criminals awaited embarkation in the galleys. Here he found the men chained to damp walls, sitting in reek and filth and mud.

Horrified, he hurried back to the Count to demand a reform. The Count assured him that he had no power to change the system which was not of his making. So Père Vincent preached and talked, until he collected sufficient funds to purchase a large house on the rue St. Honoré and secured the order for transference of the poor wretches to a clean and dry prison with a straw-covered floor.

Hearing of the affair, the young King Louis XIII, then eighteen, was delighted. Sending for the priest, he praised him for his courage and created a new office for him, that of Chaplain of the galleys, with permission to visit every detention prison at the four ports of France.

Joyously, Père Vincent set his affairs in order and journeyed to Marseilles to visit a prison as badly in need of him as that of Paris. He planned to set about preaching a crusade in Marseilles to remedy matters at once.

The fleet having been ordered to Gibraltar, the main group of galleys commanded by Count de Gondi had already embarked, but ten more ships were being manned at Marseilles with civil prisoners to fill the oar banks. Père Vincent walked beside the men as they were marched from prison to the wharf.

As he spoke cheerfully to them he saw how ill fed they were on black bread and water, ill clad, despondent at their fate, and noticed that one young chap was weeping.

"Why are you troubled, my son?"

"Because I committed only a small sin, Father, and if I must go to sea for months, what will become of my poor wife and baby?"

What indeed? Père Vincent strode along beside the wretched young slave. What could he do to help? The Admiral was out at sea. There was no time for an appeal to the King. No, but there was just time for a quick exchange of places. In the confusion of embarking, the priest contrived to slip his long black cape over the prisoner's shoulders and step into his place.

When the long galley pushed off, the young slave was a free man, tramping along the roads toward home as fast as his feet would carry him. No one stopped him or thought it strange that he wore a priest's black cape over his ragged prison clothes. But down in the ship, Chaplain Vincent sat chained in his post in the single bank, while with regular strokes, he felt the lash across his bared back.

"One-two-three-four," sang out the counter, and the

lashes fell rhythmically as the men stroked their long sweeping oars. If a man fainted, he was cut loose and thrown overboard. At the next port he would be replaced by a fresh galley slave.

In burning sun or searing wind and rain the fleet moved on, sometimes spitting fire from the guns mounted close to the water line, just to warn pirates to keep the lanes clear for the merchant ships flying the three fleurs-de-lys, ships laden with brocades from Venice, or purple cloth from Tyre or glass from Cyprus.

When at last the fleet sailed home, without an engagement with Spanish galleons, and its Chaplain was released, he knew all he needed to know about galleys. Small wonder then that when he returned to Paris he appealed at once to his sons for volunteers, and gained permission to send two men with each ship—two brothers who would listen to the men's stories, confess them, find redress for the innocent, help for wives and children, and comfort for them all.

Thus, though the Chaplain was powerless to correct the system—since steam would not be invented for another century—yet at least he did everything he could to bring comfort and help to the slaves, both physical and spiritual.

It was but one sore in the social sickness of the age. For indeed the entire seventeenth century was one of darkness and misery for France.

Henri IV had begun valiantly to heal France of her war wounds in 1589. He and Sully had brought order out of chaos, had encouraged new industries, the weaving of Gobelin tapestries, the manufacture of Lyons silk, and of cloth of gold and silver. They encouraged agriculture, and the peasants looked up at the sun and laughed. The horrors of the Medici-Valois line were ended. The House of Bourbon reigned.

Then came his assassination. His Queen, Marie de' Medici, became regent for little nine-year-old Louis XIII. Reversing all Henri's policies, she allied the crown with Spain by the betrothal of her son to little Anne, the Spanish Infanta, named for her western states, Anne of Austria.

There followed the eighteen-year reign of Cardinal Richelieu, "the king behind the throne," who revived the ancient despotism of monarchs by fighting the power of the nobles and of the House of Austria. Again he dragged in the bitter religious conflict as a foil for his political games. Thus he plunged France into the thirty years of war from 1618 to 1648.

After the death of Louis XIII in 1643, his Queen, Anne of Austria, reigned as regent for her five-year-old son Louis XIV. Now came the ministry of Mazarin to continue the struggle of Richelieu and to stabilize despotic monarchy until the boy king should gather all the despotism of ages into his own hands.

But Mazarin plus the Queen were fought even in the streets of Paris itself by the proud and turbulent nobles who were as weary of despotism as the peasants, and so wanted to gain it themselves. Aiding them was Parliament which fought to substitute constitutional for absolute monarchy. Thus the struggle of the Fronde—a word coined from the slings used by the Paris gamins—from 1648 to 1653, was followed by war with Spain, concluding in 1659 with the Treaty of the Pyrénées, by which the boy king was espoused to the Spanish Infanta, Maria Theresa.

But as this event of peace came only the year before Père Vincent's death, it is clear to be seen that during the whole of his lifetime, his country was engaged in the age-old struggle for power; one faction at the expense of another. But the good father took no part whatever in these disputes, determining at the outset of his work to be impartial and nonpartisan. All these warrings and chaos bred evils in the social life so that more calls of distress poured in upon Saint Lazare than he could answer.

ONE NIGHT Père Vincent saw a beggar beating a child in a Paris gutter, to make it cry so pitifully that passersby would give them alms. Père Vincent caught up the child, crying out to the beggar, "I thought you were a man!"

In his arms he carried the sobbing mite to the city foundlings' home. But next day, upon inquiry, he learned that out of several hundred babes and children admitted each year, most of them either died mysteriously or were sold for a franc — twelve cents — to make room for more.

With flashing eyes, Père Vincent presented the situation to his Ladies of Charity. He went himself to Queen Anne. He preached a crusade for the foundlings of Paris. The Queen gave her jewels and appointed the priest Father of Foundlings. The Ladies of Charity gathered in funds, and the sisters under Mlle. de Gras took over two large houses. Never again were babies sold or mistreated.

Yet much as he loved them, his babies became an increasingly heavy responsibility. It was not easy for women of wealth and social position to persevere in well-doing for many years after the glamour and enthusiasm had departed. Besides, during the terrible five years of the Fronde, when Paris was cut off from supplies of food and fuel, when families of nobles fled with the Queen or barricaded themselves behind barred doors and windows, who was left to carry

on the financial burden of hospitals and children's homes?

Then Père Vincent rallied together his scattered Confrerie. "I know that you, too, are suffering with all the city poor," he told them. "I know your stores of food and wine are low, and that you have no ready money. Then bring me your jewels, your gold and silver plate. Bring me your tapestries, your bolts of brocades. Let us sell them to buy bread. Our babies must starve but for you." The extremity of the need called for an extremity of giving, giving until it hurt. But he demonstrated the effectiveness of organized charity. It was not until after his death, in the year 1670, that the city fathers took over his two large and well-organized foundling homes.

Now of one class of dependents bred by the evil times, Père Vincent had a loathing. He could not abide the army of beggars. Once, when preaching in the town of Macon, he had to pass through a throng of them squatting on the steps of the church. After his sermon he sought out the town officials and presented a remedy for begging. The town police were to round up the beggars into the courtyard of the jail. Those who refused to work might be lodged in the prison on scant bread and water. Those who preferred to continue their profession must leave town. The following day there were no more beggars in Macon.

In Paris, beggars had multiplied until by 1650, in the midst of the Fronde civil war, they were legion. Père Vincent went to the Queen Regent, Anne of Austria. In the slums he had found schools to train beggars, he told her indignantly. Soon all the poor would be gluing shut their eyes and twisting their bodies out of shape to sit in the gutters and wail their alms plea to passersby. The Queen agreed with him and he obtained a grant of grounds and buildings called *La Salpêtrière*.

His experience at Macon was repeated. When the police had rounded up all the beggars – forty thousand of them out of a population of five hundred thousand – Père Vincent explained to them that any who would not work would be given nothing to eat, unless perhaps they preferred the criminal prison. But no longer could they beg on Paris streets. The ill ones were cared for in a special hospital on the grounds. A new work for the Sisters of Charity. The old people were given a home of their own. Men, women and children were segregated in separate houses and set to work at tailoring or cobbling or basket-weaving. To care for this new family of forty thousand called forth Père Vincent's genius for detail, his ability as an executive, his power of attracting the well-to-do to minister to the poor.

Yet to the good father, these were not a mere mass of wretched human beings to be herded like sheep. No, each one was an individual soul, with the stamp and beauty of the Lord upon it. It was their former calling he had despised, not themselves.

Now all France sought his help. When Spain invaded the country, and the Queen accompanied her young King to the battlefield, she sent back messengers in haste to beg the good Vincent for six of his sisters to nurse the poor wounded soldiers in Calais.

It was considered a dread thing to minister even to wounded soldiers. Peasants fled from them in terror and left them to die. They had behaved more like fiends than men. Yet Père Vincent's daughters went willingly. They found the overcrowded hospital in Calais reeking with infection. Of the four who could be spared to go, two died of the pestilence. Yet when Père Vincent read the dreadful news at the Mother House, there was a rush of fresh volunteers.

"Oh, sisters," he said to them, "behold, the Queen requests that you go to Calais to nurse wounded men. How humble you should be, seeing that God deigns to make use of you for such great ends. Men go to kill one another, and you, my daughters, are called to repair the evils which they have done; to nurse the wounded, not only in France, but even in Poland!"

Indeed, pleas came in thick and fast as civil wars grew more desperate. The five years of the Fronde were the darkest period of Père Vincent's life. The people, abandoned at last by the Queen, who fled with Louis to St. Germain, were faced with stark famine. They gnawed wood, boiled leather, ate rats. As desperately as Père Vincent labored to keep them in bread, even he came to the end of his resources. He could move neither Parliament nor the young nobles defying the Crown. There was but one other course possible. If the Queen only knew the actual state of starvation of her people, she might humble herself and consent to send aid.

Père Vincent determined to risk his life if necessary to reach her, and set forth on his horse through the storm of night. The Seine was in flood, overflowing the bridges, yet he rode on to beat at the barred gate of St. Germain and demand an audience.

His errand was fruitless of good. Anne had hardened her heart, furious at having to submit to the indignity of being barred from Paris by a Parliament demanding dangerous reforms. Let the poor starve. She hated them now, and sent her good priest back without a sou to buy bread.

The poor got wind of this visit, and thinking he had gone over to the side of Anne and Louis XIV, an infuriated and hopeless mob stormed Saint Lazare, sacked and pillaged it, and drove their best friend out of the city. In one hour of insane labor, the very poor he had given his life for destroyed the work of thirty years.

So it was that, at seventy-four, Père Vincent became an exile, forced to travel in the provinces on endless journeys among his "Missions" already established by his Lazarites. Through the bitter black frosts of that winter, in a country gripped by famine, he could see for himself, now, the heroism of his sons and his daughters. He had not multiplied himself in vain. Well might Blake have described France when he wrote:

And so many children poor?
It is a land of poverty!

And their sun does never shine
And their fields are bleak and bare
And their ways are filled with thorns.
It is eternal winter there.

In the face of stark tragedy he preached up and down the land, so that "the people might be helped through humility to give themselves to God during their miseries."

Thus this father of the poor, old and ill, saw all horrors in his travels, but kept his sanity, his simple faith, his great love.

Meanwhile in Paris stirring events were taking place. By a ruse the civil war was ended. It was a girl, Mademoiselle

Gaston, who opened the city gates of Saint-Antoine to Condé and his royal troops, a signal to the gunners in the tower of the Bastille to fire. Condé escaped to Spain. The leaders of the insurrection against the Crown were imprisoned in palaces, among them Cardinal de Retz, Archbishop of Paris, whom as a little lad Père Vincent had tutored on his father's estates. The people, subdued by starvation, watched the magnificent gilded coach of the royal family enter the city bearing the regal Mother Anne with her imperious son, Louis XIV. The court reëntered the Louvre.

But now the Queen Mother humbled herself to send for Père Vincent. Paris had need of him, and hailed him as a conquering hero. His shame-faced poor understood now that he had not betrayed them, but was their best friend, the father of Paris, the man of the century for them. So he set about raising five million francs by his appeals to the nobility to give of their jewels to buy bread.

In looking up at this great stalwart figure with his shaven head and strong square chin, with his genius for organization and his great heart for the poor, one wonders what were the springs of his power.

Surely one was his humility. As a boy fresh from tending his father's sheep, he had been proud of the fact that he alone of all his family had intellect enough to go to the Franciscan college of Dax. Here he was proud to make a place for himself among boys of wealth and good family. Whenever his farmer father came to visit him, with muddy boots and smock smelling of the barnyard, the boy was plunged into an agony of shame.

When later he realized this shame, he was stricken with

remorse. As if life had determined to help him conquer this pride, humility had been forced upon him. As galley slave, and personal slave, as one falsely accused of theft, as one exiled by his own people, he had experienced degradation indeed. But so ingrained had become the habit of humility that even when called by the former Queen Marguerite of Valois to be her almoner in 1610, or even when asked to serve on the inner Council of Queen Anne after the death of Louis XIII, Pere Vincent would always remind his royal patrons of his peasant origin. He could give no worldly counsel, only advice straight from the people.

Deliberately he made this quality of humility the foundation-stone of his life. Deliberately he taught his sons and his daughters that without it they could not do the work of the Lord. By it, he and they accomplished miracles.

With humility, this doer combined a vast knowledge of humanity gained from practical experience, plus a dose of salty common sense—peasant sense—which enabled him to choose the best way of solving the problems of his age. And beneath all wisdom was his profound spiritual life whose roots led down to the river of universal knowledge.

The eighteenth century, so concerned with revolutions, let his great works lapse, but they were revived in the nineteenth. It was in that important year 1833, the year of Lord Shaftesbury's first Ten Hour Factory Act, the year of Wilberforce's emancipation of all the slaves of the West Indies, that Frederick Ozanam and his friends determined to silence the taunts of French free-thinkers. They had maintained that the Catholic Church no longer had the strength to inaugurate a practical enterprise for its poor, and in reply Ozanam organized the modern Society of St. Vincent de Paul.

Truly did it seem then, and still does today, that the blessed *grand saint d'un grand siècle* — the grand saint of a grand century — put something imperishable into his orders. For his principles are still maintained today. The world organization involving millions in money outlay for countless hosts of individuals is still in the hands of laymen.

Happily galley slaves are no more; immense strides have been taken in the treatment of prisoners and of the sick, in the succor of country districts in time of flood or famine or epidemic. Yet many of the same needs of human beings face each new generation: poverty, sickness, adult and child crime, the care of orphans and foundlings, the need for summer camps and convalescent homes, work for beggars.

So today, nearly three centuries since his time, the blessed St. Vincent still multiplies himself, still ministers through his sons and his daughters to the needs of men.

For Mercy Pity Peace and Love
Is God our Father dear:
And Mercy Pity Peace and Love
Is man his child and care.

CHRISTINE DE PISAN

1363–1431

WITH THE exception of Jeanne d'Arc, Christine de Pisan is accounted the most celebrated woman of her age. Born in Italy, she yet lived her whole life in France. So to France is given the honor of appreciating its first woman writer in history, its first woman scholar, the first woman to earn her bread by her pen, the first great feminist, the first to glorify Jeanne d'Arc.

Christine's father, Tommaso di Benvenuto di Pizzano, was professor of astrology at the University of Bologna. Thither, to consult the astrologer as to his stars, came Charles V of France who had need of beneficent planets to guide his dealings with England, which was still pressing claims to French soil after nearly a century of war. Now, so impressive was the horoscope set up by the astrologer for his royal guest that he was invited to journey home with the king.

Before this, Maestro Tommaso had been invited by Louis the Great of Hungary to live at his court in Buda, but he had hesitated to uproot his wife and little daughter. But now his wife herself urged this travel with the French King. She, the daughter of a Councillor of Venice, where little Christine was born, perhaps felt rightly that their destiny was to be linked with France.

In 1368, when Christine was five years old, she made the long journey with her mother up over the snowy Alps, all the way to Paris, to join her father. For he had been given a house in Paris, a large pension, and a life post as astrologer to the king.

For ten years the child was the darling of the court. It did not take long to learn the new language, nor to be able to chatter with the court children and curtsy to the queen, Jeanne de Bourbon. Soon she was attending the balls and fêtes for the Dauphin Charles and his brother Louis, Duke of Orleans.

So the child grew up in luxury and beauty. For Charles V filled his palace with tapestries of Arras, and his library with rare books. Having inherited only twenty books from his father, John the Good, so long imprisoned in England, the King soon increased his library to twelve hundred volumes, all, of course, in manuscript, since printing had not yet been invented. He had one of the towers of the Louvre remodeled to house these treasures.

Here it was that his scribes were continually at work translating into French writings from Latin, Greek and even Arabic. Here it was that his court astrologer consulted his great tomes on the positions of the stars. Here hung his astrolabe, and here he set up his horoscopes. And here it was that the little Christine loved to curl up beside her father on one of the wide windowseats. She learned how to look up the notations of Venus trine the Moon or Mars conjunction Saturn. She learned even the difficult mathematical calculations necessary for an horary. With her father she watched eagerly to see how events would fulfill his prophecies.

Often the King himself would join them there, and sometimes he rested as the little maiden read aloud to him from the books they had brought from Italy — Petrarch and Boccaccio and Boethius and her beloved Dante.

With her great brown eyes, soft brown curling hair and white skin, she grew as lovely to look upon as she was wise. So it was not strange that she had suitors. Among them was a young knight of Picardie, Etienne Castel, who often joined the group in the tower library. For this young noble was secretary to the king, and wrote out his many letters and the notes for his state documents.

Christine was delighted that he, too, loved Petrarch and Dante, that he sympathized with her in her longing for knowledge. If only she could enter the Sorbonne! It was her dearest wish, but the gates were fast barred against her. She was a mere slip of a girl, with neither the rights nor the need for an education. She was only a pretty plaything, made to strum a harp, to dance and to flirt, to be amused and courted.

At least that was what the Middle Ages had taught, and was it not so written down in the *Romance of the Rose?* How she hated this poem that was read by all the court! She herself wrote verses and shyly read them to Etienne. She wanted to prove to him and to the world that a woman could be something besides a silly coquette. Etienne agreed, but he persuaded her that she could become anything she liked as his wife.

So at fifteen, with the willing consent of the King and the Queen, and the tearful consent of her mother, Christine was married. We do not know where, perhaps in St. Sulpice where so many French brides are wed, or perhaps in a chapel of the Cathedral of Nôtre Dame.

It was a deeply happy marriage as Christine tells us in her verses. And though the young people entered into the gay festivities of the court, yet Christine was free to delve in the library, to listen to her father's discussions of the planets and of how events were shaping themselves. She could listen, also, to the plans of the young noblemen for fighting against their ancient enemy and so drive the English out of the country. She met courtiers and ambassadors from other lands. She attended knightly tourneys in which she could see her own blue sleeve fluttering from the pennon of her chivalrous Etienne. She conversed with scholars, with the best minds of the age. Her life was exciting and beautiful and good and secure and happy.

But already the wheel of fortune was turning. The dire squares of Saturn which her father had predicted began threatening her own life and that of France, and nothing could stay them. Two years after Christine's marriage, the sudden death of the king ended her father's career as court astrologer. She writes: "Thus was the door opened for our misfortunes, since the large pensions now were unpaid to my father."

But a greater trouble than money-lack loomed now in the serious illness and death of her father himself. What a great figure he had been in her life, and how she missed his wise counsel now. For although her husband still retained his post as court secretary, the boy king, Charles VI, twelve years old, was being fought over by his three guardian uncles, the dukes of Burgundy, Anjou and Berry. The times were suddenly full of strife, of unrest, of uncertainty, with uprisings in Flanders and in the cities.

Yet Christine was not part of it. Sheltered, set apart, she was wholly absorbed in comforting her mother, in caring for her babies, in happy comradeship with her husband. She did not have her father to warn her to bend and meet a still heavier blow. For Etienne, traveling to Beauvais on court business, was caught in an epidemic raging there and died before she could reach him.

So at twenty-five, Christine was left alone to face actual poverty with a large household of servants, three little children, her aging mother and two younger brothers not yet established.

She felt as if her whole secure happy life had fallen about her like a child's castle made of blocks. Within eight years she had lost her king, her father and her husband. Where could she turn? How could she provide for her family? How earn enough for them all? A woman earn? Such a thing was unthinkable. What could she do? She could write verses. That was all.

The first outburst of her grief in verse, a lament, soon circulated about the court and brought her actual orders for work with her pen. Love lyrics, ballads, rounds, even plays she wrote to order. Soon it grew to be the fashion for the young knights to let the Lady Christine put into verse their pleas for a lady's hand, or to compose a new song to sing on their lutes. How Christine must have wearied with them.

As the years passed, however, her writings became more and more popular, not only with the young blades of the court but among the older men, the princes of the blood like Jean, Duke of Berry, and Louis of Orleans. They actually commissioned her to write a life of Charles V. Eagerly she set about her task as court-historian. Jean of Berry received his copy on January 1, 1405.

It was a good biography of a good and wise king who left France in a more secure and happy state than it had been for many long years. To the discomfiture of the English, he beat them at their own game of hiring mercenary soldiers, and thus drove them steadily out of the land until at his death England held only three seaports and one inland city. It was a good book to circulate in this troublous reign of Charles VI. And Christine must have been delighted with the number of copies ordered.

In seven years she had really achieved success. She was earning a living for her growing family with her pen. The whole court sang her praises. And not only French courtiers but visiting ambassadors admired her, chief among them the Earl of Salisbury, who had come over from England to celebrate Richard II's wedding to the little princess Isabeau, daughter of Charles VI and Isabeau of Bavaria. That was in 1396.

When the Earl returned to France two years later he again sought out the Lady Christine. She writes of him as "a gracious knight, brilliant in conversation and clever as a writer and speaker." Deeply concerned over her struggle to rear and educate her young family, Lord Salisbury, with her consent, took home with him her eldest son, Jean du Castel, then thirteen years old. Christine must have felt it a happy turn of fortune, even though it meant a parting, with the stormy channel between them. For Jean was to be educated with the Earl's own son.

But alas, after only two years, the good Earl was killed, and his sovereign, Richard II, deposed. Alarmed at this news, Christine next received word that Henry IV, usurper to the English throne, had himself taken charge of her son. Now he sent a messenger to France asking that the lad's famous mother come to England and settle at his court. The new king had need of her pen, of her wit and of her high scholarship.

But Christine shook her head. Not all the security of a royal court could tempt her to be disloyal to her beloved Charles V. She could not overlook the fact that England was still at war with her adopted country. So she graciously refused.

But Henry IV would take no refusal. He sent back a winning messenger, one whom she could not resist, the young Jean himself, now a tall squire speaking Chaucerian English. Christine gathered him to her heart, but she was hurt, too, that his head was so full of promises made by Henry as to his brilliant future in England, provided only that his mother would consent to return with him.

Christine was still firm. She would prove whose will was strongest. She kept her boy at home and wrote to the Duke of Orleans to beg him to take the fatherless lad into his service. Yet Christine's connection with England was not ended, as we shall see.

DURING those early days after her husband's sudden death, when she wrote love poems for money and had "to make merry when I longed to weep," she realized that if writing were to be her profession, she must have the training which she had been denied by the Sorbonne. But now, through her friendship with Chancellor Gerson of the Sorbonne, she was allowed at least to use its great library. In this, and in her own royal library of the Louvre, she set to work, leaving to her mother the care of her young children.

"I betook myself," she says, "like the child who at first is set to learn its ABC, to ancient histories from the beginning of the world; histories of the Hebrews and the Assyrians, of Romans, French, Britons, and diverse others. And then to the deductions of such sciences as I had time to give heed to, as well as to a study of the poets."

In science, as in ethics, her master was Aristotle, and she calls herself, "*ancelle de science*"—handmaiden of science. For "it is knowledge which can change the mortal into the immortal," she insists, and sets herself to a mastery of the knowledge available to a student of the early fifteenth century.

You may see for yourself how she looked in these days, poring over her books, from the miniature painted of her.* In a library she is seated before a Gothic desk, writing with a quill pen in a great folio volume. Very slender she is in her tight little blue bodice, with long sleeves falling from the elbow and ample skirts billowing about her feet. Close by lies a greyhound, perhaps one of her father's or her husband's dogs. Above her head, crowned with a snowy white coif, a window is open to show us the towers of the château.

Here, she tells us, her "heart was a hermit in the hermitage of thought."

Very attractive she must have been, very lovely in her

* Now in the Library of Brussels. Reproduced in *Six Mediæval Women*. cf. Bibliography.

grief, very appealing in her intense effort to gain knowledge to become self-supporting. Suitors were not lacking for her hand. All the royal princes offered to become her patron, to attach her to their households, to buy her pen for their own exclusive use.

But Christine made it clear with gracious candor that neither her pen nor herself could be bought. Like Erasmus, independence was dearer to her than security. She felt she must remain unattached, and free. Besides, she was conscious now of great causes to which she must dedicate her pen. One was to Dante, so little known, so mystically great. France had grave need for his spiritual quickening, his other-worldness. So one of her longest allegories was modeled on his *Paradiso*.

Another of her causes was that of peace. Why drag wearily on with war? Was not a century long enough? Now to the international conflict was added endless struggles of the older dukes of Anjou, Berry, Burgundy, Orleans. And these stirred up insurrections in the cities and rebellions of the peasants. The Maillotin insurrection swept France, a searing wind of revolt. And now the strife was between the Burgundians and the Armagnacs, even as the city of Florence was torn by the factions of Albizzi against the Medici. So Christine wrote treatises, letters, poems on peace, dedicated to Queen Isabeau, to poor mad Charles VI and to his quarreling regents.

But if her cause of peace seemed a hopeless one, her espousal of girls and women would perhaps bear fruit. Her goal was their liberation. Had she not proved to them that a woman, even one gently reared, could stand forth and make her own way with her mind and her spirit?

Yet she found women pitiably dependent on men. Even

noble court ladies might be beaten by their knights. Who but herself, of all the women of France, was free to live her own life, free to pore over precious tomes, drinking in knowledge?

So all through her writings she champions them. One of her books, *La Cité des Dames,* paints a dream city which sheltered within its high battlements all the women of all time who had distinguished themselves for goodness or for heroic deeds. Just as Europe knew and loved its *Golden Book of the Saints,* so now it seized upon Christine's *Golden Book of Heroines.*

What matter then, even if men have defamed and lowered women? she cried. They need only reread the poet Boethius to find that all souls are one, that it is not one's sex that counts, but the perfection of one's virtue. A woman may be as great as a man, yes, even wise enough to do her own pleading in the courts!

How Christine would have celebrated a woman like Catherine Breshkovsky, who wrote from her Siberian prison in 1916: "In general, I think women are the finest part of humanity. I respect and love them best of everything in the world. Almost all my correspondents are women; only the poor boys have the privilege of being answered richly, for they are little children and ought to grow big men."

How strange she would have thought it if she could have known that in far-away America, as yet undiscovered, five centuries later a woman called Sarah Josepha Hale would be met with the identical problem of earning her living by means of her pen, and that she would spend years in writing the same sort of anthology of great women, with the selfsame goal of achieving their emancipation!

Like Sarah Hale, Christine advocated education for

women. "Girls can learn just as well as boys," she maintained, "so why not educate them together?" A daring proposal, this, which she had found in her fourth-century Boethius. Little was to come of the idea just then. For it was not until the early sixteenth century that Cornelius Agrippa was to assert that "the sex of a human being is merely physical and in no way indicates the powers of soul or of mind." How his defense of women, dedicated to his patroness, Margaret of Burgundy, would have delighted our Christine!

For she found few to agree with her. The age was still too fond of its *Romance of the Rose*. And against this long poem, she took up cudgels, begging her readers to substitute Dante instead.

Today, whenever a book is put under the ban, the public rushes to read it. So we too must see what it is in this old romance that so irritated Christine.

In her book of proverbs written for her son Jean, she admonishes him:

> *So well and chastely live*
> *That you do not read the book of the Rose.*

The long allegory in the first part of the *Romance of the Rose* is a summary of the whole love philosophy of the Troubadours. In a dream the Lover visits a fair park into which he is admitted by Idleness to find Pleasure, Delight, Cupid & Co., and at last the Rose. Welcome gives him permission to kiss her, but now a crowd drives him back: Danger, Shame, Scandal, and above all Jealousy who spirits Rose away and imprisons Welcome, leaving the Lover all disconsolate.

There was nothing that could be found wrong with this allegory in the Middle Ages, nor in Christine's period of the early fifteenth century. Love was the game of life, and a lovely lady an alluring siren. Nor could Christine quarrel overmuch with its author, Guillaume de Lorris, because there was much sheer beauty in his poem.

But the second part, running into some eighteen thousand lines, was another matter. Completed in 1270 by Jean de Meung, it was still the most popular French romance of Christine's day. Why? Not because the Lover finally wins the Rose, but perhaps because of its biting satire against women and marriage. For in fables, he exposes with brutality all the vices of women, all their pretty tricks and wiles and flatteries and false prides and deceptions, without giving them one redeeming trait, nor allowing one serious thought to enter their pretty but empty heads.

No wonder that Christine revolted. If men were to think it fun to treat women as toys and to keep them so, she for one was going to rebel and to rebel vigorously. In all her writings she combats Jean de Meum. And she does more.

For he wrote a treatise called *Le Livre de Vegèce de l'art de chevalerie*, a translation from *De Re Militari* of fourth-century Vegetius. Christine herself was very much interested in this art of chivalry, in the whole system of arms, and also in the international complications arising out of war: prisoners, attack and counter-attack.

Her son would one day have to fight, and when this dread day came, she would like, at least, to know that both sides were willing to abide by certain fixed rules. For many years there had been no revision of medieval tactics. So now, she set herself the task of combating De Meum's scorn of women by writing her own book of chivalry, an annotation of five earlier sources, including that of Vegetius, and with most excellent observations and arrangement of her own.

She would show the men of her age that a woman was more than a toy. And she did. For even in her lifetime the book was widely acclaimed, becoming at once an authority. After her death it so delighted Henry VII of England that he ordered William Caxton to translate and print it in 1489. And on into the reign of Henry VIII it was still an accepted authority on military tactics and international law.

Fifteen copies of this work still exist, all in fair manuscript form, in nine of which she acknowledges authorship. But it is sad to relate that due to a rain of criticism at accepting such a work from the hands of a woman, in the remaining six copies her invocation to Minerva, ending "I am as ye were, a woman Ytalien," is deleted.

Of the copies in the British Museum, one is especially interesting, since it was a wedding gift to the young bride, Margaret of Anjou, who crossed the channel to become the queen of Henry VI (that same tragic king who, as a child knight at the age of ten, was actually and shamefully crowned King of France in the cathedral at Paris, in 1431). John Talbot, first Earl of Shrewsbury, was sent over to France to bring home the girl bride in 1445, and he it was who, knowing of the fame of Christine de Pisan, now, fifteen years after her death, ordered this very beautiful copy made. A great book it is, eighteen and three-quarter inches by thirteen, on fair vellum. The frontispiece is a miniature painting showing the Earl in the very act of presentation, holding up the book in its ponderous iron clasps, to the young king and queen who are seated on carved thrones behind which hangs an arras diapered in the arms of England quartered with those of France.

How merciful it was that its author did not live to see it!

In Caxton's translation of 1489 he begins Book One thus: "Here begynneth the chapytres of the fyst book/ the first chapitre is the prologue in whiche Chrystyne excuseth her/to have dar enterpryse to speke of so hye matere as is conteyned in thys sayd book/"

And translating in turn from his quaint English; we find Christine's own apology for the book:

"Because that hardiness is so necessary in order to undertake these things, which, without that could never be undertaken, it is wise for me to put forth this present work without further excuse. Seeing the smallness of my person, by which I have not deemed me worthy to treat of so high a matter, nor dare not think what blame hardiness causes when she is false, I then, moved not at all by arrogance in false presumption, but admonished by my very affliction and the good desire of noble men in the office of arms, am exhorted after my other writings to attempt this work. . .

"I supplicate humbly the said high office and noble state of chivalry that, in contemplation of the lady Minerva born in the country of Greece of whom the ancients, for their knowledge reputed to be a goddess of war, as the old writings say, and I have at other times said, and so the poet Boëtia recited in his book of clear and noble women. . .

"The art and manner of making harness of iron and steel, which many would not have me undertake, I, a woman, charge myself to treat of. . . But my answer is from the teaching of Seneca which says, 'Take no thought for the sayer, so the words be good.'"

And now she addresses Minerva, whom she invokes:

"Adored lady and high goddess, be thou not displeased that I, a simple and little woman, deign to implore thy protection. . . For since greater Greece is now Italy, I am as ye were, a woman Ytalien."

Who can say how many men used her book, but strangely enough, at least one woman profited by it; that was none other than the very Margaret of Anjou to whom the book was given by John Talbot. For in perilous times to come, Margaret was to defend her mad king, and vainly seek to establish her young son Edward on the throne by means of many battles.

So throughout her numerous books and writings, Christine continued her revolt against the accepted ideas about women. Besides her Utopia for women in a city all their own, she wrote one other book directly to her own sex, to "all women high and low."

This book she dedicated to the Dauphine, Margaret of Burgundy, wife of the Dauphin Charles, later Charles VII. Amid all the court intrigue and scandal, she appeals to this princess to set the true tone to the life of the court.

All well-born women she counsels not to put too much faith in possessions. The wheel may turn and the high be brought low. She begs them to give time to charity, care to the education of their children, and above all, to study themselves so as to take the place of their lords and husbands while away at war or at court. Then she pleads with them to have pity on the poor. For the poor were in a pitiable state in France then, after a hundred years of wars, of being all overrun with soldiers, and burdened with taxes.

Townswomen she bids not to be afraid to go down into their own kitchens and have a care to their management, and to avoid all luxury. A sage bit of advice which Sarah

Hale was to repeat almost word for word five centuries later.

With servants she pleads not to take bribes, since God sees everywhere. They must do their best and have a good heart, knowing that the misery of earth will be recompensed in heaven.

The wives of farm laborers she counsels to guide well the flocks and herds, and to urge their husbands to work.

To the men of her age, the Lady Christine must indeed have been an astonishing creature. Reared at court among scholars and gentles, she yet had a largeness of heart for the people. Again and again in her writings she urged princes and nobles to have a mind to their care. In her life of Charles V, she advocated a principle of Aristotle that "a strong middle class is the basic hope of a nation" — a principle to find complete agreement only in our twentieth century. Certainly to her own age the idea was preposterous.

One of the most charming English reprints of Christine's many books is that of her *Moral Proverbs*, translated by Anthony, 2nd Earl Rivers, and at his request printed by William Caxton in 1478, now one of the rare Incunabula prized by book lovers. *

These *Proverbs* must have been so thoroughly read and reread in France that they were literally read to tatters, since no public library in Europe possesses a copy. Fortunately, in England three copies came to light in private libraries.

How happy would Christine have been to see the little book printed by Caxton — the second dated book from his press — and all the more so since she wrote it for her own son Jean, and this translation was made for the use of the young English Prince of Wales over whom the good Earl Anthony was appointed governor by Edward IV in 1473.

* cf. Bibliography.

Moreover, small as the little book is, it is famous because at the end of it, Caxton wrote his first colophon in rhyme:

Of these sayynges Chrystyne was aucteuress
Whiche in makying hadde suche intelligence
That thereof she was nureur & maistresse
Hire werkes testifie thexperience
In Frenssh languaige was written this sentence
And thus Englisshed dooth hit rehers
Antoin Widenydle therl Ryuers
(Anthony Woodville or Wydeville, 2nd Earl Rivers)

Go thou litil quayer/ and recomaund me
Unto the good grace/ of my special lorde
Therle Ryueris, for J have enprinted the
At his comandement. followying eury worde
His copye/ as his secretaire can recorde
At Westminstre of feuerer the XX daye
And of Kyng Edward/ the xvii yere vraye (truly)

Enprinted by Caxton
In Feuerer the colde season

It seems astonishing that, though scarcely fifty years had elapsed since Christine's death, the English should have been made so readable to us, and so charmingly admixed with French words. But lest it prove tedious, we might ask Earl Rivers for the liberty of transposing his rhymed translation of the *Proverbs*:

A happy house is one where dwelleth prudence.

Neither that land nor country may long rule
Where there is no justice.

And to God no man may be acceptable
Be he not charitable.

A cruel prince, grounded in avarice,
Should his people not trust.

One ought to work while he hath liberty;
For time lost can never be recovered.

He that often blames another
Has reason to be blamed himself.

Happy is he that can dispose his life
Justly, in truth, without envy or strife.

To win worldly riches wrongfully
Doth bring danger both to soul and body.

It is better honor to have a good name
That rich treasure, and none shall endure so long.

Humility is the grace of nobility;
The lowlier the heart, the higher will men account him.

Reverence is the heart's own balm
For the soul, for women, and for God.

Thus it was that the Lady Christine counseled her son Jean.

Now it seemed to her, after a life full of books and of years, as if once more her house of human life were built of child's blocks and that it came crashing down about her. Only whereas before it had involved her personal life, now it carried with it in its fall the whole social structure of her world. For with civil war and revolts of the peasants and nobles alike, England had seized her advantage to encroach nearer and nearer to Paris, demanding not only the return of her ancient rights to Normandy and Aquitaine but to the whole of France as well.

Finally came Agincourt, the flower of France mown down, and Henry V victorious.

Again the streets of Paris ran red with rioters.

And in that shameful Treaty of Troyes in 1420, Christine's own Queen Isabeau — to whom she had addressed a hundred of her ballads and many pleas for peace — Isabeau turned against France to sign away the inheritance of the Dauphin Charles, and Henry V was declared regent on condition of his marriage to the Princess Catherine, daughter of the mad Charles VI.

Surely the Queen herself was mad — nay, and all her counselors too. With the flight of the Dauphin and his followers to the south, and the absence of all the old courtiers who had made her life so gracious and purposeful, Christine herself fled. Her children no longer needed her; France was beyond her help. She fled to Poissy — a suburb of Paris — to the dear sisters in the convent where she had educated her daughter.

So now that her house of France had crumbled, she went as Lady Recluse to "*un très doux paradis*" — a very sweet Paradise — to mourn like Rachael for her children, and could not be comforted. All she had striven and longed for seemed utterly undone — war and strife in place of peace, and the ancient nobility of her childhood all fled or perished; France about to be swallowed up by that neighbor across the narrow sea, and her people crying out for bread.

The Lady Christine entered the silence and laid down her pen. She prayed and she read her Dante, she meditated on the mad folly of men, and she waited with longing for the sweet Paradise of Heaven.

Then it was, in that year of 1429, that a passing pilgrim brought tidings of great joy. A maid had come forth out of Lorraine, a simple child bidden by her Saints to raise up the Dauphin into his kingship, and to restore France to her people.

Christine lifted her head to listen, a new light in her wondering eyes. The nuns nodded their white-winged heads, remembering an ancient prophecy of a Maid of Lorraine. And she had begun, the stranger declared. Already she was commander-in-chief of the army—of those same lawless ragged unpaid mercenaries that were the terror of the countryside. By now they were marching to raise the siege of Orleans, with Charles wakened at last by a new faith in the Maid and in himself.

Breathless days of waiting for more news! When it came, Orleans had fallen, and they were marching on to Reims to crown their king.

What a wild rush of joy this was now to the heart of our Lady Christine. A woman—at least a slip of a girl—had saved France; had redeemed the work of Charles V by crowning his grandson Charles VII. Her own faith in girlhood, in womanhood, was at last vindicated.

Blessed year of our Lord, 1429.

L'an mil quarátre cent vint et neuf
Reprint a luire le soleil. . .

The year one thousand four hundred and twenty-nine
Begins the sun to shine. . .

And with this burst of spring sunshine in her heart, Christine caught up her pen once more to write a poem to Jeanne. It was in fifty-six strophes of eight verses each, making four hundred and forty-eight verses of eight lines each.

In the prologue of her poem she acknowledges (prose translation):

"I, who have wept for eleven years, in the convent where I have lived ever since Charles, the King's son, fled from Paris, now for the first time I am laughing, laughing for joy. In this year, fourteen twenty-nine, the sun begins to shine. For the King's son, who so long has suffered much and great trouble, is coming as crowned king, with great and fair power and shod with spurs of gold."

So she must have imagined herself in that great press in the Cathedral of Reims waiting to greet them when they came, the Maid with stars in her eyes, and her blue banner waving and her young "king all fair and shod with spurs of gold."

This poem to Jeanne was the last writing from Christine's pen, her swan song and the first cry of glory for the Maid.

Mercifully, it is thought that Christine did not live to know of the burning by the *gent avugle*, as François Villon called the poor blind English.

No, Jeanne was still winning her battles when the poem ends, and through her the gentle Lady is healed of her own grievous woe for France. Through Jeanne d'Arc, the honor of poor Queen Isabeau, as of all France, was redeemed. The Lady Christine had not lived in vain.

Her poem continues:

Jeanne d'Arc

Jeanne, ordained the Maid of God,
Created in a blessed hour,
The Holy Spirit pours His flood
Of grace upon thee, as thy dower.
In bounty all high gifts are thine.
Praise be to God who grants thy prayer,
Rewarding thee with deeds divine,
Of victory and mercy rare.

Of God's bestowal who shall tell,
Honor to women! Stricken lay
This land where knaves and cowards dwell
Helpless to find out freedom's way.
A woman did what none dared try,
Brought us high faith and hope once more;
Drove the vile traitors hence to fly.
Scarce could we hope such things before.

A maiden, sixteen summers old,
On whom arms weigh not over much.
(How can the child's endurance hold?)
Meseems that, by the iron's touch
Nurtured she is, in ruggedness.
Before her, fly in wild array
Her enemies. Their sore duress
She wrought, in all the fray.

Of Englishmen she frees all France.
Castles and towns recovers still;
Never such force in sword or lance
As in the power of her will.
Of all our heroes she at length
Is head and chief, since she alone
Has Hector's and Achilles' strength;
*All this thro' God who leads her on.**

* The translation of four stanzas of the long poem are given by courtesy of the History Reference Council.

FRA ANTONINO
1389–1459

Marco Polo left an impress not alone upon his own age but on each succeeding one, by writing the story of his travels and adventures in far places. We are as fascinated by his tale today as were the boys and girls in all the six hundred years since his time.

San Antonino—for he was canonized as a Saint in the sixteenth century—left an impress on the city of Florence which has endured for five hundred years. Never did he travel out of Italy, but spent most of his life in the street where he was born, the street called now the *Via Ricasoli*, which leads from the convent of San Marco to the Duomo.

Little did the boy Antony Perozzo dream that he was one day to become Prior of San Marco and Archbishop of the Cathedral, with two homes for life, his cell in the convent and his palace beside the Duomo.

Antony's father was a notary, one who, in the fourteenth century, drew up legal papers and plead cases.

His mother died when he was very small, and he liked best to spend his days curled up on a wide windowseat in his father's library among the big law books, folios written by hand on parchment or vellum, and bound in pigskin or wooden boards. Eagerly he would question his father when there was a case to be tried between merchants of the cloth or wool guilds, or a suit for taxes brought by the city magistrates.

His favorite book was a big tome on church laws. One day when his father came home the boy was still poring over it.

"Well, well, Antonino *mio*, have we got a future lawyer in our family?"

It was true that the child seemed to have a legal mind. He could be corrected only by love or by reason. Yet he was much too frail and slight for his age. For this, the name Antonino clung to him all his life. It was true that instead of romping with other boys, he liked best to pore over books.

The second love of his childhood was for processions. Never a feast day at Santa Maria Novella, never a saint's day at Santa Maria di Fiori, but a boy with an elfin chin and great brown eyes, his hair falling to his shoulders, surmounted by a round scarlet cap, watched wide-eyed as the procession came down his street. He would run along beside the Dominican monks, watching as their black mantles blew out to reveal their white habits. He would look down at their sandaled feet, and wish he might be walking there among them. On to the Cathedral he would follow, to see the Archbishop in his gorgeous vestments and to hear the choir boys sing the *Te Deum*.

Out from the Medici palace close by Antonino's home

would come a small boy exactly his own age, called Cosimo, for he too loved to see processions. Although a serving man always accompanied him, so that he could not play freely with the other boys, still the two boys became friends.

They both went often to service at Or San Michele. Cosimo sat dreaming of what he would do when he came to power as a great man of Florence, and he wondered why that Antonino knelt on the cold pavement so long. Whatever could he be praying for?

The neighbors also wondered, for the boy came so often. Especially on the days when the prior of the black and white friars from nearby Fiesole came to preach. To Antonino he seemed a splendid and wonderful hero. His voice was like a trumpet calling to the boy, stirring him to dreams of what he would do for his "city of flowers" if ever he could stand up there preaching to the people.

He knew now what he wanted to become, not a notary like his father, but a Dominican friar. If only he were old enough! He begged his father not to apprentice him; and the moment he turned the corner of fourteen, he trudged out of the Croce gate, up through the olive groves to the convent of Fiesole.

At the gate he rang the bell and asked to see Fra Giovanni Dominici. And he lifted a slight, boyish face and great eager eyes to this prior who was his hero.

"I have come, my father," said Antonino simply. "I have come to stay."

The good prior must have been astonished enough, though he hid it from the boy. But he explained that he was still too young, too frail looking to enter the strict discipline of the brothers. They must rise at midnight for service, and again at four in the morning. They must study hard and work hard and eat simple food and think high thoughts. It might be several years before he was ready.

Then seeing the disappointment in the boy's face, he asked him:

"What is your favorite study?"

"Canon Law," answered Antonino.

The prior must have been secretly amused. What, a boy of fourteen interested in church law? He would set him a hard task then, and let him see for himself how impossible it was for him to enter here.

"Go home and learn the whole Decretal of Gratian, and then come to see me again."

It was the kindest possible way of saying, "Wait ten years and then come back to me."

Once outside the gate in the early spring sunshine, Antonino drew a long breath. He looked down on the fair city lying there at his feet in the valley of the winding Arno. Giotto's tower and the domeless mass of the cathedral showed him plainly where lay his own house. He had hoped with all his heart to be able to stay on here in Fiesole. But now that he had been set a big work to do, he would go back home and do it. And he ran down the olive slopes, and in through the Croce gate, past the old convent of San Marco, and so to his house.

From a shelf he took down a big folio tome, written by some monk-scribe in Latin, on parchment. Opening to the title page he read, *Decretum Gratiani*. It was like an encyclopedia of all the decrees and laws of the Popes, of the Church Councils, with quotations from the early church fathers, St. Jerome and St. Ambrose and all. Compiled by Gratian in the twelfth century, it was so well done that there has never been another; only many annotations and commentaries have been added by scholars of every age.

Down through these eight centuries, it has stood in all the libraries and universities of the world, copied and recopied, printed countless times on many presses, always in Latin. But how on earth could a boy of fourteen memorize it, all this mass of laws for abbots, priors, clerks, priests, bishops; with all its decrees for cases against criminals, and its penitences and its dry-as-dust judgments from the Laws of Rome?

But Antonino never wavered. If this was all that stood between him and his heart's desire, then he would simply command his extraordinary memory to serve him. He had only to begin. So he turned to the very first line and read:

Humanum genus duobus regitur, naturali videlicet inre et moribus. . .

What a task! Surely it would be unfair to compare it to a command given a boy or girl today to memorize the Bible from cover to cover, or the works of Shakespeare, for there would be story, drama, rhyme, meter to aid the memory. Perhaps it would be equivalent to learning by heart a bulky three-volume grammar, or the entire history of the United States, or a textbook on logic or economics, or Chaucer and Langland and Froissart's *Chronicles* in archaic English.

How hard that young Antony must have worked! On hot summer days, when the boys of his street called for him to go swimming, or to lie under an olive tree, he had to say no, and shut himself up with his big book. Or on crisp winter days, when the Arno had frozen over, and the boys went off to play a game called *palla*, he could only loan them his balls and his wooden bat, and put his head back into his book.

His father must have been amused at his questions as to the justice of the conflicting decrees sent to Spain and to Carthage. For above all, the boy had a passion for justice. He must look at both sides of a dispute with absolute impartiality, until he could decide on a fair settlement. The boys valued him for this. And this was why he loved Gratian, who always stated both sides of a case.

Well, on he went, through the hundred and one *Distinctiones*, and the thirty and six *Causæ*, on to the very end of the laws bearing on church ritual. Just one year from the time of his first visit, Antonino again mounted the slopes of Fiesole.

This time his feet had grown wings. His eyes were alight. He was fifteen now, and he had done it—had fulfilled the whole requirement. The Canon Law was in his head.

Naturally, the kindly prior was astonished. He led the boy to the library and took down a bulky *Decretum*. Turning here and there at random, he began quizzing the lad, who answered easily and eagerly.

So, he had actually accomplished this astonishing feat of memory! What could the prior do but keep to his word and accept him? That was in the year 1404, just at the turn of the wonderful *Cinquecento*, the Italian Renaissance.

ALTHOUGH the good brothers of Fiesole took the boy to their hearts, they were obliged to send him off to a branch priory at Cortona to study. Other boy novices of his own age were there, among them one who became his dearest friend, Guido da Vecchio, whom the world was to know as Fra Giovanni Angelico da Fiesole. This friend, who had magic in his fingers and heaven in his heart, amused his comrades by drawing saints and angels and their own faces on the margins of all his books, and even on the white convent walls.

Antonino set himself to master his lessons as he had the Gratianus, so that in a few years he had not only been admitted to the order but was chosen prior of Cortona. Now he could admit the boys who came knocking at the gate.

From Cortona to Naples, then to Siena, to Gaeta, and to Rome he was sent, as prior in each, always to bring order and serenity and justice to his Dominican brothers. Then he was called home to Florence to remain all the rest of his life.

This time he entered the convent of Fiesole as its new prior. So there he stood in the sandals of his boyhood hero, Fra Giovanni. And there below him lay the lovely city of Florence with its Giotto Campanile, and its massive Duomo, with the new dome which Brunelleschi was busily building, and the sun shining on the river Arno, ribboning away to the blue hills of Tuscany. He drew a deep breath of content.

Now of course there must needs be a procession to the Cathedral, winding down beneath the gray-leaved olive trees, through the very street where he was born, with his sisters and his father looking proudly from the windows. But this time he, Antonino, led his preaching friars, his black mantle blowing out to reveal his snowy habit. And beside him ran small boys—shouting for joy of the procession, just as he had once.

At the Duomo, a boyhood friend greeted him, Messer Cosimo de'Medici, now the richest man in Florence, and the most powerful.

Through his influence, the Fiesole Dominicans were soon invited to return into the city. They had been driven out years before, in one of the sudden upheavals so common to Italy. Now the Signori turned over to them an old convent called San Marco. Prior Antonino knew it well. Was it not at the head of his own street? Had he not played as a boy outside its high white walls?

Now Messer Cosimo determined to rebuild it in a grand style, and offered a prize to the young architect who should bring in the best design. Among them all he chose the plan of Michelozzo—who was later to build the great new Medici palace, now the Riccardi.

By 1439 the convent library was finished, and the black and white friars moved down from the hills, with Prior Antonino at their head, into San Marco. Now Fra Angelico joyously set to work with his brushes and his paint pots. How the white walls called to him, all along the cloisters, in the refectory, above the doorways, over the altar, in each cell. The others might go out and preach. Fra Angelico praised in color and line. The exquisite paintings of San Marco were to be his life-gift to Florence, and to the whole world for hundreds and hundreds of years to come. And none was more truly appreciative of his paintings than his prior brother Antonino.

In fact, the prior was delighted with his new home, with its simplicity, its beauty. He loved to walk in the cloisters and watch Fra Angelico at work, marveling at where he found his pure colors for the gowns of his angels. He could have spent the live-long day in the spacious library among the four hundred folio volumes. How lovingly he must have reached down a big copy of Gratianus, and smiled to think where he had brought that boy who had once memorized him by heart.

Yet he must not spend all his time in this sheltered convent, sitting in meditation as he loved to do; no, he must go about the busy streets of his city, getting acquainted with its citizens. And from each excursion he would return to converse with his patron, Cosimo.

For fifty years these Medici bankers had been now powerful, now exiled. Cosimo the Elder and his brother Lorenzo were to found a dynasty which was to rule or be ruled in this Florentine republic for three hundred years to come; which would furnish Italy with four Popes, Tuscany with countless dukes, and to France a Queen Catherine who would become one of her most powerful tyrants.

Just now, Fra Antonino realized that Messer Cosimo was bent on amassing wealth and tightening his power over his enemies. As he kept a cell for himself in the convent opposite that of the prior, the two friends had ample time to discuss the affairs of Florence and of the world.

For Florence was not just a small medieval walled town, but mistress of a province and owner of cities: Cortona, Siena, Pisa. She had her seaports and her trade roads and a finger in world politics.

Fra Antonino drew from him his own version of his struggle for power. It had begun fifty years before, this battle between Medici bankers and wealthy merchants of the Greater Guilds, or Arti, headed by the Albizzi family. In turn, each house dominated the city, even though in government Florence was a republic.

In the 1370s, when the wind of the revolt led by Wat

Tyler and John Ball had swept over England, blown through France and down into Florence, the people themselves rose to overthrow the Albizzi. For the seven Greater Guilds, risen to power on their looms, dominated world trade in cloth of wool and brocade of silk. Against their unjust taxes and too low wage, the fourteen Lesser Guilds rose in revolt, and their wool-carders led by Michel Lando swept the people with them to demand reform. These *Ciompi* were championed by none other than a Medici called Salvestro, who thus made himself popular and broke the power of the Albizzi to seize it in his own hands.

Fra Antonino shook his head. Poor people, used as a tool, with no voice in government but a cry! Must the city continue forever the old struggle between rival houses? It had been so for a hundred years and more. The feuds of the Guelphs against the Ghibellines were succeeded by the Blacks against the Whites, by the house of the Cerchi against the Donati, they who exiled even Dante the beloved during the last twenty years of his life.

Yet he understood now that it was but natural that Cosimo, inheriting his father's quarrel, and himself banished to exile by the Albizzi, should now on his recall, in turn banish the house of his old enemy. For Cosimo was determined to secure, without a revolution, the balance of power in this city which had long been acknowledged the foremost commercial democracy of Europe. But though he refused the office of Gonfalioniere, and remained all his life a private citizen, in reality he was slowly gaining such power over the Signori that he was soon to become an absolute monarch within a republic.

Yet Fra Antonino found great good in this man, a liberal, generous nature, which delighted in befriending young artists: Ghiberti who had won the contest for the doors of the Baptistry and was spending forty years in their creation; Donatello who was carving his David, his prophets and his saints; Brunelleschi, who, in his cathedral dome, was acheiving one of the greatest works of architectural genius in the world; Luca della Robbia, whose singing angels and dancing boys still adorn the Duomo.

Moreover, when Constantinople fell, Messer Cosimo filled his new palace with Greek refugees and thus acquired priceless classics not yet translated. When he first heard Plato read to him, he determined that the whole world must know his greatness, and sought out a young writer, Marsilio Ficino, whom he had trained in philosophy and languages to translate all his works. Thus through his Academy of Plato, Cosimo de' Medici gave Socrates and Plato and Aristotle to the Latin world, and through Italy in turn to France, and through France to the whole Western world.

Aye, Fra Antonino mused, much could be forgiven this man. But yet no amount of art patronage could make right his mismanagement of the city. For the magistrates, instead of representing both factions, the Medici and the Albizzi, the bankers and the Greater Guilds, were now all men of Cosimo's choosing. Which meant that he alone controlled the purse-strings.

He had determined not only to exile the Albizzi house but to crush thoroughly the power of the Greater Guilds. For this means he used taxes where his predecessors had used daggers.

In the just tax system called the *catasto*, set up by the Albizzi, each citizen was taxed seven per cent of his annual wealth, which he himself might declare. Now Cosimo, working secretly behind his Signori, swept aside this *catasto* to substitute the older system of assessment of income based on the opinion of the rulers. Thus by grossly over taxing the rich merchants, at one stroke Cosimo gained the popularity of the people and ruined his enemies.

When Fra Antonino got wind of this, he went at once to each of these old families to see for himself. Behind barred gates he was admitted by servants in frayed livery into once splendid houses. He found the great rooms drafty and cold. For their tapestries had been sold one by one to buy food. When they hastened to bring out wine for their guest, it was not as formerly in rare Venetian goblets on a golden plate, but in the cheap glass sold in the marketplace. The city pawnshops held the glass and plate of these families.

Little by little he drew out the confession of their ruin. Daughters gently bred were unmarriageable for want of a dower. Lads and young men could not set up for themselves in the Guild for want of the price. He found grave illness in mansions where no doctor had been called because they could not pay the fee. Their large fortunes had been swallowed up by the State through grossly exaggerated appraisals by the clerks of the Signoria.

The great wheel of fortune had turned, and they who were once at the top now lay prone beneath it.

And between these factions, as always, were caught the people. So Fra Antonino went among them, up and down the crowded narrow streets, along the river where floods had left houses unsightly and tumble-down but cheap of rent, into the quarters where every few years the dread plague raged.

Life was hard, they told him. Corn was high and the

price was often raised still higher by the commune. There was a new tax on wine. In fact, taxes took all they could make. Wages were too low. But what could they do without the power of a vote? Abandoned waifs, left in doorways, were cared for by kind-hearted mothers who had too large a brood of their own. In every house were too many mouths to feed.

Now the good prior went home to his clean white cell and thought of the need of all these, the rich become poor and the poor who could never be rich. Nothing hurt him so much as injustice. So he prayed and he thought. He must not antagonize Cosimo, nor stir up strife or resentment among the Signori. Clearly he reviewed all sides of the problem. There must be some impartial solution. After many days he found it.

He summoned twelve citizens to confer with him in the convent library. These twelve he chose carefully, friends of both houses, the Medici and the Albizzi. Some were bankers, to represent the wealthy class. Two were notaries, of the professionals, as his own father had been. The Greater Guilds were represented by a silk mercer and a draper, and the Lesser Guilds by a shearer and a bootmaker. To these twelve Fra Antonino presented his plan. He had divided the city into six districts, and now appointed two of his men in charge of each. It would be their duty to collect funds and disburse them. They were to seek out cases of distress and above all to help the *vergognosi*, the shamefaced poor, so called because as former heads of the guilds and wealthiest merchants of Florence, they were now too proud to beg, so lived on in their mansions in poverty and shame.

They were to model their deeds on that of St. Martin

who had slashed his own cloak to share with a beggar. It was to be a society of sharers. Their headquarters would be the tiny church of San Martino—where Dante was married. Their directors were to be the friars of San Marco. Their title: *Proveditori dei Poveri Vergognosi*, the providers of the shamefaced poor; this the people shortened to *Buonomini di S. Martino*, the name by which they are still known today, the Good Men of Saint Martin.

And not one of those twelve men but answered Antonino, "We are with you." Not one but knew well that with another great turn of the wheel, perhaps he and his whole family and servants and workmen might all be in the same position as these *vergognosi*.

Above all, the small society was to be a secret one. They were to make no noise about their deeds. No one need know but themselves. The monies collected were not to be refunded nor put out at interest, but promptly spent. Nor were they to be under any authority, civil or churchly. For Fra Antonino thought it safer to let neither Cosimo nor the Signori nor the Archbishop administer these funds. These twelve whom he trusted implicitly were to go forth impartially as knights on a crusade to heal Florence of her wounds.

Now for the poor, our good prior organized the *Spedale degli Innocenti*, which he opened for waifs that were left as a burden on the poor: a foundling home, with women to look after each bambino. And thanks to the generosity of Messer Cosimo, Luca and Andrea della Robbia were commissioned to adorn it. So they made the *Bambines*, those adorable babies bound in tight linen cloths which we know in replica as small plaques of blue and white terra cotta. There they are to this day, all along the outer walls of the cloister, holding out their arms to us, all wreathed in wheat or in fruits.

For orphan boys and girls, Fra Antonino opened a home in the Bigallo, just at the corner near the Baptistry, under the bells of the Campanile.

These three charities still carry on today. For five hundred years the *Buonomini* (*buon' uomini*) the Good men of Florence have sought out those who need help. They have paid doctors' bills, provided nurses for the sick, furnished doweries for girls and apprenticeships for boys; they have redeemed pawn tickets, and made gifts of food and clothing and beds and money. They have sent people on journeys, and have paid fees for burials, for christenings and for weddings.

Oddly enough, whenever during these centuries the civil or church authorities have insisted on taking them over, the society has failed. So they keep the original laws of Prior Antonino. It was not for nothing that he knew by heart the principles of justice and fair dealing. To him love was but a higher octave of justice, and passionately he loved all those in need.

For five years the building continued at San Marco until the cloisters and refectory and church were finished. And during these years while Prior Antonino was caring for the city as best he could, his brother Angelico was painting his Annunciation, his Peter, his Gifts of the Magi for the cell of Cosimo.

At last, in 1444, the convent was ready for dedication. And since Florence was the heart of the intellectual and cultural life of Italy, Messer Cosimo determined to make of this dedication a grand affair. He invited the Pope and

Cardinals, neighboring Bishops and all manner of dignitaries. He was now a very rich man, and could afford a gift of four hundred gold florins for more books.

And every guest who came oh'd and ah'd over Angelico's paintings, for not in all Italy, nor in all the world, had they seen anything so lovely.

The Pope, Eugenius IV, decided that the Vatican must know his work, so he carried the shy, round-faced friar off with him on his return to Rome. And while Angelico painted, they used to chat.

"So Florence is asking for an Archbishop? Why not take it yourself, then?"

"I! Mercy no, Your Holiness," cried Angelico. "The city is troublous with strivings. I know only my painting. Why not ask my brother Antonino? He has a level head for disputes. No man on earth's so just as he."

"Well then, why not Antonino?" And the Pope dispatched a letter-carrier with the news of the appointment.

The whole city was delighted. Not for long years had they had a citizen as Archbishop, but always a foreigner, who lived like a prince.

But Prior Antonino was terrified and tried to flee to Sardinia. He had to be persuaded by a petition from the Signoria.

"And what though a tranquil and quiet life be more to your mind?" they argued. "You ought to remember that we are not born for ourselves alone, but that our country, our friends, our associates, and even the whole human race have certain rights over us."

So it was that early one spring morning in 1446, there came walking barefoot down through the olive groves from Fiesole a friar in a simple white habit and black mantle.

Alone he entered in through San Croce gate and paused at the old fifth-century church of San Pietro Maggiore. For here he must enter into his archbishopric through the quaint ceremony of marriage to his city, *la città dei fiori*. Then on into the city, followed by all his brothers of St. Mark's, down the very street where he was born, with all the neighbors leaning out to wave and to cry out glad greetings. And so into the Duomo, Our Lady of Flowers.

You may see him for yourselves, entering the west door of his cathedral, for Fra Angelico painted it all on the cloister walls. The choir boys sang a glad *Te Deum*, and the new Archbishop Antonino preached his first sermon to the crowds thronging to hear him. Rich and poor, all Florence knew and loved him.

But they were to know him better as the years wore on. For first came the plague, that dread thing recurring at intervals, no one knew why. During the heat of summer, when flies were busiest, the whisper would spread: "Plague in the Via Pitti—a man died in the Via Sforza." And at the alarm, all who owned villas or farms in the country fled.

Who then was left to care for the sick? To find them when they fell in the street? To bury the dead?

Who but good Antonino and his *Buonomini*, young and stalwart and unafraid? For the Archbishop neither fled to Fiesole nor sat at home in his palace. He obtained from the magistrates money to use for medicines and doctors. Up and down the streets he trudged behind his donkey whose panniers were laden with wine and bread and medicines, and for those who could no longer eat, the "bread of angels," as he called it.

After the plague had abated, there came an earthquake which broke houses and chimneys and opened holes in the earth. And close upon the earthquake came a rain of comets and meteors, so that the people grew terrified and thought it the end of the world. What terrible and evil power threatened Florence?

Now the scholar Antonino went to his library at San Marco and searched the ancient tomes, and those newly translated by order of Messer Cosimo. From the logic of Aristotle and the science of Albertus Magnus, he composed a scientific treatise on the natural laws of comets and of heavenly fires. This he had his brothers copy and spread broadcast by his Good Men of St. Martin. For he reasoned that fear and superstition had a great part to play in spreading infection of the plague.

The poor were half starving. What was he to do about it? He walked back and forth in his beautiful garden. How fragrant the flowers were, and how velvety the green in his cathedral close. If the earth could produce such luxuriant grass and flowers, it would yield vegetables. But he had no land. The city was close-walled and crowded with houses and palaces. He had only this—this garden here by his Duomo. Yet even this would help.

He called to his gardener and asked him to spade up all the flower beds, all the smooth lawn. The poor man was horrified. But the Archbishop knew what he wanted, and sent a servant to market to buy cabbage plants and leek and garlic seeds. In a few weeks his donkey's panniers were bulging with green tops.

Then he invited Tommas Tommaso and Pietro di Grasso and the boys of their crowded street to come up and each choose a garden plot. Other families followed, and the city fathers were aghast to see the poor busily digging and hoeing and watering in the Archbishop's own garden.

What next? For the good man had reduced his elaborate and princely suite to six, and lived as simply here in his palace as in his narrow white cell in San Marco.

Now that the whole city was his parish, and all its citizens, rich and poor, his children, he began to educate them by his sermons, going in turn from one to another of the many parish churches crowded within the walls. He had much to say to the rich, for many in the city seemed to think life was meant for nothing more than feverishly to hoard money and goods.

"Riches are of no value in themselves," he told them, "but are only to make beautiful our city or to use or to give away. Riches should lead a man nearer to God, not farther away. You miss the whole point of life if you care only for the adornment of the outer man, and nothing at all for the enrichment of the inner."

Again and again he beseeched them to "earn only enough for yourselves and your families, and give the rest to the State and to the poor for hospitals, for the old, for the babies and the helpless ones."

Another day, he summoned to the cathedral all the guilds. He had much to say to them. There were so many ways of making money in honest trade, "then why go out of your way to cheat and to steal?"

He reminded them that if they stretched cloth too tight, it would split after they had sold it. Or if they did not properly shrink their woolen cloth, then they were giving false measure. He knew all the tricks used in city barter: padded weights, short measures. Some men in the building trades made roofs so faulty that they let in the rain, and walls so thin they let in the cold. Wood merchants often sold wood for carving which was so ill-seasoned it warped.

Paper merchants sold paper on which no pen would leave a mark, and ink too thin to last. The bookbinders too came in for a scolding, for he said that books were often badly bound, or with such wide margins that the price asked was exorbitant.

How they must have hung their heads, one group after another in his audience.

"Now barter, trade," he told them, "is good if it binds together men of all nations. We here in Florence send our iron work, our statues, our carvings, our cloth, our brocades all over the world. How shall men have confidence in us if we are not honest? How is any social life possible among men, except as each one trusts the other to speak the truth? So deceit and lying and falsehood in commerce, or in banking or in trade are destructive of human society, while justice and truth and courtesy will preserve society and make of our city one of the foremost of all nations."

In their hearts, they knew that he spoke the truth, this simple preaching friar who still wore his black-and-white robe, and refused his gorgeous vestments except to officiate at the altar.

Next he talked to his poor. They came crowding humbly to hear what their father had to say to them. For news of his reproof of the guilds had got round the city. The poor knew that he loved them.

"Poverty in itself is not good," he told them. How well they knew that! "But it may lead to good if in it you find yourself or your God."

They must study their trade, must give an honest day's work, must try to do that work best suited to each one. It was not enough just to earn one's bread. No, each man must follow his own bent, develop his own latent capacity, and use his own individual talent. Then he would not only earn for himself and his family, but contribute to the harmony of the city and nation.

No one trade was better or nobler than another, he made them see, but each thing produced or created depended for its value on the labor of head or hand that went into it.

How could they know, as they listened, that a man called Karl Marx was to seize upon this same principle five hundred years later, and that an entire nation of people were to adopt it in our own time?

"Things in themselves are useless," the good father went on, "unless the silk cocoons, the iron ore, the timber, the marble and the clay have either been completed by human industry or transferred to other markets by human labor."

Therefore, the poor must lift themselves out of poverty by fitting themselves to do useful work in one of the staple trades of the city: metal or building or cloth-making, in the tending of sheep or the cultivation of the soil.

How modern he sounds, and how he would have rejoiced in our trade and evening schools today!

Nor did St. Antonino hesitate to address even the Signori and the city magistrates. Out of their pride and love for Florence, they would continue to befriend the arts, to pay well for the treasures created by Ghiberti and Brunelleschi and the Della Robbias.

Yet they had a greater rôle in protecting the citizens against trusts and monopolies. It was not unnatural that a few merchants should put their heads together, buy up corn or wine and then hold them for a high price. "But the Canon Law calls such profit immoral," thundered the Archbishop. To break up such trusts was to avoid future friction and to protect people against poverty.

"For God did not create the poor from the earth and nobles from precious metals," he reminded them. "No, all alike come from a common source, with a common soul."

Even as all should contribute to the State in the form of tax, so the State must provide for its own, the sick, the old, the poor, the unfit. These are its special care.

Never did he suggest that rulers should abdicate their power in favor of the poor, for he regarded the relationship of ruler and ruled as part of the harmony of the universe. Some who are the most industrious are often the least successful, while the idle often abound in good things. This is because some are best fitted to rule, and others to follow and to be ruled. But this gives opportunity for those who have much to give to those who have little.

The State and the Prince must rule poverty out of the city, and should also punish those who refuse to work according to their ability.

Thus he anticipated Rousseau in his insistence that the citizens and their welfare should be the chief concern of the state, but he says it seems to work best when the few rule the many.

Again and again he speaks of "the great law of content," of well-being, with none too poor and none too rich.

Nor did he fail to rebuke the magistrates. They must obey the laws and respect the liberties of the people. They must allow free elections and correct their false counting of the black and white beans used in balloting.

When in return for this frank speaking, they threatened to dispossess him of his high office, he smilingly pulled out the big iron key to his cell at San Marco.

"Gentlemen, how gladly would I return to its peace."

Once, when he actually left his palace, with a message

to the *Balia* that he left the city in their safe hands, he remained in his cell until Messer Cosimo came and urged him back.

But men learned that he had no price. He could not be bought or sold because money meant nothing to him but as a gift for his poor.

After hammering long on the matter of false taxation, he had the joy, the year before his death, of seeing the *catasto* restored, so that a man's tax was again fixed on his own word of honor as to the amount of his wealth.

Nor did he forget his children in all this care for his city. They must be taught early and late, knowledge of God and letters, and the arts and crafts useful to them in earning, and obedience and above all honesty. The little book of catechism he wrote down for them was published after his death by the Aldine Press in Venice, one of its earliest works, and another Incunabula beyond price.

Now all of these principles and precepts for the conduct of a city and of its citizens, St. Antonino gathered together and wrote down in four big volumes called *Summa Morales*. Written during the last eleven years of his life, in snatches of time, this work represents his major contribution to his city—a kind of social utopia—a city of just and upright men; a great commercial republic, noble, beautiful, godly. These books, put into practice in the Greater and Lesser Guilds, have left their mark on the glory of Florence through the ages. A work of a legal mind, this, turned to the ethical service of his birthplace.

Indeed, this quality of justice, of balance, made his busy life possible. Never was he known to lose his temper or even to show irritation. Nothing and no one had power to disturb that deep peace of his inner life.

Moreover, in all his dealings with men he was so just that he was sought as an arbiter in disputes and his court decisions were never appealed. Nothing disturbed his judgment, nothing prejudiced him.

A story is told that one day a citizen brought him a basket of apples. Busy at the time, St. Antonino thanked the man, and sent him away with a blessing: *Dio tel meriti* — May God reward thee. But the man was cross and went off scowling. Poor thanks to be so quickly dismissed.

Seeing him disgruntled, St. Antonino called him back. Then he sent to the kitchen for a pair of scales. On a sheet of fair parchment he wrote the words of his blessing — *Dio tel meriti.* On one pan he put the apples, on the other the blessing, which drew down the scales.

"So you see, my friend," St. Antonino said with a smile, "the blessing weighed most, after all."

When his busy life drew to the end, he returned to die in his white cell at San Marco, with its walls painted by his brother Angelico, surrounded by his friars. He left a will, giving his body to the convent and all his money to the poor. Alas, a diligent search of his belongings brought forth only four ducats. He had given away all he possessed.

Back along the *Via Ricasoli* that leads from San Marco to the Duomo they brought him for the last time — the street where he was born, where Giotto once lived, where Donatello was later to come to die — a street lined now with sorrowing people. His poor, his friends among the *vergognosi,* his dear Good Men of St. Martin, were led by Cosimo and the whole City Council. For well they knew that a "just man made perfect" had lived among them, laboring for the good of their souls and of the city he so loved. All joined in calling him *Beato,* the Blessed.

His message to the fifteenth century brings him strangely close to the need of our own time:

And when the time comes, as come it will, when society as a whole recognizes that big fortunes and starvation are alike intolerable, and must be put an end to, God grant it may discover at the same time that the mad rush for wealth is folly and sin, and that a life of greater leisure in which to cultivate the higher faculties of our being and the sweeter sides of our total experience is infinitely to be preferred to the life of fever and tumult, and of the base and sordid values that so many of us are living now.

BIBLIOGRAPHY

I. *Henrietta Szold*

Jewish Year Books.
Pamphlets and Reports covering 20 years: Hadassah, New York.
Translations by Henrietta Szold, all published by Jewish Publication Society.
from French: The Renascence of Hebrew Literature, by Nahum Slouschz. Phil., 1909.
from German: The Ethics of Judaism, by M. Lazarus. Phil., 1900. The Legends of the Jews, by Louis Ginzberg. Phil., 1913. History of the Jews, by Heinrich Graetz. New York, 1927.
from Hebrew: The Talmud, by A. Darmesteter. Phil., 1897.

II. *Catherine Breshkovsky*

Hidden Springs of the Russian Revolution: Personal Memoirs of Katerina Breshkovskaia. Stanford University Press, 1931.
Message to the American People, by Catherine Breshkovsky.
Russia and the World, by Catherine Breshkovsky. New York, Russian Information Bureau, 1919.
The Little Grandmother of the Russian Revolution, ed. by Alice Stone Blackwell. Boston, Little, Brown & Co., 1919.
Magazine Articles of 1905, 1928, 1934: notably, *The Outlook*, Jan. 7, 1905; June 15, 1927.

III. *Malwida von Meysenbug*

Malwida von Meysenbug, by Romain Rolland, tr. from the French by Thos. J. Wilson. New York, Henry Holt, 1933.
Malwida de Meysenbug—Sa vie et ses amis, par Gaby Vinant. Bibliotèque de la Revue de Litterature Comparé, V. 81, 82.
Rebel in Bombazine: Memoirs of Malwida von Meysenbug, tr. by Elsa von Meysenbug, ed. by Mildred Adams. New York, W. W. Norton & Co., 1936.
Writings of Malwida von Meysenbug:
Briefen an deiner Mutter. *Deutsche Revue*, 1908, V. 1, 2.
Der Lebensabend Einer Idealistin. Berlin, Schuster & Loeffler, 1908.
Himmlische und Irdlische Liebe. Berlin, Schuster & Loeffler, 1905.

IV. *Don Bosco*

Don Bosco, by Johannes Jorgensen, tr. from the Danish by Ingeborg Lund. London, Burnes, Oates & Washbourne, 1934.

The Blessed Friend of Youth, by Father Neil Boyton, S.J. New York, Macmillan Co., 1929.

Ven. Dominic Savio, 1842–1857, by St. John Bosco, tr. from the Italian, by Mary Russell. London, B. Herder Book Co., 1934.

The Secret of Don Bosco, by Henri Ghéon, tr. by F. J. Sheed. New York, Sheed & Ward, 1936.

V. *Lord Shaftesbury*

A Life of Anthony Ashley Cooper, 7th Earl of Shaftesbury, by W. D. Christie. London, Macmillan Co., 1917.

Lord Shaftesbury, by J. L. and Barbara H. Hammond. London, New York, Longmans, Green & Co., 1933.

The Ten Hours Bill, by Philip Grant. Manchester, J. Heywood, 1866.

Studies in Biography, by Sir Spencer Walpole. New York, E. P. Dutton, 1907.

VI. *Hannah More*

Hannah More, A Biographical Study, by Annette M. B. Meakin. London, Smith, 1911.

Hannah More, by Charlotte M. Yonge. Boston, Roberts Bros., 1890.

Memoirs, Life and Correspondence of Hannah More, ed. by William Roberts. New York, Harper, 1834.

Letters of Hannah More, ed. by K. B. Johnson. New York, Dial Press, 1926.

Pioneer Women, by Margaret E. Tabor. New York, Macmillan, 1927.

VII. *William Wilberforce*

British Slavery and Its Abolition, by Wm. L. Mathieson. London, New York, Longmans, Green & Co., 1926.

Correspondence of Wilberforce, ed. by his sons, R. I. and S. Wilberforce. Phil., H. Perkins, 1846.

Eulogium of the Life and Character of William Wilberforce, Delivered and Published at the request of the People of Color of the City of New York, October, 1833.

Journal of a Lady of Quality from Scotland to the West Indies, 1775–1776. New Haven, Yale University Press, 1934.
Journal of a Slave-Dealer, by N. Owen, ed. by Eveline Martin. London, G. Routledge & Sons, Ltd., 1930.
The Life of William Wilberforce, by his sons. London, 1843; Phil., H. Perkins, 1839.
The Speech of William Wilberforce on the Abolition of Slave Trade. London, 1789.
William Wilberforce; A Champion of Freedom, by Wilfred Jenkins. London, Epworth Press, 1932.

VIII. *Thomas Paine*

Damaged Souls, by Gamaliel Bradford. Boston, Houghton, Mifflin Co., 1923.
Life and Writings of Thomas Paine, ed. by Dan Edwin Wheeler. 10 vols. New York, V. Parke & Co., 1908.
Thomas Paine and American Independence, by David S. Muzzey. *American Review*, v. 4 : pp. 278-288.
Thomas Paine, Bridge Builder, by Don C. Seitz. *Virginia Quarterly Review*, v. 3 : pp. 571-584. Charlottesville, Va., 1927.
Thomas Paine, Prophet and Martyr of Democracy, by Mary A. Best. New York, Harcourt, Brace & Co., 1927.
Six Historical Americans, by John E. Remsburg. New York, Truth Seeker Co., 1906.
Who Wrote the Declaration of Independence? by William M. van de Weyde. New York, Thomas Paine Historical Assn., 1911.

IX. *Sarah Josepha Hale*

Editorials of *Godey's Lady's Book*, 1850–1890.
The Lady of Godey's, by Ruth E. Finley. Phil., Lippincott, 1931.

X. *St. Vincent de Paul*

Heroes of Modern Crusades, by Edward Gilliat. Phil., Lippincott, 1909.
Heroic Life of St. Vincent de Paul, by Henri Lavedan, tr. by Helen Y. Chase. New York, Longmans, Green & Co., 1929.
History of St. Vincent de Paul, by Emile Vougand. London, New York, Longmans, Green & Co., 1908.
The Life of St. Vincent de Paul, by Henry Bedford. New York, D. & J. Sadlier Co., 1865.
Vincent de Paul, Priest and Philanthropist, by E. K. Sanders. New York, Longmans, Green & Co., 1936.

XI. *Christine de Pisan*

Christine de Pisan, par Fernand Demeure. *La Revue Mondiale.* July-August, 1930, Paris.

History Reference Council, Bulletin no. 167. Cambridge, Mass.

Livre des faites et bonnes moeurs du sage roi Charles V., by Christine de Pisan: Reprint, Paris, Petitot, 1819.

Six Mediæval Women, by Alice Kemp Welch. London, Macmillan Co., 1913.

The Book of Fayttes of Armes and of Chyualrye, tr. and printed by Wm. Caxton from Christine de Pisan. Reprint: London, Early English Text Society, 1932.

The Epistle of Othea to Hector of the Boke of Knyghthode, tr. from the French of Christine de Pisan, by Stephen Scrape. London, Nichols & Sons, 1904.

The Moral Proverbs of Christine, tr. by Anthoine, Earl Rivers. Reprint by Wm. Blades, London, 1859.

XII. *St. Antonino*

A Florentine Diary, 1450–1516, by Lucca Landucci, tr. by Alice de Rosen Jervis. London, Dent & Sons, 1927.

S. Antonino and Mediæval Economics, by Rev. Bede Jarrett. London, Manresa Press, 1914.

The Makers of Florence, by Mrs. Oliphant. London, New York, Macmillan Co., 1903.

The Story of Florence, by Edmund G. Gardner. London, Dent & Sons, 1910.

Decretum Gratianus.

INDEX